PHILOSOPHY, QABBALA AND VEDANTA

Owing to the antiquity and rarity of this book, certain pages are regrettably absent, and readability is compromised due to the blurring of the original text. If you possess any insights regarding the availability of these missing sections, kindly inform us. Your assistance is crucial in ensuring the completion of this significant work for the benefit of future generations.

PHILOSOPHY, QABBALA AND VEDANTA

MAURICE FLUEGEL

GYAN

Published by

GYAN

Gyan Publishing House
5, Ansari Road
Daryaganj, New Delhi-110002
Phone: 011-47034999, 9811692060
E-mail: books@gyanbooks.com

Distribution Network
gyanbooks.com
India, USA, Canada, UK, Australia

ISBN: 978-93-7097-178-3 (PB)

First Published, 1902

2nd Impression 2025

Printed at: Gyan Press, Delhi.

PHILOSOPHY, QABBALA AND VEDANTA
Arthur MAURICE FLUEGEL

PHILOSOPHY, QABBALA AND VEDĀNTA.

Comparative Metaphysics and Ethics, Rationalism and Mysticism, of the Jews, the Hindus and most of the Historic Nations, as links and developments of one chain of Universal Philosophy.

BY MAURICE FLUEGEL,
Baltimore, Md., U. S. A.

Author of "Religious Rites and Views."—"Spirit of the Biblical Legislation."—"Messiah Ideal: I. Jesus' Ethics; II. Paul and New Testament; III. Mahommed and Koran."—"Zend-Avesta and Eastern Religions."—"Israel, the Biblical People," etc.

PUBLISHERS, H. FLUEGEL & CO.

BALTIMORE:
THE SUN PRINTING OFFICE,
JANUARY,
1902.

To the venerable and distinguished President of Harvard University, Professor, Dr. Charles W. Eliot, Cambridge, Mass., a leading Promoter of American Education, Learning and Liberalism; in token of sincere reverence,

Dedicated by

THE AUTHOR.

Contents of this Volume.

This volume continues the series of the "Biblical Legislations" and the "Messiah Ideals," on the great social, intellectual and ethical issues of history; since Manu, Zoroaster, Kapila, Buddha, and Sankara, to Plato, Philo, Plotin, Apochryphae, Talmud, Gebirol, Maimonides, Qabbala, Zohar, Spinoza, Schelling, Hegel, etc. It treats of the Qabbala in juxtaposition with Hindu philosophy, the Vedãnta, and most of the leading philosophical systems of the world.

Chapter III—Philo.

Chapter IV—Yezira.

Chapter V—Gebirol.

Chapter VI—Hindu Philosophy.

Chapter VII.

INTRODUCTION.

THE VALUE OF PHILOSOPHY.

In his first lecture on the "Vedanta Philosophy," the late Professor F. Max Mueller, of the Oxford University, a scientific representative of the nineteenth century, recently demised, after a long, glorious career, introduced his subject with the following timely remarks (Ibid., p. 1): "I am fully aware of the difficulties which I shall have to encounter in trying to enlist your interest and, if possible, your sympathy, for an ancient system of philosophy. It is no easy task to obtain a hearing for philosophy, whether new or old. The world is too busy to listen to theoretical speculations. . . . And yet I remember one who ought to be well known to you, . . . our dear friend Tyndall, rejoicing over a new theory, because, as he said: "Thank God, it will not produce any practical result; no one will ever be able to take out a patent and make money by it." Leibnitz, I suppose, took no patent for his 'Differential Calculus,' nor Sir Isaac Newton for his 'Theory of Gravitation.' Trusting in that spirit, I hope that there may be some friends who are willing to listen to mere speculations, though not securing any tangible results, in the ordinary sense of the word. For though not money-producing, nevertheless these speculations are bound up with the highest and dearest interests of our life."

Reader! Even such are the thoughts and considerations I suggest in offering to your perusal this work on "Philosophy, Vedanta, Zohar and Qabbala." No doubt, neither of these themes presents any practical scheme, be it of rapid transit, steam or ocean navigation, Suez or Panama canals, tunneling the Atlantic or Rocky Mountains, etc. Philosophy and Qabbala, Zohar and Vedanta offer no lucrative patents, nor any money-making opportunities. They are purely theoretical, intellectual, scientific, ethical. Yet they influence in the highest degree, purely speculative and abstract as they may appear, our entire destiny, our daily life, our aspirations, our omissions and commissions, our motives and hopes, here and hereafter. "They are bound up with our highest and dearest interests," more precious than money, patents and railway projects.

RELIGIONS AND PHILOSOPHY.

Is it of interest to study other religions and their philosophy than our own? In reply let us quote an old and venerable writer, Bishop Beveridge (1636-1707, "Private Thoughts on Religion," I., 2): "Naturally there is implanted in my soul a desire for religion. But since there are so many religions so I desire seriously to examine them all. Not that I am dissatisfied with that I have already embraced, that I am born in, which the Supreme Authority has enjoined and my parents educated me in; but because it is natural for all men to have an overbearing opinion of that religion they are born and bred up in. In order not to seem to be biased by education and prejudice, therefore I am resolved to be jealous, suspicious and make sure not to entertain any opinion without being convinced by solid and substantial arguments of the truth of it. . . . . Indeed, there was never any religion so barbarous and diabolical but was preferred by them who professed it. That therefore I may make diligent and impartial inquiry into all religions and so be sure to find out the best, I shall for a time look upon myself as one not at all interested in any particular system, but only as one who desires, in general, to serve and obey Him that made me, in a right manner, and thereby to participate in that happiness my nature is capable of . . . ."

PHILOSOPHY, QABBALA, VEDANTA.

Philosophy as Qabbala and Vedanta treat of God and universe, of soul, mind and matter, man and woman, right and duty, objects of life, success and failure, home, state and society, truth and happiness, here and hereafter. Such are the themes treated by the sages of all climes and all times, in either Philosophy, Vedanta or Qabbala, and discussed in the following pages. For these I crave, reader, your kind attention and your sympathy, your thoughts and your feelings. These pages will reproduce before your mental vision, the meditations of the sages of the world's great nations and of the sages of Israel, in juxtaposition to each other; they will pass before your gaze the philosophical, ethical and sociological systems of the Hindus, Persians, Assyrians, Alexandrians, Greeks, Romans, the mediæval ages and the modern times, in rapid and succinct outlines, and in orderly, logical succession, from a bird's-eye view, representing the philosophical centers with their bright constellations of intellectual suns and ethical planets, surrounding their nucleus, gradually evolving one from the other and all from one common stock, one pivot, peaceably, logically and harmoniously; mankind no longer arrayed in opposition, nor Israel as the prophetic whip of the nations, but all working out sympathetically the sociological progress, the honey of civilization in the great bee-hive of human endeavor; all marching together under the ægis of monotheism, its ethics and its logic, the inheritance of Israel-mankind.

The pioneer philologist and philosopher, Frederick Schlegel, correctly surmised, in his linguistic studies, that "human speech, human thought and human motives have really but one root, one sap and one goal, all basing and all culminating in monotheism." In his work on "Indian Language, Literature and Philosophy" (p. 471), he says: "It cannot be denied that the early Indians possessed a knowledge of the true God. All their writings are replete with such sentiments and utterances, noble, clear and austerely grand, as deeply conceived and reverentially expressed as in any human language." The same writer, again, speaking of Hindu philosophy, says: "The divine origin of man is there continually inculcated to stimulate his efforts, to animate him in the struggle to consider a reunion and reincorporation with his divine origin, as the one primary object of his exertions."

This view of God, world and man, claimed by Sanscrit scholars for the Hindus, and by European thinkers as lying deep at the bottom of all philosophies, this Hindu-European philosophy is the one taught in the whimsical, enigmatic and versatile folios of the Qabbala also. The representation of Vedanta, Qabbala and Philosophy, in unison, as derived from one root, as different varieties and phases of the same paramount truths, that is the scope of the present labor. Heretofore Vedanta was little known, and the Qabbala was noticed only as Oriental supernaturalism. The striking affinity of both, their important influence on ancient and modern thinkers and the fact that they are necessary links and integral parts of general philosophy, will be demonstrated in these pages.

Concerning the Qabbala and its preceding Hindu philosophy, our immortal F. Max Mueller wrote me on last June (1900) the following: "If you could trace Indian influences in the Qabbala and the other Hebrew philosophical works, that would be very important. Indians certainly came to Alexandria and taught their philosophy. Why should they not have come into contact with Alexandrian Jews, even with Philo and his friends?" This contact will be shown in these pages. Here the influence of the Hindu Upanishads and Vedanta philosophy will be clearly retraced to Hebraic and to Teutonic thinkers. The intimate connection between the hoary philosophy of the Upanishads and Vedanta and that of Philo, Qabbala, Gebirol, Maimonides, Zohar, Spinoza, German mystics and philosophers, down to the nineteenth century, will be made clear here. To show this influence of the Orient upon the Occident, as well as the succinct representation of universal philosophy from that standpoint, viz: as one organic whole and one continued growth, is the task of this work; that the human mind is ever developing one system from another, ever connecting with antecedents, as do the circles of the cylinder; that it is ever producing by evolution, not by arbitrary, accidental and abrupt starts; that each system is the fruit of the preceding and the seed of the succeeding system; that this holds good for the several schemes of philosophy, be they Hindu, Persian, Assyrian, Alexandrian, Greek, Teutonic or Jewish; that "Indian influence is undoubtedly to be retraced everywhere, and especially in the Qabbala, the Zohar and the other Hebrew philosophical works;" that, finally, the Upanishads, the Qabbala and the other Hebraic thinkers have greatly influenced the Arabian, Teutonic and Neo-Latin sages of the middle ages and of modern times down to Jacob Boehm, Spinoza, Schelling, Hegel, Schleiermacher, etc., that will be shown and proved in the following pages.

MAURICE FLUEGEL.

BALTIMORE, July, 1901.

CHAPTER I.

PHILOSOPHY AND QABBALA.

In the course of our studies on the several bibles and their contents, the legislations, sociological schemes, ethics and doctrines of the world, we have first surveyed the western biblical codes in their relation to the East and to Parseeism, especially. Then subdividing this vast theme, we have treated successively of the laws of Sinai, of Nazareth, of Tarsus, of Mecca and of Media-Persia. We have now arrived at the discussion of the deepest problems in the religious and political domains; at the hidden layers of man's mystic intuitions, on one hand, and on the other at the highest social and metaphysical conceptions framed by the largest hearts and the strongest intellects of the human kind. Mysticism stands to metaphysics in the same relation as feeling does to thought; feeling is the mother of thought. The contemplation of and the contact with the external world creates the first, and out of the chaos of that dim sensation arises the clear conception, the definite, logical idea. Hence are metaphysics nothing else but mysticism pruned, verified, scientifically expressed and formulated.

Mysticism is metaphysics in embryo, as feeling is thought in a crude, unclarified condition. It is drawn from the deepest strata of the human self. It is the veiled, chaotic and mysterious source of all the genuine impressions and holiest intuitions of mankind. But it is also the spring of the very reverse of that. It is a most dangerous brute force. It is an abyss paved with pearls and corals, swarming with monsters and frights, as also full of common pebbles and mire. It challenges the bold diver to bring forth the one or the other. As the famous Egyptian sphinx used to offer a riddle with a costly reward if solved, or with destruction if failed; even so is mysticism. It offers the greatest prices and the direst disappointments. The noblest thoughts and the most childish notions have arisen out of that chaos. Abraham found there the scheme of reforming state and church by reason and justice. Moses saw in the "burning bush" the liberator and legislator of his race. Isaiah and Ezekiel discovered there purified ethics and a new statescraft. So Jesus of Nazareth drew from mysticism the scheme of reforming the world; Simon Magus, the glittering sands of self-glorification; Sabbatai Zebi contrived there his own deification; Spinoza saw there the divine omnipresence, God, as the only reality, and the world as less than the wavelets on the ocean. Thus is mysticism the great reservoir and treasury of man's mind. But it must be used cautiously. The greatest good and the direst hallucinations have come forth from that very same abyss. Religion, philosophy, ethics, laws, new nations and sociological schemes, etc., are pearls fetched from that ocean. Fanaticism, superstition, the devil, Baal-worship, etc., are its mud and mire. Originally they all rested in the same bosom of the deep—mysticism; beware of it!

METAPHYSICS AND MYSTICISM.

At a lower stage of civilization are all metaphysics but mysticism. Brahman, Zeus and Ormazd, Baal, Merodach or Ahriman, no less than Elohim, Shaddai and Ihvh, are gradually developed conceptions, purified and corrected ideas, each transcending the other. Religion, science, art—all is a growth, evolving from lower to higher; all from kindred seeds and roots; a scale of ever progressing human education. Higher developments differentiated them and discriminated between substance and shadow, between philosophy and mysticism. Originally they were one. We find them yet united in Plato, Philo and Plotin; we find them so in Qabbala and Zohar. In some sense is, even now, philosophy in part mysticism; even Spinoza's "Ethics" are not free from that element. Any philosophy is transcendental, and things transcendental belong to mysticism. Hence do we treat here of that and of metaphysics under one heading.

We are thus about, in this volume, to occupy our attention with religion in the broadest and the highest sense of the term; with that phase of religion not yet promulgated from mount and temple, but in that stage as it dawns in the intellect of the best, as it looms up and illumines the heart and the brain of the greatest thinkers and the noblest propellers of the race. We have to do here with the philosophy of religion; what the Germans call: "Religions Philosophie," religion, ethics, sociology and philosophy identified in the highest sense. True religion, in its objective sense, is philosophy, and true philosophy is ever religious. They are really different names for one and the same thing. Philosophy in the highest sense is a scientific hypothesis, rendering account of the universe to the human beholder, connecting all its parts, making it an organic whole and giving each thing its appropriate place therein. Religion in the highest sense is an authoritative doctrine, combining all existences, the world, man and things, into one whole, assigning to each its place and substantiating all by stating its first cause and its final object. Both try to solve the riddle of the universe: the one does it by authority and tradition, the other by speculating reason; the one mostly by supernatural postulates, the other by natural proofs. Both aim at the same object to demonstrate the physical connection and the logical, reasonable co-ordination of the universe. Their methods appear different, their object is identical. Now this object, viz., to explain the universal existence, is and will remain beyond our experience, transcendental. Hence religion, philosophy and metaphysics try to show what we, in last instance, must accept on authority, not by proof. Their objects and their methods are substantially identical; for each deals with things beyond our ken and apprehension, each must be accepted or rejected on authority. We are drawn to it by a certain irresistible craving of our moral nature; and this craving again is mystical. Hence is mysticism as rationalism, religion as philosophy, eternal ingredients of man's moral nature. Such philosophy and such religious philosophy are the themes of this present volume.

QABBALA.

Religious philosophy has in the Occident a central doctrine, vaguely known there after the epoch of Maimonides, since the 13th century, by the name of Qabbala. It is a vague and dark term of various and ambiguous significance. It meant originally tradition and reception, a theory delivered and accepted upon venerable historical grounds. It meant then a doctrine handed down from a well-established old authority. It meant at last a divine revelation, a tradition derived from a holy source; a code of teachings come down from high antiquity, with a claim to a supernatural origin. This Qabbala really is a philosophy, an eclectic system to explain all, to systematize existence, to say what it is, what is its cause, its essence and its objects. We shall see that Qabbala is not, as popularly believed, exclusively Jewish philosophy, a specially Judaic mode of explaining the universe. No, it reflects the universal philosophy; it is a rough, eclectical way of combining the several views on that vast theme into one homogeneous system. Indeed, it almost seems that from Hindostan to Media, Persia, Greece, Italy and western Europe, the same system was handed around from race to race and from sage to sage, growing and developing with each generation. The Jews in the middle ages, the industrial and commercial agents of the world, were also its intellectual and ethical brokers; they were the middle-men between the East and the West, between Christian and Moslem, the Occident and the Orient; they were the best situated to bring about that amalgamation and unification of philosophical doctrines. We find the Qabbala deeply settled among thinking Jews of Europe and Asia during the entire long cycle of the mediæval ages. No doubt the form, the canvass, the figures of speech, the texts, etc., are Semitic, Biblical, Talmudical, Jewish mystical. But when looking deeper into the very core and kernel of its theories, we shall find the Qabbala wonderfully bold and cosmopolitan. We shall see there ideas and views hailing from India, Bactria, Media, Persia, Grecian Asia Minor,

European and Egyptian Greece, Italy, Spain, France, indeed the entire globe, West and East. Even so shall we find there a confluence and fusion, a harmonizing of the views of all creeds, nationalities and countries. The Qabbala contains elements unmistakably derived from, besides Bible, Talmud, Aggada, etc., also from Zoroaster, Pythagoras, Plato, Aristotle, Philo, Plotin, the Christian and the Mohammedan scholastics, the Book of Creation, Saadia, Avicebron-Gebirol down to Abulafia, Mose de Leon, Corduero, Luria, inclusive of leading traits which Spinoza and Hegel borrowed from it.

THE ZOHAR.

The very center of the Qabbala is universally recognized to be the work, called the *Zohar,* meaning splendor, light. It is really a collection of books, a compound and a series of treatises not sure if written by one hand; at any rate, not flowing from one mind and one inspiration and following up one method. The Zohar appears to be a compilation of the current thoughts on past and contemporaneous religious philosophy, roughly collected, systematized and shaped into one, apparently, not really, coherent system of doctrines. The Zohar, the bible of the Qabbala, partakes of all the good and the bad sides of the Qabbala. Mose de Leon did not copy his work from the writings of his fictitious R. Shimeon, nor from any later worthy. He did not copy at all. He was the author of his work. But he was not the author of his thoughts. He was not a plagiarist, but he was not the thinker of his doctrines. He was their compiler. Did he create, was he a man of genius, did he shape scattered elements of thought into a system, firm, logical, consistent? We shall see further about that. Professor Franck told me personally "He was a man of genius." Professor Graetz thinks him but a smatterer, without any substantial ideas of his own to be retraced to his work, the Zohar. It is written in minor part only in biblical Hebrew but mostly in the Arameo-Chaldean idiom, often incorrectly and with many confusing readings. It is now generally and correctly believed as having been composed, or rather compiled, by a Spanish Jew in the middle of the 13th century P. C., Rabbi Mose de Leon, though it bears the name throughout the text and on the title-page, of Rabbi Shimeon ben Jochai, a revered Mishna teacher of the first century. The Zohar has during many centuries assumed and held the important rank of a bible, the bible of the Qabbalistic system, the bible of metaphysicians and mystics, the central book of religion and philosophy, with the claim of having come down from antiquity and by tradition handed to modern times. The Zohar is really the bible of mystic philosophy of the middle ages. It holds its own views on all things of import to human inquiry. It has its own construction of history, of theology, of religion and worship, of law and society, of marriage, of life, of social science. It has its own Messiah-Ideal, viz: its own way of solving the great problems of the destiny of man here and hereafter, of the aspirations and the future of the human race. Nay, more; this ideal is so tenacious, so realistic that it has embodied itself in a human aspirant in nearly every age. This Messiah-Ideal electrified enthusiastic natures to the greatest deeds a century before Jesus of Nazareth and a century after him. Therefore the Christian believer and the Christian unbeliever will find great interest in that study. So will the Mohammedan. That doctrine has really had its adepts and admirers among Jew, Christian and Moslem. Josephus mentions quite a number of such leaders who had assumed that part. The very last and gigantic struggle of Judæa against world-conquering Rome was under the lead of such an impersonation of the Qabbalistic Messiah-Ideal. Since that remote epoch hardly a century has passed without the reappearance on the scene of the world's history of such a messiah realized. Their doctrines, aspirations and claims are strikingly similar to those held forth in the Qabbala and its central book, the *Zohar*.

This book and its world-embracing system has thus represented a sort of religion, yea, it is such, even to this day, to thousands in the East, the "Hassidim." It is the religion of united metaphysics and mysticism, a combination of radical rationalism and symbolic ceremonialism; of pure metaphysics and exploded popular notions; of real philosophy and eschewed superstitions; a compound system from all ages, creeds, races and regions; the bible, the central code and legislation of mediæval times. It had ages and centuries of undivided sway over Christian, Jew and Moslem; it held in awe popes, nobles and illiterates; several times it raised the bold claim of being the Bible, the only and last mysterious word of God, yea, it hinted at its role of mediating between the several religions and of actually unifying Church, Synagogue and Mosque into one Zoharitic worship. It practically tried it in Turkey and in Germany. This book, a necessary link in the history of human thought, in the systems of philosophy and ethics, having its own construction of world-history, its own solution of the great social and humanitarian problems, its own way of realizing human destiny, its own Messiah-Ideal, representing a religion, a philosophy, a bible, a sociology, a historic world-conception, claims its place in our studies on the world's great systems. Thus is this volume dedicated to these mental and ethical studies, to Qabbala, Hindu and religious philosophy; to religion and philosophy, to metaphysics and mysticism; with their construction of human history, the future and the destiny of the human race, the hoped-for realization of the Messiah-Ideal, viz: the brightest phase in the development of mankind; the summit of all human aspirations; the object of all religion and all civilization. We shall follow up these ideas, from grey antiquity to the threshhold of modern times; as they developed and came down from age to age, ever vaster and nobler, gathering in the Qabbala all their elements; a variegated chaos of grand and petty, true and false, divine and unholy conceptions; until later thinkers distilled out of these heterogeneous materials the elements of modern philosophy and actual, ethical thought.

SOURCES OF THE QABBALA, PLATO, PHILO.

In our foregoing volume on the Zend-Avesta and Zoroasterism, we could easily detect a general outline of that religious philosophy, later, in part, embodied and elaborated in the Qabbala and Zohar. We have seen there Infinity of Space and Eternity of Time as the highest definition of Deity, developing from its own abyssmal bosom the two Supreme deities of Good and of Evil, and their two-fold realms, hierarchies of genii, with their legions of subordinate angels and demons. The student of Qabbala will see in these pages how closely that system utilized the Zoroastrian doctrines, though giving them other names and more gorgeous draperies.

In Pythagoras' system, we meet many more parallel elements of both philosophy and mysticism, of bold rationalism combined with enthusiasm and credulity, aspirations to higher sanctity and distinction; secrecy and mystery; the divine soul, its transmigrations and purifications, the ten heavenly spheres and the *ten Numbers,* intermediate between the Origin of All and the single, actual bodies of the universe. These elements we shall meet also here, in the Qabbala and the Zoharitic system.

These metaphysical categories we find further elaborated in Plato, who, connecting by his doctrine of the "Ideas" with the mystic eastern "Infinitude of Time and Space, as the Father of All," postulated the Eternal Mind and the Eternal Matter, as the origin of all apparent existence. To him the ideas are the eternal types, the realities; the apparent things grasped by our senses, are but the shadows of the ideas which alone are substances and eternal. According to that philosopher is matter ever and instinctively rebellious to mind, its prime-ordeal partner. Mind is personified by a hierarchy of types, an infinitude of ideas, all scaled and contained in the highest idea; this Supreme Idea is God. Matter is the dark and ephemeral substratum of all the sensual existences of the universe. These are the short-lived bodies, the incarnations of the eternal types; those ideas or divine types are the souls, living together with the body in a forcible union, an involuntary partnership. This Platonic dualism is but another version of the two eastern antagonistic supreme deities, Good and Evil, and their two creations ever opposing each other, illustrating the universal struggle for existence. These two systems combined are taken up now in the Qabbala and elaborated as the "holy Sephiroth-world and the unholy Sephiroth-world," the extreme poles of the universe. We shall later see their Vedanta origin.

We come now to the several phases of Judaism, viz: The simple Abrahamic version thereof, the Mosaic legal version, the prophetico ethical version, the elaborate Talmudic version, and, lastly, the Aggadic and Apochryphal version, respectively and successively representing religion, first as a system of doing good; then doing good and worshipping the only One God; then this with an addition of elaborate public worship, rites and observances, and at last with a superabundance of ceremonies, accompanying man at every step and moment of his life, as invisible strings connecting him with the spiritual world—all these phases are duly considered and minutely enlarged upon in our Qabbala and Zohar.

The metaphysics and the mysticism of Zoroaster, Pythagoras and Plato, of Abraham, Moses and the Prophets, we shall find in these pages to be further developed and elaborated, altered, yet fully utilized by their successor, Philo Judæus. Both their bold metaphysics and their dreamy mysticism we shall find continued in the vague and scattered philosophems of that versatile Alexandrian thinker and writer. He accepted the mind and matter theory of Plato, but he openly altered them, made them to be the powers of Good and Evil of Zoroaster and identified them with the doctrine of Ihvh and of Satan, of the Rabbinico-Mosaic system. He utilized the blocks taken from the quarries of his Greek and his Biblical masters, and built up that theory which later became the starting point of his successors, the Neoplatonists. This eclecticism of Philo can be followed up step by step in our pages on the Zohar. His rationalism hailing from Greece, his piety derived from Rabbinism, his mysticism coming from the further Orient, all can easily be retraced in the Qabbala. Even so will be found the unmistakable influence of Neoplatonism upon that system. Its doctrines and ideas were entailed upon its successors, the Jewish, Christian and Mohammedan scholastics. Such views, modified to a certain extent by their own religious tenets, influenced the Jewish philosophers and mystics, the authors of the "Book of Creation," of Shiur Qoma, etc., of Saadia, Gebirol, the rabbinical rationalist Maimonides, and a host of others. They brought them down to the Qabbalists and then to Mose de Leon, the Zohar, Corduero, Luria and their successors.

Qabbala and Vedanta, distilled by the pitiless logic of Bacon and Descartes, Spinoza, Hegel, Shlegel, etc., at last produced the "Ethics" and modern philosophy. Thus from Manu, Zoroaster and Plato to the Qabbala, etc., there is but one long, unbroken chain of development of both rational metaphysics and abstruse, yea, popular mysticism. We shall treat of each of them at some length, having as our central theme the Qabbala and the Vedanta; while the Part II. will treat of the Zohar. Finally, all these metaphysicians and mystics were philosophers and sages; they were no empty dreamers; they had their definite doctrines not only about God, creation and duty, they had also such about human society, its means and objects, its struggles, drawbacks and aspirations; its Messiah-ideals, its socoilogy, its hopes and destinies, its ethical, intellectual, physiological and economical goals and developments. The Part II. will closely discuss these various problems and their solutions, and will thus conclude our studies on the "Messiah-Ideal," viz: the historical developments of those human capacities and aspirations, the goal of all progress, science, religion and philosophy, of all human endeavors and hopes.

OUTLINE OF PHILOSOPHICAL QABBALA.

The Qabbala is the theosophy and philosophy of the Jewish middle ages, historically and logically connecting with the philosophy and mysticism of preceding ages, schools and creeds. It treats of God, creation, universe, spirit and matter, of nature and its phenomena, of man and his position in the world, his duties and rights; of religion, soul, immortality, hereafter, etc.

The Qabbala has its leading book, its bible; it is the Zohar.

It is a commentary on the Pentateuch, inclusive of the books of the Bible and the entire rabbinical Aggadic Literature. It follows the chapters of the five books of Moses, commenting on their verses, connected with some other parallel biblical verse and some rabbinical analogous passage, thus interweaving Pentateuch, Bible and Talmud into one frame of philosophical and mystic speculation. The Qabbala has its complete and full version of divine and human affairs. It has its version of the final aims of history or the Messiah-Ideal. It claims to hold the key to religion and Judaism; to unlock its inner sanctuary, its higher and real import. It has its own ideal of life, virtue and objects of human existence. It aspires to represent the religion, the universal religion, to be alone saving; to be the heir of the hoary past, to bring down the best ideas and teachings of all ages and sages. It reaches out a fraternal hand to Christianity and Islamism, showing a mode of amalgamating and fusing all the sects into one. It is cosmopolitan and Jewish; it is all and everything. It was for centuries reverently looked up to by Christian, Jew and Moslem as the fountain of all wisdom, religion and true theology. During the period of the Reformation it absorbed all attention. The noblest intellects in all the camps, the proudest church dignitaries occupied with it as the great source of revelation, as the balm for all spiritual and social ailments. Nor has its influence vanished to this day even, and its effects are not yet effaced. Hence its place here in this series of treatises on the bibles, doctrines and influential systems of the world.

Its foremost work, the Zohar, which in its time greatly influenced theologians, popes, princes and cardinals, as well as the authors of the Protestant Reformation, is accepted to be the product of the thirteenth century, since it hints at the Messiah as about to come in the fourteenth century.[1] We shall later spread before the reader the many proofs of its compilation late in the thirteenth century during the hottest of the crusades, just in time to announce the advent of the Messiah who was to

1 Zohar II. 7—Zohar III. 19.

leave his secret abode in paradise, the sacred bird's nest where he had been hiding in beatitude since the beginning of time. He would vanquish the nations and redeem Israel. Atrocious and bloody wars would be waged among the peoples. Edom and Ishmael would wage cruel wars against each other, and at last both will be annihilated by the messianic third party, the model of the new Social Order, the "Kingdom of Heaven." Wonders and monstrous things will precede, resurrection of the dead and universal Qabbalistic divine worship will form its climax. The new social order, history's goal, the messianic ideal pervades the very center and core of the system of the Zohar. It is a treatise of metaphysics, of mystics, of ethics, of sociology and of worship, all in one combined. It occupies itself with the highest and with the humblest things. It is often sublime, grand, poetic, profound, abounding with the best and noblest thoughts of all times, systems, creeds, sages and philosophers; boldly and successfully it fathoms the thoughts of Abraham, Moses, Isaiah, etc., of Manu, Zoroaster, Kapila, Plato, etc. It is, side by side with that, the very reverse of all that. It abounds in bombast, nonsense and pretense, in superstition, hallucination and thaumaturgy, in low effect to catch the veneration of the ignorant and satisfy their hankering for the wonderful. It is a complex work, a compilation of the old and the new from prophetic teachers, pagan sages, religious enthusiasts, rabbinical mystics, bold philosophers, reaching the wing of a Spinoza or Plato; with a strong admixture of old and modern spiritualism, of empty claims and hollow affirmations advanced by contemporaneous mystics and the author himself; of his own additional, personal sophisms and small, far-fetched combinations; exorbitant allegories, twisting and torturing the biblical verses and commandments, narratives and persons to mean any and everything they and he wanted, under the screen of the Sacred Writ, used as a protoplasm for often vain theories; making use of scriptural verses, words, names and figures of speech in its ethics and metaphysics, the Zohar produced a compilation of treatises, all forming a body of theosophy. This theosophy is denominated Qabbala,[1] a Hebrew word used often in aggadic and halachic rabbinical literature to mean tradition, oral doctrine handed down from the fathers, in contradistinction from the written law of the Sacred Writ, as also from reasoned doctrines arrived at by the use of human argument. The method of the Qabbala and the Zohar is therefore not to reason and give proof of the teachings, but dogmatically to affirm on authority, to reveal. A leading rabbi, a Mishna teacher of the first century P. C., is claimed to have received it by revelation and to have handed it down before his death to a few companions, in secret conclave, in a cave of Palestine, overshadowed by the frowns of Rome and illumined by the smiles of angels.

DOCTRINES, GOD, AIN-SOPH.

According to that system is the Deity forever hidden from and unknowable to human understanding. God is the Infinite, Unknowable, Substance and Source of all existence.[2] God, Ain-Soph corresponds to Zrvana-Akarana of Persia; to Brahman, All, of the Vedas; to the Biblical Ihvh Elohim; to the Supreme Cause of philosophers. That is all we know of Him. Zohar II. 20 a (Ed. Wilna, 5655) says: "When the creative thought arose in the Holy One, blessed be He, all the worlds arose in that one thought and by that one and same thought they were all created."[3] The nature of God is thinking, and the thinking of God is creation, a known view of Vedanta, Yezira, Aristotle, Maimonides, etc. He created the original light, a luminous point,[4] the emanated essence which contains in potentiality all the types and germs of subsequent creations. This is the light-habiliment, the lustrous atmosphere of the Deity. It is ever radiating light and force. It is developing and calling forth the universe. Now, this first creation, or emanation of the unknowable Supreme Being, this first ideal world of light, the

---

1 The root is קבל to receive something handed down, a tradition קבלה, in Aramaic it further means hidden, secret; while Zohar means, lustre.

2 אין סוף, אין

3 כל העולמות עלו במחשבה אחת, ובמחשבה נבראו בולם

4 Zohar II. 20—Zohar III. 128, נקודה ראשונה

Zohar denominates *"the primordeal Man, the higher Man."*[1] It corresponds to many kindred notions of myth and philosophy, as the Greek Makrokosmos, Demiurgos, Logos, later on discussed. The system argues on, as a tradition, dogmatically:[2] "The human form is the prototype containing the types of the higher and the lower creations." Creation was called forth by that Spiritual form through further emanations in different grades, which emanations the further they distanced the Supreme Deity the less they were luminous, spiritual and pure; until at last they became the opaque matter of this our sensual world. The Zohar counts four gradual creations or emanations of worlds, the highest of which, the most spiritual one after the Deity, he denominates *Adam Qadmon,* the first man, or the heavenly man.—That theory fitted the Trinitarian dogmatics admirably, and this explains why Christian scholars at the close of the middle ages were so eager to study our book in question that offered such excellent material for christological speculations. This explains the enthusiasm of Reuchlin, Pic de Mirandola and the host of other Christian writers on the Zohar and the Qabbala.

ADAM QADMON. PROPHETS.

Thus, according to the Zohar, the Infinite, Unknown and Unknowable God—Ain-Soph—began by manifesting and revealing himself as the Primeval Man, Adam Qadmon, this form containing the types of all further creations or emanations. Our book gives no reason why the first divine manifestation was the human figure. I offer it simply as my own guess whence the Qabbalists borrowed that metaphor. It is first an heirloom from the past. Man wishing a concrete, tangible image of the Deity, naturally shaped it after himself, giving it first his own shape and form, then his own passions. Next it is from the biblical anthropomorphic figures of speech concerning the Deity,

---

[1] אדם קרמון—אדם עילעה. [2] דיוקנא דאדם הוה דיוקנא דעילוין ותתאין דאתכללו בהו . . ובגין כך אתקין עתיקא קדישא תקונוי דהאי דיוקנא . . . Idra Rabba 141 b, Zohar III. Wilna.

the "face, heart, head, foot, the wrath, satisfaction and love of God"—all that calls forth the idea of God under a human image. The genesis of "Adam in the image of God" (I: 26 Gen.), etc., no doubt went in the same direction, as further on shown. The prophets continued that impersonation. So Isaiah VI. suggests such a metaphor: "The Lord sitting upon a high throne and his folds filling the temple." More so is the divine vision of Ezekiel, the mysterious Mirkaba, the divine chariot, carried by four mystic angels or Hayoth, with the *man-vision* on the throne, the "likeness of the divine Glory."[1] This tendency goes on in the book of Daniel; there the poetical visions are condensed to anthropomorphical conceptions of the Deity. Such they are there in Chapter X., as also throughout the book, here frequently alluded to; so, too, in Chapter XII., with a revelation concerning the end of Israel's tribulations; so especially in Chapter VII., 12: "I saw the mighty vision and beheld; with the clouds of heaven came a man-likeness which stepped forward to the Ancient of Days." . . . . From such passages, it seems to me, the Qabbalists have taken their metaphors about the God-Infinite and his first emanation, the "primordeal man," the "higher man," the "Adam Qadmon." The whole is a human figure of speech. When man desires to describe the Infinite as revealed, he will lend him a human figure; the bees will imagine the Omnipotent under the shape of a queen bee, and the birds as the condor of Chimborazo. The later awakened philosophical mind could not accept those anthropomorphical and anthropopathetical expressions as referring to the Deity and belittling it. So the Rabbis taught *"the Thora speaks in human or popular language."* While the speculating Jews assumed that they applied not to God-Supreme, unknowable and purely spiritual, but to his first creation, to God-revealed, the first divine manifestation, as further developed in this volume.

ADAM QADMON, THE VEDIC BRAHMAN AND MANU.

In the course of these studies we shall show that the Qabbala is not isolated in this conception, as generally, in its entire sys-

---

[1] במראה אדם עליו מלמעלה, hence the Zohar's literal אדם עילעה.

tem. We shall see that this stupendous figure, Adam Qadmon, pervading the Qabbalistic theory, finds its parallel in the Hindu *Brahman,* the first manifestation of the Supreme, and in *Manu,* one of the first creations of the *Self-Existent.* Brahman is the creator and *Manu* assisted the Deity in producing the world. The Brahmanic *Self-Existent* is without attribute or shape; he is not differentiated even as to matter and mind; he is embracing all, the boundless space and the eternity of time and described as unknowable and inconceivable; he is the God Supreme of the Vedas and the Origin of all existence. That Vedic *Self-Existent* corresponds to the Zohar's *Infinite, Unknowable, Ain-Soph.* Brahman, the unknowable Origin of All, first produced the waters; he deposited there the seed which produced the *Golden Egg* of the universe, and therein he was re-born as the revealed Brahman.[1] This born-Brahman is the Creator, and he corresponds to Adam Qadmon. Another myth narrates that Brahman began with bringing forth the man-god, Manu. We shall later enlarge upon these Vedic themes and see how they were elaborated in our mystic system. Out of the materials of the Hindu born-Brahman and Manu, the Qabbalists constructed their Adam Qadmon, the revealed Supreme, the II., the Deity manifested in human shape; the actual creator, containing all the types of creation. The parallel is complete: The born-Brahman creates Manu, and in the Qabbala the celestial Adam emanates the Ten Sephiroth and creates the earthly Adam, father of man, a great figure in Jewish mysticism. So is Manu the father of mankind, the Hindu lawgiver, and assistant in the divine creation.

I believe Manu is the first intimation of that mystico-philosophical conception of a divine man, a god in human form. Though a creature of the Supreme and Unknowable, Absolute God, the mysterious Source of all existence, he was the right hand, the grand vizier of the Unknowable and the effective assistant in creation. Manu in Brahmanism is but one of the gods. He is father, patron and lawgiver of men and the oracle

---

1 Laws of Manu. Creation.

of the Deity. As all such philosophical myths, it expanded and grew in time. It developed in Magiism to the greater role of Zoroaster; then to the yet vaster one of Buddha, the incarnation of the Supreme Spirit. The Hebrew Genesis reduced it to that of Adam, "made in God's image to rule and domineer." The Talmud gives the *first Adam*[1] gigantic proportions and a miraculous importance. Hebrew and Christian legendry allow him a divine role similar to that of the Messiah. Philo declares: "Adam is like the Logos, the mediator between God and the world,"[2] commenting upon Genesis iii: 22: "Behold Adam is like one of us to distinguish between good and evil."—The Neoplatonists further increased the part of the Logos as "Nous." The Gnostics had their Demiurgos, the actual creator of the world. The later theosophists evolved their *Divine Intelligence;* so even the Hebrew-Arabian thinker, Gebirol. Thus was the role of the Vedic Brahman and Manu growing and ever gaining in importance, until with the Qabbalists and the Zohar, it assumed the immense proportions of Adam Qadmon, the great arch-type, the Creator of the spiritual and the material worlds, son of the Unknowable Infinite. The first embryo of all these speculations is the Vedic *Self-Existent,* reproducing himself in Brahman and then in *Manu,* the lawgiver. These are the parallels of the Persian Zrvana-Akarana, the unknowable All, Infinitude in Space and Time, split and reproduced in the dualistic Ahura Mazda and Ahriman, and revealed by Zoroaster. In Christology can be retraced the same evolutionary ideas, symbolism and doctrines. Further, mark that the diverse divine assistants at creation, belonging to the several philosophies mentioned—Brahman, Manu, Logos, Nous, Sophia, etc.—up to the Qabbalistic Adam Qadmon, all mean, etymologically, word, *wisdom,* mind. Hence they are all but names for and personifications of Divine Intelligence, all intend to say that creation was

---

[1] Hagigah 12, a, "Adam Harishon first occupied the space between heaven and earth, until he sinned."

[2] De Confus. Ling. 339, etc.

effected by the wisdom of the Supreme Cause. In conclusion, I venture to say the following: As the *Ain-Soph* and *Adam Qadmon* are no original ideas of the Qabbala, but imitations from Hinduism, Parseeism, Gnosticism, etc., even so are most of the leading features of that system, but later developments and adaptations from Oriental and Occidental doctrines; derived from gray antiquity and elaborated in modern times, comparatively.

TRINITARIAN DOCTRINES. MESSIAH.

No doubt the mystic theosophy of the Qabbala is offering many analogies to Trinitarian conceptions about Messiah, Redeemer, Son of God, primordeal Man, the first begotten Son, emanation and incarnation, etc. According to the blessed H. Graetz, the *Zohar* actually contains speculations and mystical phrases that are striking parallels to Christian orthodox dogmatics.[1] Nevertheless it seems to me that, upon closer examination and after hearing the testimony of Professor Ad. Franck, in his Qabbala, of Dr. Yellineck, in his revised edition of Franck's Qabbala, of Dr. Hamburger, in his "Real Enclycopædia," and many other writers and scholars, any such supposition must be discarded. It is a fact that Mose de Leon, the ostensible author and, at any rate, the compiler and editor of the older portions of the parts of the *Zohar*, has lived and died a Jew, that his books were thoroughly imbued with Jewish spirit, that he hinted at the near advent of the Messiah; hence could he not at the same time accept Jesus of Nazareth as that personality. But there is no doubt that Zohar's many-colored, glittering, sonorous and often repeated Trinitarian formulæ give rise to such a view; his vague and abstruse doctrines are offering aspects, vistas and striking analogies, running in parallel lines with Trinitarian views. As such they were joyfully conceived and accepted at the close of the middle ages by many Christian writers; as such they were looked upon by many Jewish ones. Soon after our book was made known among Christian theologians, they were carried away by that new and unexpected ally

1 "Graetz's History of the Jews," vii., 249.

from Jewish quarters. There was a rush for the study of Hebrew and Aramaic, with the sole object in view to fathom the Qabbala, and especially its central work, the Zohar, and bring to light newly discovered mysteries, treasures of hidden wisdom and faith bearing upon Christianity.

PAULUS DE HEREDIA.

Paulus de Heredia, in the fifteenth century, and many other converts from Judaism, were the first to claim the discovery that the authors of the Talmud and the Qabbala were adherents to the teachings and the Messiahship of Nazareth. The grain of truth in all such affirmations is, that some of the Talmudical teachers and more Qabbalists were entertaining ideas in some sense parallel to Christian Gnosticism, hailing from Neoplatonism, as we shall further see, and that the Jews expected a supernatural liberator, as Jewish orthodoxy does even now. Again, it is true that for several centuries, until the beginning of the fourth one P. C., the difference between Jews and Christians was solely on that point, that the former were expecting the Messiah to come, and the latter claimed he had come, has disappeared, and is about to come again and realize his "kingdom of heaven." It is only after politics had taken the place of ethics and soldiers that of philosophers, viz: with the Cæsars and the Patricians dictating dogmatics, that the antagonism between them became fierce and radical, that two creeds came out of the strife and that Jews and Christians were divorced from one another.

When the courts of Byzantium and of Rome took the helm of the Church, they dropped the real points at issue, viz: the teachings of Nazareth; they ignored and hushed the real questions raised by that school, viz: whether Jerusalem or Rome, God or Cæsar, monotheism or polytheism should reign; whether right and duty, or force and selfishness, should be the rule of conduct. All that was thrown out of sight. Rome, with its old policy, etc., remained mistress. Only from prudence and by way of accommodation and policy, it inscribed upon its banners the name of the "Christ," exalted in words the Son of God and worshipped the "Mother of God" and the Saints, with their relics and shrines, etc., while the old Cæsarian regime remained under new names. From Nazareth to Moriah the gap could yet be bridged over; it is Cæsar who handed the letter of divorce; he who made the gulf impassable.

Paulus de Heredia had written many books to prove his standpoint. Pic de Mirandolia, of world-fame in his age, studied Hebrew, busied himself with Qabbalistic books, became infatuated and charmed with that study, claiming it to be the great science, the reservoir of the doctrines of Christianity: so especially in his "Apologia" (p. 42, etc.) At about the same time Reuchlin, the great German scholar, was deep in the study of that new scientific discipline, laboring under the same illusion of new truths discovered, revelling in the empty mysteries of the Zohar, with its *"Sephiroth* and *Gematrioth,"* the divine emanations, numerical combinations and notarikons, believing there to find the hidden head-waters of the great theological Nile, the Victoria-Nianza Lake and source of Christian dogmatics. The renowned Reuchlin wrote his work, "De Arta Qabbalistica" in 1517, in which it is tried to show that Christology is to be found in the Aggada and especially in the Qabbala; that in this latter one Judaism and Christianity are at one. That was a strong illusion, though it is true that the sources of Christianity are derived from Jewish mysticism of old, as shown here and further on.

EGIDIO DE VITERBO. GALATINUS.

The general of the Augustine Order, Egidio de Viterbo, thought the same thing and zealously studied that hidden lore. He, as also Pope Sextus IV., had many Qabbalistic works translated into Latin to serve for the same purpose. In 1518, another book was written to prove the same hypothesis, so important it seemed during the epoch of the dawn of the Reformation. Under the name of *De Arcanis Catholicae Veritatis,* Petrus Galatinus, a Franciscan monk, compiled all those passages of the Qabbala that might bear a Trinitarian construction, and of which, apparently, there are many in our book. Nor could it be otherwise, since Jew and Christian were permeated by the same hopes and the same ideas: the amelioration of the human condition, and both were expecting ethical and social improvement, not from individual efforts and personal deeds, not from education, scientific, moral and intellectual; not through peace, righteousness and wisdom, as proposed by the prophets, by other great ethical leaders and by philanthropic scientists, but as taught by mysticism, or as claimed by men of nostrums and charms, awaiting it gratuitously, by miraculous intervention. Neither party could help wandering off the right path and losing themselves in the clouds of supernaturalism. As the Christian world bowed at the shrines and to the dry bones of Saints, even so did their Jewish contemporaries, the modern mystics and *Hassidai* worship the "Qabbalist," the "*Zaddiq,*" the "holy man," who could by supernatural charms and puerile combinations of letters, etc,,[1] dictate even to the Deity and raise entire nature out of its hinges. Though a mystic himself, Abraham Levi, afraid of the mystic craze proceeding to excesses, exclaimed: "The Qabbalists pray not to God, but to the Sephiroth (divine emanations)."[2] Christians and Jews, in place of hastening the advent of the true Messiah, viz: human improvement through righteousness and wisdom, as taught by the prophets and by Jesus himself, imagined to achieve that through mystic formulæ and supernatural spells. Hence we need not wonder at their coincidence on this point, for the same cause brought about the same effect. So, too, as the non-arrival of the Jewish Messiah had several times induced wholesale conversions to the ranks of the surrounding majority, even so the non-realization of the Christian Messianic hopes is now causing daily lapses into scoffing infidelity and materialism, the majorities of the majority. Mysticism is a dangerous arm, it cuts both ways: him who upholds it as him against whom it is raised. The Christian theologians used the Qabbala as their auxiliary. Jewish mystics exalted it as their salvation. It became a source of superstition to the thoughtless among both sets of adherents.

---

1 נמטריות נטריקן צירוף and cameas. 2 See "Kerem Chemed," ix., 141.

The Jews were speculating to learn from its premises the time and advent, the signs and events of the Messiah. Stupidity urged on cunning wickedness. In 1502 a certain *Lammlein* claimed that Messiah part. Many more individuals followed him in that role. Elia del Medigo (fifteenth century) rose against the craze. He and several other enlightened men openly declared that the Zohar is spurious, without authority, and that its emanation or Sephiroth doctrine is Neo-Platonic—neither original nor Jewish.

MESSIANIC PRETENDERS.

What we have seen explains the most amazing appearance of Sabbatai Zeby, the latest Jewish claimant to the Messiahship, who in the midst of the seventeenth century P. C., could mislead the Orient and the Occident, Jew, Christian and Moslem, to such a degree as to set the world into a commotion for more than a decade. He lived in Smyrna in 1625 and was a narrow Qabbalist of the school of *Luria* and the *Zohar*. His scheme was as follows: In order to restore the world, according to the original divine plan, before the fall of Adam, the Deity had created a great personage, the holy king, Messiah, the Adam Qadmon, whose special task it was to annihilate sin and bring about the epoch of grace—the Christian "kingdom of heaven" upon earth. This Messiah is an incarnation of God. He is the Redeemer and to him worship is due. This modest role he modestly assumed, was his. He as modestly signed himself: "I am Ihvh, your God." One of his successors, Jacob Franck, and his numerous adherents in Poland and Germany, practiced what they taught and passed into a kind of Qabbalistic hybrid Christianity. Later on they established themselves in Offenbach, Germany, near Frankfurt, A. M., ostensibly as Christians, with a Qabbalistic drapery. Another of Sabbatai's successors, a kinsman of his, played that doubtful role in Turkey, inaugurated a Jewish Mohammedism under a hereditary messiah. Both the leaders claimed that the messiah soul of Sabbatai had entered their bodies and given them dominion over men. They motived their conversion with the assumption of thus unifying the three religions of the world, a task imposed upon them by Providence.

MONOTHEISM AND MYSTICISM.

The development of the religious ideas, their doctrines, forms and formulæ are interesting to contemplate. They are as a river with ebb and flood, overflowing and retreating, encroaching and receding, according to the sober or the imaginative bent, the scientific or the poetic moods and tastes of the respective ages. Human history began with fetichism, ancestor-worship, hero and king, star and nature adoration, with an infinity of ceremonies, religious notions and forms. Such was Greek and Hindu worship. Zoroasterism seems to have made the first advance out of that religious chaos. Abrahamism, Mosaism, Prophetism appear to have been further reactions and reforms against such polytheistic cults and theories. Instead of the multitude of gods, temples, priests, rites, worships and offerings in order to propitiate the divine powers, Mosaism reduced the cult to one God, incorporeal, eternal, omnipresent and omniscient—ever present, never visible. It reduced it to one national temple with three holidays and a comparatively simple ritual, with but few sacrifices, at a single place, by one set or family of priests and one tribe of preachers, teachers, judges and temple ministers, the Levites. The original Mosaic cult was a marvel of simplicity. It was a telling protest against Egyptian, Hindu, etc., priestcraft. The spiritual needs of man were well taken care of. The ideas of God and Providence, manhood, womanhood, right and duty, earthly reward for good and punishment for wrong, etc., were well established and utilized as the very foundations of society and made to be the levers of the right conduct of the citizens. But just as much care was taken against encroaching superstitions and priestly usurpations. The lawgiver had the Oriental, powerful hierarchies before his eyes. He did all he could not to let them invade his own politico-religious creation. He limited therefore the religious institution to one temple, to but three yearly holidays, originally, to but few sacrifices, to a plain cult by one responsible, fallible class of priests, thus discarding chances and possibilities for priestly overbearing and the selfishness of hierarchs. In parallel with Mosaism ran Prophetism. The work began by Moses, the reaction against Assyrian and Egyptian priestly encroachments, was continued by the prophets. As every honest reaction it was at times overzealous and radical. The neighboring priesthoods insisted so much on forms and so little on deeds; so the prophets taught the contrary: "What is it that God asks of thee? But justice and truth, mercy and modesty"—I desire mercy, not offerings; "kindness and justice thou shalt practice"—" for God loveth mercy." Mosaism appears to have been the compromise between those two extremes; it was the moderator of the prophetic radicalism. It insisted on the essence, but left space for the forms, too, as the body of the essence. It mediated between the priestly ceremonialism and cold, philosophic rationalism.

But Mosaism had made its reckoning without the host. Man craves for more pomp and more cult than that. He needs such from ever-increasing, real, religious yearnings first, from superstition, hyprocrisy and sheer desire for the marvelous next; and there will always be priests enough to administer to that, to real spiritual needs and to superstitious needs. "Man craves contact with the Deity," says Achilles. He is feeling his constant dependence and helplessness, and wishes God close by, as the child feels best when nearest to the mother. So three times yearly worship was not enough. The women and the young, too, desired to come in contact with the divine. Good deeds, justice and humbleness are too costly prices for reconciliation with the Maker. Ceremonies, sacrifices and fasts are more readily resorted to. The Prophets taught religion essentially to consist in the performance of our duties towards our fellows, as children of the same one Father. But man needs ever more contact with the divine. Gradually the sacrifices were increased, religious pomp added, and at last, side by side with the Moriah Temple appeared the Synagogue, with the many-fold daily prayers, the one hundred daily benedictions, the host of ceremonies and symbols. In place of the one national, central temple in the national capital, arose the many synagogues in every city and every street. Soon came the many churches and many mosques in Christendom and in Islamism, etc. Now look to the multiplicity of gods, goddesses, genii and inferior supernatural beings in Homer, Hesiod, the Orphic and Druidic cults, etc., among Greeks, Romans, Teutons, Gauls, Northmen, Slavs, etc. What a free, wild career to nonsense and superstition! As in hygiene, all that is necessary for health is plain living and following up the natural instincts; while man created for himself an interminable variety of wants and habits with an arsenal of drugs and *nostrums,* in health and in sickness; even so are our religious needs. Instead of reverence to God and justice to man, man created sects and cults and dogmatic worships and propitiations to satisfy his cravings for the marvelous, the mysterious; and selfish, cunning over-reaching is satisfied.

QABBALA'S METHODS.

Even such is the cause and the origin of the modern Qabbala; such it is of old, new and all mysticism. Let me illustrate that by an example. In psalms civ: 2, we read a fine poetical metaphor: "He, God, envelops himself in light, as a habiliment, and spans out the heavens as a tapestry." This the psalmist engrafts upon, as the expounding of, the grand verse of Genesis (i: 3): "And God bade: Let there be light, and there was light." Thereupon the Qabbala, further speculating, builds up its creation system: Light is emanated from God. Light is the substance out of which the universe is shaped. God beamed forth light and impressed into it the forms of existence. So the Talmud and especially the Qabbalistic bible, the *Zohar:* Light is the origin of the world. God spread out a tapestry of light and marked there unto all the existences. Theses are the *Sephiroth,* the ten emanations, the successive creations intervening between the Unknowable, Supreme Being and this our material world. We read in Gen. i: 26: Let us make man in our own image and in our own likeness. The Zohar says: This means the ten *Sephiroth,* all contained in the chief and first Sephira, *Adam Qad-*

mon. The Alexandrine mystics identified that biblical figure of speech with the *Sophia, Logos,* Verb and divine Word or Wisdom. The Judean Essenes and the Christian Gnostics identified it with the Messiah and "Son of God." Many names designate in the Bible the Deity. They are God's attributes; they are identical with the Sephiroth. But in the Qabbala these divine attributes are abstracted and personified as independent entities. They are assumed to be subordinated deities, each with a particular sphere of activity, just as were the Persian Ameshas Spentas. No wonder that in some popular quarters a body, too, was attributed to them. In such a manner came out polytheism, idolatry, anthropomorphism, man-gods and anthropopathism—God with human passions. John's doctrine about Jesus as the Verb, or Logos, had a kindred evolution of thought; and the *Qabbala* with its *Ten Sephiroth* and the heading *Adam Qadmon* had the same origin; all hailing from the Upanishads, Vedanta and Avesta. Hindu-Zoroastrian conceptions came to the Qabbalists by the way of Alexandrine Neo-Platonism, as we shall show further on.

AIN-SOPH. TEN SEPHIROTH. THEIR ORIGIN.

In the preceding pages we have seen the Qabbala teaching that the Supreme One is the Ain-Soph, the All, the Infinite in space and time, unknowable and hence non-existent, Aïn, to human intelligence; that He first brought forth the *celestial man,* with the Ten Sephiroth or divine emanations, intermediate between the Supreme Essence and this world of matter. Let us now look closer to the Sephiroth, their analogies and derivations; these are ten in number, viz: "Crown, Wisdom, Intelligence, Majesty, Grace, Justice, Foundation, Firmness, Splendour, Dominion." Let me premise here that these ten Qabbalistic Sephiroth may well turn out to be identical with the ten fiats of Gen. i. with the ten "sayings" מאמרות of Mishna Abboth and Talmud Hagigah, etc., spoken of in these pages; with the Ameshas Spentas, etc., the divine companions and assistants of Parsee mythology. These latter were shaped after the pattern of the chief grandees of the Persian kings, the Achæmenidæ.

The *Ameshas Spentas* were the genii and patrons, but really personified abstractions of the different parts of the universe and Ahura's divine attributes. We shall later on find more analogies with the Ten Sephiroth.

The following will show the striking kinship of these ideas. We read in Babli Berachoth 16 b: "R. Saphra used to conclude his prayers with these words:[1] "May it please Thee, O Lord, that Thou makest peace in Thy heavenly Council and in the earthly Council." The commentator, *Rashi,* correctly explains "this to refer to the *Divan,* or Senate, of the heavenly genii, the patrons of the respective nations on earth; when these genii are at war, their clients below are so, too." This is a Zoroastrian view, accepted by the Babylonian Talmud and R. Solomon Izhaki. The same permeates later philosophers and mystics down to our present time.

Such are the Ten Sephiroth of the Qabbala. Indeed, each of these sets of divine beings reflects the many sides and features of the Infinite. They are His forces and His attributes. Looking closer to the names and doctrines of the Zohar, we shall find them not original. We shall see, as mentioned, that the Qabbalists took their cue, consciously or not, from earlier thinkers, the Talmud and Jewish mystics, and these in their turn derived their wisdom from more ancient sources, as far back as Brahmanism and Parseeism. Philo and the Alexandrine Platonists teach that God, the Unknowable, first created the Logos, *Sophia,* the only begotten Wisdom, which brought about the world. Aristobul, an earlier Jewish thinker of Alexandria, preceded him in that train of thought: God is the Infinite embracing the unbounded space and time; matter is uncreated; and the *Intellectus Activus,* Logos, shaped the universe. Plato's system is not far off, either; he had taught: God is the highest Idea, and His emanations are spiritual prototypes of all material, existing beings; these types he called Ideas. There is an infinite scale and gradation of such Ideas; all are contained in, and emanations from, the highest God-Idea. Brahmanism

---

[1] י״ר שתשים שלום בפמליא של מעלה ושל מטה.

teaches: The Infinite, or All-God, as unfolding in Brahma, Wishnu, Shiwan and their myriads, the creative, conservative and destructive forces of nature. Parseeism teaches: *Zrvana-Akarana,* Infinite space and Eternity of time, produced Ahura Mazda and Angro-Mainyu, each emanating his court of grandees and his own world. Modern materialism thinks God, the Unknowable, is unfolding in matter and force, and both are eternal. Greek Polytheism taught: Fatum and chaos, differentiating into Ouranos, Chronos and Zeus; Zeus is the brother of Posseidon and Hades; the earth belongs to all, heaven is the empire of Zeus; the sea and the nether-world belong to his brothers. That means, in plain words: boundless space is Ouranos; infinite time, Chronos; and Zeus as the living existence. He, Zeus, gives birth to Athene, wisdom and force, Logos. All the gods are the genii of the material universe and Zeus is the father of gods and of man, the ruler of all. We shall later enlarge upon this topic. Each of these systems had an infinity of inferior powers, deities, agents. We read in Talmud Bably, Hagiga, 12 a: R Zutra, son Toby, in the name of Rab, said: "With ten words was the world created: Wisdom, intelligence, knowledge, force, terror, power, justice, judgment, grace and sympathy."[1]

These are simply attributes of the Deity. The Zohar assumed them as semi-independent, divine beings, under the pompous name of *Sephiroth,* retained some of these and took some other epithets, so as to hide his dependence upon this and other Talmudical and foreign sources. That these *Sephiroth* and Words are essentially identical with the Persian *Ameshas Spentas* and the other genii, we have shown in our treatise on Parseeism.

In the same Talmudical context are marvelous things told of Adam, the first man: "He first occupied the space between earth and heaven, and after he had transgressed, God placed His hands upon him and made him small." Another teacher there repeats: "He was occupying the space from end to end of the universe, and after he had sinned he was reduced to small pro-

---

[1] בעשרה דברים נברא העולם. בחכמה ובתבונה בדעת ובכוח בגערה ובגבורה בצדק ובמשפט בחסד וברחמים.

portions." In Midrash Bereshith Rabba 8 we read alike: "When God created the first man, his body measured from end to end of the world." In the same Midrash and in the same place, we read in reference to Gen. i.: 2: "And the Spirit of God was hovering over the waters." "That was the spirit of the King Messiah."[1] Here we have the origin of the Qabbalistic Sephiroth and Adam Qadmon. Even the expression and term *"Sephiroth"* is not original with the Qabbalists. "Sephiroth" has several meanings. It signifies numbers, of Hebraic origin, ספר ; next a sphere, globe, realm, of Greek origin, σφαιρα ; it means irradiation, emanation, beaming forth of light, from the Latin *sapphirus,* σαπφειρος, in Greek, ספיר in Hebrew; sapphire, etc. Now, in this threefold meaning the term, Sephira, was known long before the Qabbala, as now before us. Pythagoras (540 B. C.) taught that, the principles underlying the universe are not bodies or elements, as assumed by the Ionic naturalistic philosophers, but numbers, ten numbers, are the archtypes of all existence, the proportions, combinations and symbols of the sensual bodies. Here are the Ten Sephiroth, as meaning *numbers.* As to Sephira denoting a sphere, globe, the word recurs most often among the Greek thinkers after Pythagoras, for it is well known that the Pythagorian school taught the earth to be a globe revolving around its own axis and around the sun. They preceded Copernicus and assumed the planets as *spheres.* Finally, Sephira, as light-irradiation, or emanation from the essence of the Deity, that idea pervades all the Platonic, Neo-Platonic and Philonic philosophical systems. It is their very backbone, and from them it came to the Qabbalists.

Here are some further rabbinical analogies: We have seen Adam Qadmon, the first Sephira, is called, as such, *Kether, Crown.* He is presumed to be the divine Viceroy, God-manifested, in contradistinction to God-Unknowable, *Ain Soph.* Now, we find in the following passage the origin of that name and conception. Evidently that goes to prove that the mystics did not draw upon their own imagination, but had Talmudical and Aggadic authorities behind them, and that there may well have existed a Qabbala, a secret philosophy handed down by tradition. In Berachoth 7 a, R. Johanan says: "How do we know that God prays? For we read (Is. lvi.), I shall bring them to My holy mount and delight them in My *house of prayer.*" What does God pray? Rab said: "May I be pleased to conquer My own anger and treat My children rather with My attribute of mercy than with that of justice." Here we have *Akathriel* as the second God, who is expressly surnamed Iah, Ihvh, Zebaoth. Next, we have two further powers, mercy and justice, which later developed into semi-independent divine beings. According to Talmudical mystics, God has mercy and justice as His two leading attributes in the world's dominion. He wears philacteries with proper inscriptions. Such attributes condensed into the Sephiroth, in Qabbala and into Ameshas Spentas in Parseeism, its analogy. The passage continues: "So have we learned, R. Ishmael, son Elisha, said, 'Once upon a time I entered the Holy of Holies to offer incense, and I saw *Akathriel Iah, Ihvh, Zebaoth*[1] sitting upon a high and sublime throne. . . . He said to me: "Ishmael, my son, bless Me," and I said: "Mayest thou be pleased to conquer Thy anger, display Thy mercy and treat Thy children with Thy attribute of love rather than with that of justice." And he nodded with his head. . . . That means to say: "Let not the blessing of a common man be light in thine eyes," modestly closes the Aggada. Now, *Akathriel,* etc., means Kether-El, the divine Crown, Ihvh, Lord of Hosts, viz: of the universe of the Sephiroth. That is the Adam Qadmon, the first Sephira of the Qabbalists. These justly thought that R. Ishmael could not have seen the Unknowable God whom "no living man can see." He saw His Alter-Ego, the first Sephira. Interesting, too, is: "He nodded with His head." So in Homer, Zeus nods assent. Thus the name and conception of that Sephira is rabbinic. Indeed, it is hardly conceivable that the Talmudists imagined God as praying, with philacteries on, asking for man's blessing and nodding assent to a mortal. But some of them have entertained, as Philo, etc., the idea of emanation, of a divine Alter-Ego, a Logos-Metatron. These passages may apply to such,

---

1 וראיתי אכתריאל יה יהוה צבאות ונענע לי בראשו.

be less derogatory and congenial to Persian views. The Aggada abounds in such tales, which the mystics applied to the Sephiroth to avoid irreverence. The prophetic epithet *Zebaoth* may imply, too, the idea of a Sephiroth world. All that is to say that the creative power of the universe was not God Himself, but His derivation, the emanation, called elsewhere Logos, Verb, Sophia, Demiurgos, the Primordeal man, Mithra, Metatron, Brahman, Zeus, etc. Out of such materials scattered in Talmud and Aggada, Greek and Alexandrine philosophers, Hindu and Persian teachers, etc., the comparatively modern Qabbalists have constructed their quaint mystic system of the Infinite or Ain Soph, the Unknowable God, the Ten Sephiroth, his emanations with their sublime, heavenly man, the primordeal Adam, the first and highest Sephira, the Crown Kether, containing all the ten in his bosom, the prophetic Zebaoth, the Logos or Intellectus Activus, the Demiurgos, the working mind of the universe, "the Spirit brooding over the waters" and calling the universe out of chaos. These ten *creative words* of the Rabbis, originally meaning, at the utmost, attributes of the Deity, or its forces, were gradually abstracted, personified and rendered independent *Sephiroth,* divine hypostases in the Zohar with the leading emanation, "Adam Qadmon, Crown," containing them all. Hence the metaphor in Talmud: "Adam the first occupied the space between heaven and earth," quoted above. All that huge chain of reasoning is hanging upon the simple verse in Gen. i. 26: "Let us make a man after our image and likeness." All these mountains of mysticism are hanging by that one hair; Talmud, Parseeism and Upanishads, polytheism, Plato, Philo, Qabbala and Zohar express essentially but that one and same thought.

The Midrash narrates further: "When God had created the first Adam, the angels mistaking him for God Himself, were about entuning the hymn: 'Holy! holy! holy!' To prevent it, God made him fall asleep. . . . That may be compared to a king in his triumphal chariot, accompanied by his Grand Vizier. The people, not knowing which of the two was the king . . . . What would His Majesty do? He ordered him out of the chariot and the people learned to distinguish between the two."

Here is a fine intimation that people should learn to discriminate between the Deity and the Messiah, often confounded in mysticism.

TRIADS IN QABBALA AND ELSEWHERE.

We have seen: The Talmud counts ten creative words; the Qabbala counts ten Sephiroth. Each two Sephiroth have a third one, as intermediate or connecting power. The *system of Ten* is thus identified with the system of three. Two extremes, two poles; one positive, the other negative, the third intermediate. There are thus three triads. The tenth Sephira, *Yessod,* contains the material world. We find such triads, or three united divine powers in all the mystic systems. In India, Brahma, Wishnu and Shivan; in Persia, Ahura Mazda, Agro Mainyu and Mithra; Osiris, Isis and Horus in Egypt; in Judæa, Ihvh, Metatron and the *Holy Spirit,* רוח הקודש or שכינה; in Christendom, the Trinity of God, the Father, the Messianic Mediator and the Holy Ghost. Here, in place of the Rabbinic Metatron stands the Essenian divine Messiah. Its trinity was: God the Father, Christ the Son, and at first, the goddess Mother, later making room for the Holy Ghost. Islam kept clear of mystycism. Nevertheless, later Arabian mystics gave, too, to Mohammed, the last and greatest prophet, a supernatural position. He, too, was primordeal, existing from all eternity, remembering both the mystic Christ and the Qabbalistic Messiah. The identical mystical place was bestowed upon Mohammed, most naturally. God, the Prophet, and Eblis, or Satan, made up the Arabian Trinity, in imitation of the Avesta Trinity. All the Egyptian deities and priesthoods had their triads. Closely seen, the Greek and Assyrian mythologies might be also reduced to the trio system, Ouranos, Chronos and Zeus; the deities of Olympos, of the ocean, and of the Nether-world; Zeus, Poseidon and Hades; Zeus, Athene and Phoibos, later corresponding to Mithra. Dimly conceiving the agents of nature to be three, male, female and offspring; active, passive and combination; attraction, repulsion and compromise, the priest-philosophers formulated their Triads in accordance: first, God, the Unknowable; second, His potentialities, emanations or attributes;

third, the visible, material universe, the object of our senses. So our mysterious, ethical and physical forces, nature's positive and negative magnetism, electricity, etc., with their centripetal and centrifugal properties and their equilibrium, all form a triad in symbolical language. Even such is the Zoharitic mysticism. It is simply poetry, symbolism, imitating all other triads, new names for old ideas. So the Ten Sephiroth have nothing new besides their names. They are figures of speech, dialectics. God is the unknowable substance. Its different aspects, as manifested to the human mind, are cunningly described as ten, for reasons mentioned, and yet to be enlarged upon later. These ten consist of three triads, and the last one is the symbol of the material creation itself; there is "nothing new under the sun." As to be discussed yet later, the Zohar assumes *ten* as the number of his emanations, in imitation of similar theories. But these ten, it claims, are contained in the first *"Kether Crown, Adam Qadmon,"* who is but a reflex, a radiation from the Unknowable God Supreme, *Ain-Soph*. Thus the Zohar teaches an eclectic system; it has phases of monotheism, dualism, trinitarianism, decadism, polytheism, pantheism, rationalism, mysticism and anthropomorphism! It has a good word for all systems and malice to none. It is a compilation of all.

CREATION. MESSIAH. PAUL. JOHN.

Curious enough! Pure, prophetic Mosaism appears to be the only whole-souled monotheistic doctrine. Where ever else we look, the ethical teachers seem to shrink from it. They are bewildered and oppressed by the multiplicity, variety, heterogeneousness of things, all in apparent clash, battling for existence. Failing thus to see unity, they are substituting for it dualism, trinity; decades, polytheism, pantheism. Everywhere they declared the Supreme Deity unknowable and too sublime to create this material universe. Everywhere they imagined the Godhead emanating an agency intermediate between mind and matter. Prophetic Mosaism alone makes an exception. The Gospel of John i: 3, states: "All things were made by the Word." Paul was brimful of the Alexandrine Logos doctrine, the saving Son and Verb, a reflex from imbibed Philonian eclecticism. As Philo attempted to square Greek intermediate divine powers with prophetic monotheism, even so Paul tried to identify Philonian Platonism with Talmudic Judaism. His doctrines that "grace" saves, not work, not practical good deeds and not law; his gloomy view about man's total incapacity to act correctly and attain a salvation by fulfilling his duties, the Thora; hence his only reliance upon God's mercy, and therefore the need of a "Redeemer," the sacrifice of the "divine lamb" as a propitiation, etc., all that hails from Philo's eclectic philosophy.

The Mediator, Logos, Verb, Son, the emanating Power, was to bridge over the chasm between mind and matter; the one reflected in our consciousness, the other perceptible to our senses. Mosaism alone simply states: "In the beginning God created heaven and earth," viz: the intelligible and the material universe. The Talmudists mostly have their intermediate power, Metatron, agent or angel. According to them, the Ten Commandments were delivered by an angel, a voice primordeally created for that purpose. Let us adduce our authorities and references proving this. We read in Talmud Bably Pessachim 54 a: "Seven things were created preliminary to the world: The Thora, repentance, paradise, hell, the divine throne, the temple, the name of the Messiah."[1] In Pirke Abboth v.: 1, we read, similar to Hagiga 12 a: "With ten words was the world created."[2] Could not the Deity create with one fiat? Modestly the Rabbis give no answer, but say: "We learn by that how great must be the wickedness of those that destroy, and the merit of the just that preserve the universe, created with ten words." These two versions differ slightly in the wording. In Hagiga it reads: "With ten words, *debarim*." In Abboth quoted we find: With ten sayings, *mamaroth*." Now, this latter version closely alludes to the ten "sayings," biddings or fiats of Gen., chap. i., where it is ten times repeated: "And God said."[3] The meaning simply is: God effected the creation

---

1 תניא שבעה דברים נבראו קודם שנברא העולם. תורה תשיבה גן עדן ונהינם, וכסא כבוד ושמו של משיה.

2 בעשרה מאמרות נברא העולם, ומה תלמוד לומר....אלא להפרע מן הרשעים וליתן שכר לצדיקים

3 ויאמר אלהים יהי—Gen. I

in *ten fiats,* repeating ten times: "Let there be," and the universe sprang into existence. The Talmud changed the "sayings" into words; mysticism changed the "words" into the "*Word,*" Verb, angels, emanations; so did John i. 3. Dogmatics made out Christ; the Essenians, Messiah, and the Zohar, Adam Qadmon and the Ten Sephiroth; all are evolutions of the biblical "God *said.*"

GNOSTICS, MAIMONIDES' COSMOLOGY AND SEPHIROTH.

Let us further elucidate. Utilizing the same material and the same methods, the Gnostic [1] Semi-Christians taught: The Supreme Deity has nothing to do with this lowly, perishable, material world. God radiated out of His own luminous substance subordinate divine beings, emanations, *Aeons,* His attributes. These are the creative powers of the material existences. Apparently following the version of our quoted ten creative words of the Talmud (Hagiga 12 a) and the other mystics, Asian and Alexandrianian, they described them with approximately identical metaphors: "Spirit, Intelligence, Wisdom, Love, Truth," etc. The immediate Creator of the world they designated as Demiurgos, world-builder. They stated that the Supreme Deity, the Demiurgos, and the primordeal matter, are the three eternal substances of all existences, the essence, and gave Jesus the role of the Demiurgos, or world-creator. These Gnostics had each their own theory about the Christian founder and his relation to God and man; they had each their own gospel, rejecting all the other ones, and each of their doctrines was claimed as taught by Jesus himself.

Maimonides[2] in *"Yad," "Mada," Foundations of the Law,* ii, 7,

---

[1] Gnostics (gnosis, knowledge). The common name of various semi-philosophical and mystic sectarians during the first centuries P. C. later absorbed by the church, mostly, holding the doctrine of Emanation from the one incomprehensible Divine Essence, "*Ouk on,*" the Qabbala's "*Aïn.*"

[2] Maimonides or Moses, son Maimon, flourished between 1135 to 1204. He was born of renowned Jewish parents, at Cordova. Successfully he studied the sciences of Judaism, Talmud, Greco-Arabic philosophy, especially Aristotle, medicine, and was master of nearly all the knowledge of his century. The religious persecutions by the Moorish princes com-

says on the subject in discussion: "Creation had to do with three kinds of objects: beings with mortal bodies and souls; beings with immortal bodies and souls, as the stars, etc., and, lastly, beings, pure souls without bodies, as the angels. These are the highest in the scale of creatures and are divided into ten categories, or ranks, one higher than the other; their names are: Holy Hajoth, Ophanim, Aralim, Chashmalim, Seraphim, Malachim, Elohim, Bnai Elohim, Cherubim and Ishim.[1] The lowest rank, the Ishim, are those angels that speak with the prophets and appear to them in inspired visions, they being nearest to man. Each order of these angels conceives God according to their respective capacities; less than those above them, more than those below them. Whilst the full and adequate knowledge of God has only God Himself." Plato declares each *Idea* immortal, rising in the scale of existences, reflecting the bodily universe; the highest Idea is He, God. Plato's Ideas appear to be the angels of Maimonides. The latter continues: "God alone knows Himself; He sees the universe within Himself, all beings of the universe drawing their existence from His substance." This theory was followed up by Spinoza to its last consequences, in *his Ethics*. Thus the rationalistic Maimon-

---

pelled him to interrupt his studies, leave his country and flee, first to Fez and then to Jerusalem (1165), and soon he took up his definite abode in Fostat, opposite of Cairo. He first occupied with commerce for a livelihood, but soon became the body physician of the Sultan of Egypt and the chief of the Hebrew community there. He was the greatest Jewish erudite of his time and, decidedly, the most lucid writer on the Biblical, Talmudical, theologico-philosophical and natural sciences. By his wonderful erudition, his noble and brilliant spirit and character, his vast and various works, composed in Hebrew and in Arabic, on Jewish law and ethics, on philosophy, medicine, etc., he became a leading philosopher, to this day influencing Arabic and Christian thought. But he has acquired a domineering influence upon Judaism especially, and counts among its greatest teachers. Conservative in his Rabbinical works, he was a rationalist in his philosophical ones (More Nebukhim, etc.), and after his death was fiercely attacked by the zealots and his works were excommunicated. At last common sense and justice prevailed, and he became a leading authority on Jewish science. "Between Moses and Moses (Mendelssohn) there was but Moses (Maimonides)."

1 Zohar II, 43 b, gives the identical list of angelic beings.

ides shapes the *Ten Words* of the Talmud and mystics into ten categories of immortal, spiritual beings, all forming the throne and chariot of the Deity, the Prophet Ezekiel's *Mirkaba* being his nearest illustration. He holds yet, quasi, to the Mosaic doctrine of the world's creation as being achieved by God immediately and spontaneously. Whilst Apochryphae, *Aggada,* Qabbala and Zohar especially, assume that He is the Creator only through his emanations. This idea followed up, seems logically to show that creation means emanation, gradual development; that evolution is the eternal law and essential nature of God, identical with His holy Being; that He was not long resting, and then pleased to create, but that evolving worlds from His own existence is His office, His being, from all eternity; the manifestations of His Supreme Self is not accidental nor arbitrary; no, it is one of His many divine attributes; eternal activity, creation, is inherent in His essence. Divine essence, activity and creation are synonymous. From all eternity He has been manifesting Himself in creating, *i. e.,* emanating the beings of the universe. This is the logical consequence of all emanation theories in Aggada, Philo, Maimonides, Qabbala and Zohar down to Spinoza's "Ethics."

Maimonides assumes not only ten ranks of angelic beings, but also as many heavenly bodies or spheres, with the central globe of the earth; they count just *ten* together. He says (Ibidem iii): The spheres (Σφαιραι) are: Shamaim,[1] Raqia, Sebul, Araboth, etc., nine in all. The nearest to us is the moon, the next is Kokhab,[2] then Nogah,[3], then the sun, Meadim,[4] Kokhab Zeduk,[5] Sabbethai,[6] the visible heavens with the stars; the ninth sphere revolves daily from east to west, making all things revolve with its own motion. These spheres, radii, "galgalim," contain and envelop each other and are arranged one above the other (around the earth their common nucleus and center), as the peelings or coats of an *onion,* surrounding their kernel.[7] All these spheres are circular as a globe and the earth hangs in the center,[8] making up the number *ten,* with the other nine spheres. The ninth sphere is divided into the 12 signs of the Zodiak (*the*

---

[1] שמים רקיע זבול ערבית [2] Mercury. [3] Venus. [4] Mars. [5] Jupiter. [6] Saturn. [7] כמי גלדי בצלים [8] והארץ תלויה בעמצא

twelve months of the year.) All these spheres are endowed each, with a soul, knowledge and reason; they are living organisms, conscious of themselves, of the higher angels and of the Deity, offering worship to their Creator. They are inferior in knowledge to the angels, and superior to men. . . . Beneath the sphere of the moon, God created a (golem̃) lifeless body, different from the spheric bodies mentioned; into this body He engraved four forms; each form combines with a portion of that terrestrial body and makes out the elements of fire, air, water and earth, one higher than the other, enveloping one another and filling out all space. These four sublunar bodies are soulless and lifeless, each having its own leader to be guided by . . . . . and all on earth is a compound of these four elements. Maimonides gives here a rough outline of the old rabbinico-scientific universe, inclusive of its astronomy, cosmology, physics and theology. A creative God "in whom every creature is contained"[1] emanated ten ranks of spiritual beings, with ten spheres of heavenly bodies, endowed each with soul and reason; each rank and sphere is gradually, in descending order, enclosing the earth as their common nucleus, and man as its final center.—Closely considered, the Zohar is but a Midrash and commentary on that world-conception, a clumsy, overstrained paraphrase thereof, a diluted and awkward development of that rabbinico-neo-platonical scheme. The emanation theory, the ten Sephiroth, the triads, viz: God manifested through his emanations; the spiritual, cosmological and terrestrial worlds are here. The aggadic and mystic anthropomorphism (Shiur Qoma) alone are the Zoharitic infusion and addition. Later on we shall elucidate that more fully.

MEANING OF SEPHIROTH.

Whether these emanations or *Sephiroth* are but abstractions and divine attributes of the Supreme One, or real independent, divine beings, distinct, subordinate deities, the mystics are not plain and explicit about it, nor consistent with themselves; less so are they at one with one another. On the whole, we shall come

---

[1] כל הנמצאים מכוח אמתתו נמצאים, ולפי שהוא יודע עצמו הוא יודע הכל, שהוא אינו יודע בדיעה חוץ ממנו.—Yad II, 9-10.

nearest to the truth by taking their average opinions, so to say. As Plato's Ideas, Philo's Logos, the rabbinic Metatron, or the Essenian Messiah, so the Qabbalistic *Sephiroth* may be assumed to be spiritual substances and potencies, condensed light, irradiations from the Supreme Unknowable; they are primordeal principles, sun-rays, departing from their Supreme Source, gradually leaving their pure spirituality and verging toward opaque growing materiality; until *Yessod,* the lowest *Sephira,* condensing, becomes the world of matter. Or, in other words, the *Sephiroth* are divine forces emanating from the Supreme Existence, the inconceivable Infinite, *Ain-Soph,* slowly darkening and materializing, the farther they depart from their light-source, until at last they become this bodily, sensual world. The systems of Vedanta, Zoroaster and Buddha, Platonism, Neo-Platonism, Philonism, Eessenism, Talmudic mystics, Midrashim, Yezira-book, Gebirol, Maimonides, Qabbala, Zohar, etc., may be well understood by such an interpretation of their common God and creation, etc. ideas. So, too, according to them, when the Bible says: "God's word or God's hand or heart or His love or anger," etc., all such anthropomorphism and anthropopathism must be understood as referring to some of His emanations and hypostases, the Supreme One Himself being too sublime to be affected, to change and to concern Himself with world, man and their affairs. All divine changes and attributes, physical, local, moral, etc., refer to such *Sephiroth* alone, not to the Deity proper. The several biblical names of God, His thirteen attributes or *Midoth* (Exod. xxxiv.: 6), the Talmudical *Ten words* of creation, the Gnostic emanations, the Maimonian and Qabbalistic Ten Sephiroth, etc., just as Plato's Ideas and the Neo-Platonic Logos, Verb, Sophia, etc., are assumed as primordeal, original, divine substances. The irradiated rays from the Deity gradually condensing into this sensual world of matter, have as their opposite pole the demoniacal world, the *Qeliphoth,* the shells, spiritless, lightless matter.

SOUL-RESERVOIR AND MESSIAH.

Abstruse metaphysics will soon be turned to the good account of incomprehensible mysticism. The overdrawn theories of Logos,

Emanations, Demiurgos, Metatron, Sephiroth, Adam Qadmon, etc., became the building material of the Messiah doctrines. They were the elements and the pattern for gradually developing the Messiah-ideal into a concrete, socio-political personage of the grandest dimensions. Thanks to mysticism, the Logos-Demiurgos left the heavenly abode and descended to earth to redeem man and the world from their original taints. That mystic part of the leading Sephira, Adam Qadmon, as Messiah, has been claimed before and after the Christian founder even in modern times, by many: Abraham Abulafia, Lammlein, Isaac Luria, Caro, Sabbatai Zeby and others. The Zohar asks of his followers to be pious, in order to empty the heavenly tabernacle of its pre-existing souls; when the Messiah, the last soul will have the opportunity to make his descent unto this sublunar world. As long as that soul-reservoir is not emptied, that advent cannot take place. The Qabbalists namely assume that all souls are pre-existing, awaiting their turn to animate their respective bodies and make their pilgrimage through the world, called transmigration. The Messiah is the very last and greatest soul of that spirit-receptacle. Of course, that is a new view; it clashes strongly with the original claim that he is the very first and holiest divine emanation, the *"Crown."* The argument is: the leading Sephira is the spiritual and perfect pattern of the universe. But this latter one was spoiled by the earthly Adam's fall. At the appointed time the perfect original will be reinstated, by the redeeming celestial Adam Qadmon. That Messiah is the last soul, is a later idea of the Qabbalists. In this sense the pious are thus asked to perform divine worship according to the Qabbalistic rites and methods; in order to empty the soul-reservoir and hasten the advent of the redemption of the world. Particularly is it asked to pray to the Sephiroth themselves. So prays the Hindu to his gods; the Parsee to the Ameshas Spentas; so the Greek to his divinities; so does the Trinitarian to the Holy Mother, the Saints and the Redeemer. This part was claimed in modern times by Sabbatai Zeby who signed himself "I am Ihvh, your God." He pretended to be an incarnation of the Ancient of Days, viz: *Adam Qadmon,* the *"holy king"* of the Zohar, who came to redeem Israel

and the entire world; to gather the first from their dispersion and lead them to the holy city, etc. Similar claims had raised Rabbi Caro. They had all the claims, trappings and paraphernalia of the messiah minus the substance.

not clearly state it; or it expresses freely both opinions, however opposing each other. Nor is it intelligible how they can be separate and distinct from God and yet make one unity with Him. Here is exactly the same difficulty as with the reigning church trinity. Ten Sephiroth distinct from God make altogether eleven, not one. Next, why are these attributes *Ten,* why not myriad, as Spinoza observes? The number ten is arbitrary, or borrowed from elsewhere, as we shall see later. This unison is shown by different metaphors and illustrations. "Who wishes to have an insight into this sacred oneness, let him contemplate, says the Zohar poetically and quaintly, the flame rising from the lamp or the burning coal. At first he sees a twofold light, a clear white one and a dark or purple one; above is the white light rising in a straight line; the dark one appears to be its seat and basis; yet both are intimately connected and form but one flame. This base, the dark light, is connected with the burning material beneath it. The white light never changes its color; it ever remains white. While the dark light beneath it offers several shades of color to the beholder. The dark light below has two opposite directions; it is connected above with the white light, and below with the burning matter. This matter is ever being consumed, and the lower light ever rises to the upper one; in that way is all connected into one unity."[1] This illustration is very quaint and graphic, popularly speaking. But it nearly upsets the entire theory. If the emanations are but the logical irradiations from the Divine Essence, as the flame is from the coal, or the ray from the sunlight, then what for so much ado about them? Then they are no entities at all, no divinities and can have no real conscious influence; they are but God's lustre, or rather shadows; God is the cause and creator and they the effect and creatures. Again God is the cause of innumerable effects; why then ten Sephiroth and not innumerable ones? Thus the entire Sephiroth doctrine is upset and shown to be a fata-morgana, a castle in the air. Besides, that illustration rather illustrates too much and might as well be

---

1 מן דבעי למנדע חכמתא דיחידא קדישא, יסתכל בשלהובא דסלקא מגו נחלתא או בוצינא דדליק"— Zohar I, 50 b. Ed. Wilna.

quoted by materialism. In a vessel with burning coals emitting a flame, the coals are the root and efficient cause, and the flames, dark and white, are the effect. Hence is the material world the reality and the spiritual one its effect and reflex—the very contrary of the Zoharitic doctrine. While the Qabbala and religion postulate just the contrary.

The first three Sephiroth are especially considered as the spiritual, primordeal Substance, and the oneness of the three is illustrated in this manner: Thought is at first a vague and inarticulate feeling; arriving clearer at our consciousness, it *becomes mind,* reason; at last it becomes voice or word. Here are three stages: thought, reason and speech; nevertheless all three are one.[1] Or the three highest Sephiroth may be compared, the first one to knowledge, the second one to the knowing Subject, and the third one to the known object. These three, different in man, are but one in God who is the knowledge, the knowing subject and the known object; yet are all three contained in the same divine Subject. So is all existence centering in the Sephiroth, and all the Sephiroth center in God.[2] It is interesting to remark that this passage about: "God being the knowledge, the knowing subject and the known object and that in Him all three are one,"—is literally taken from Maimonides and Aristotle, later shown as leading to Pantheism.

ZOHAR'S TRIADS AND CHRISTOLOGY.

Let us quote yet one more interesting illustration from the Zohar: "The Ancient of Days has *three heads,* (viz: He reveals Himself in three arch-types, all three forming but one. He is thus symbolized by the number *Three*). They are revealed in each other. (These three heads or arch-substances are): first, secret, hidden *Wisdom;* above that is the (Crown) *Holy Ancient One.* Above that is the Unknowable One. None knows what He contains. He is above all conception. He is therefore called, for man, Non-existing, *Aïn.*"[3] — These three lights radiate their

---

1 Zohar I, 246 b. הוא מחשבה הוא בינה הוא דבור וכלא חד 2 Pardes 55 a.

3 Zohar III, 288 b. בגין כך אקרי אין

light to the other Sephiroth, receiving it all *from the same place.* When the Ancient of Days reveals Himself, they are illuminated and all form one Unity."[1] Further we find the three principles in God denominated as father, mother and son; or wisdom, intelligence and knowledge.[2] The Ancient of Ancients himself, is designated at times also as the *Crown,* the highest Sephira, and has three heads. The other Sephiroth form likewise triads; altogether counting three triads; and above them is the Crown, a sort of Supreme duplicate of deity. Another time the Ancient of Days is designated as dual, viz: the Crown and the Infinite. Again is He there represented as One: the Crown. So too all the Sephiroth form but one unity. The *Crown,* as emanation, is designated in the Qabbala as Creator and Law-giver; just as the Demiurgos of the Gnostics. Thus the formulas of trinity are often enough found in the Qabbala.

Elsewhere we have seen that such formulæ abounded everywhere, with the old religious mystics, therefore also in Jewish mysticism. Hence they entered the Church and became her dominant feature. The formulæ continued in mysticism their own way. Therefore we find them in the Qabbala, where they have retained a certain family likeness with the church trinity, though not fully identical. So the ten Sephiroth form three triads, each of the triads is really but a split unit. All the three triads are united in the first Sephira, the *Crown;* while *The Crown* is but another name for the Infinite; it is the Infinite in His first concentration or revelation. That Infinite or Most Ancient of Days reveals Himself in three arch-types, three heads, and is symbolized by number three, all making but one, The first three Sephiroth form the spiritual primordeal Substance; they are really but one as sensation, thought and word. The remaining seven Sephiroth are further irradiations from the Unknowable, all ten forming with their inscrutable source but one indissoluble Unity.—These are the sonorous formulæ of the Zohar. Wonder that mediæval divines so eagerly caught

---

[1] אלין תלת נהורין. נהרין לאחרינין. וכלא נהיר מאתר חד. כד אתגליא האי עתיקא כלא נהור. וכלא אשתכח בחד שלימתא.—Zohar III, 290 a.

[2] והאי אב ואם ובן, אקרין חכמה בינה ודעת והאי בן אקרי בוכרא, כלא חד מלה.—Zohar III, 291 a.

after these glittering glass-pearls! They but remind one of Goethe's remark: "They look for gold and catch worms. . . . When ideas are lacking, words take their place!" Yet must we not overlook the great and essential difference between the trinity of Qabbala and that of Christology. In the first, it is but a formula, a mystic heirloom, a speculative theory, a metaphor. It is but a numerical illustration to explain the process of mind becoming matter, of one growing into many. It is a screen for human ignorance. In Christology it is a doctrine, positive, concrete. Here the term Crown, Logos, Verb, Sophia, etc., is posited as a concrete person, a man-god, and claimed as a historic fact, an *incarnation* to whom worship is due.

But even such found its initiation in Jewish mysticism. Abraham Abulafia, Sabatai Zeby and others assumed the part of such incarnations of the highest Sephira, the *Crown,* the messiah, the son of God, the primordeal man, Adam Qadmon. We have spoken of Sabatai Zeby of the seventeenth century, in Smyrna. Abulafia exhibited in Italy during the thirteenth century. He did not only speculate in mystics, he practiced, too, the Qabbalistic art in combinations and Notaricon, in letters, initials and words, with their arithmetical value, exchange, transposition, etc. It was a sort of spiritual *alchemy.* By such combinations of letters and numbers, *Gematrioth,* he imagined to be master of all nature and able to influence God, angels and world! He led an adventurous life and tried many bold experiments. Soon he pretended to have revelations, to be the messiah and a divine incarnation. He edited a book claimed to be inspired by God, as Mohammed did the Koran. He announced the end of the exile. After him his disciples continued the same mischief and deluded many simpletons.

SPIEGEL, ASSYRIOLOGY AND GRAETZ ON THAT.

Among others the late noble and great Jewish historian, Prof. H. Graetz, is of the opinion that the Qabbala contains really many trinitarian views. Dr. J. Hamburger thinks, not. Many of the above quotations, I annotated according to them. The latter one remarks that the Christian dogma posits trinity in God himself, while the Qabbalistic triads are but in the Sephiroth, especially in the first one. Yet we must remember that in the Zohar the first Sephira is termed the Ancient of Days and also Ancient of Ancients, originally applying to God only; either of them is called *Crown,* the divine *Alter-ego,* and in either the Triad is claimed to exist. Here is a sort of Christian Tri-unity.—According to Fr. Spiegel, (Avesta Vendidad, p. 271, Ed. Leipsic 1852), the Assyrian mythology too differentiated Bel, Baal, Supreme Lord, from Bel the younger, the Demiurgos. *Zrvana-Akarana* of Hindu-Persian origin means the *Ancient of Days, who,* at the creation, developed into Ahura Mazda, the Creator in fact. Fr. Spiegel says that *Zrvana Akarana* is a discord in the Parsee system, the Avesta hardly ever alluding to him. He claims that mysterious deity to be introduced from Assyria. To me it appears rather a remnant of universal pantheism and nature worship. Pantheistic nature was denominated Zrvana Akarana, viz: Eternity of Time and Infinity of Space. So it was in Assyria. So later Judæan mystics called the Supreme Deity, Maqom, the space of the world. From there Daniel and Qabbalists took their *Ancient of Days,* viz: Eternity of Time. So the first Sephira, not God, became the Creator, Demiurgos; and so in Assyria, not Bel the old, but Bel the younger, had that part. I find rather the salient distinction between Qabbala and Christology in this: Church dogmatics teach messiah as a real, historic person, while in the Qabbala he is an abstraction, a speculation, a theory. At any rate the Zohar following the same models, as other mystics, had given free career to trinitarian philosophems and many have taken such vague dreams for real doctrines. No less than six leading scholars are counted by Dr. J. Hamburger, who have claimed to find in the *Zoharitic* system Christian trinitarianism. Thus it cannot be denied that the Qabbala gives scope to such ideas.

QABBALA AND MESSIAH. KANT.

Let us resume the above said. The ten times repeated verse: God said: "*Let there be,*" of Gen. i., poetically developed in the

Talmud into *Ten Creative Words;* in the Aggada, Midrashim and Maimonides, into ten angels or divine agents; in the Qabbala, Jewish philosophers and mysticism, into ten Sephiroth, the Supreme divine emanations creating the universe. No doubt Philo and the Essenians, Persian, Hindu and Greek thinkers were intermediate links in that chain of reasoning. They speculated in the same line and brought out their Athman, Logos, Verb, Sophia, etc., as in the old tongues "to *think* and to *speak*" have but one word. So too John i, 1, etc.: "In the beginning was the Word (emphasized), and the Word was with God, and the Word was God. In the beginning it was with God. . . . All things were made by Him. . . . In Him was life." Critically looked at, all these various mysterious names and speculations, Verb, Logos, Athman, Manthra, Spenta, Bel the Son, Mithra, Metatron, Christ, Angels, Messiah, Sephiroth, Emanations, etc., that mountain of speculations hangs on the simple, salient, rational verse, repeated at each creative evolution in Gen. i.: "*And God said let there be,*" which tractate *Abboth* introduced with the wise remark: "Could not God make the world with one word?" And modestly answers: "It but intends to teach man the importance of the world and of duty; to come up to its universal laws and not to infringe upon them." Why did not our philosophers take an example from that sober, solid, common sense and save for mankind so much waste of brain with their meteor-like speculations! The great and honest Kant (1724-1804) destroyed all these pompous idols. He showed conclusively that we know nothing about these matters; all such speculations transcend our faculties; we can affirm nothing about the first cause or the final cause, the universe with or without an end, eternal or created; only, for all practical purposes, we may say, existence has a cause and universal laws that must be respected. Mosaism affirms no more than this salient common sense view.

ARISTOTLE, MAIMONIDES, QABBALA AND CORDUERO.

I shall give here a closer literal and full translation of a passage hinted at above, showing pantheistic phases in the Qabbala after having looked at its trinitarian formulæ. It says: "The three first Sephiroth, Crown, Wisdom and Intelligence, form one unity. The first is the knowledge, the second is the knowing one, and the third is the known thing. These three are different things in man; for in man is knowledge different from the subject of the knowledge which contains the object, and which object again is different from the subject. The terms here are: the thinking, the thinker and the thought of object. But God, who does not think anything outside of Himself, *since everything exists within Himself,* sees and knows but Himself; He knows and sees all that is. God is the type of all knowledge and of all beings. Thus the form (viz: the spiritual essence) of all existences in the universe is derived from the Sephiroth and that of the Sephiroth is contained in the Source whence they flow.[1] Now this is a pantheistic view of the universe: "Everything that exists, exists in God, and God thinks and sees nothing but what is in Himself."—That is the logical conclusion of the Sephiroth or emanation theory. Another remarkable fact is that this entire passage is remorselessly copied from Maimonides. He says in Yad, Mada, foundations of the Thora ii.: 9-14: "All created things, the highest as the lowest, draw their existence from God's essence; hence He knowing Himself, fully knows all that is. We, men, and our knowledge are different things. But as to God Himself, His knowledge and His being are all one and the same and absolutely identical. . . . He is the knowing subject, the known object and the knowledge; all three are one in Him. . . . Therefore does He know the creatures not as we do, outside of ourselves, but because He knows Himself, He needs must know all, all being derived from Him . . . ."

Had Maimonides been a layman, a rigid logician, a simple philosopher and not at the same time a pious Jew and a Rabbi, he would have concluded: "Therefore does He know the creatures not, as we do, as existing out of ourselves, objectively; no, He knows them subjectively, as contained within Himself. He being the essence of all existence and containing the forms or types of all the creatures. Such plain words we shall see in the bold argument of Aristotle. Maimonides avoids, dexterously,

---

1 Pardes Rimonim 55a—the most scientific Commentary of the Zohar.

this pantheistic reasoning; he does it dialectically; he concludes: "God knows all because all derives from Him." Maimonides postulates thus God as being outside of and above creation. He believes by dialectics to satisfy his biblical conscience. He feels the difficulty and concludes: "These are abstruse things and the uninitiated should not meddle with them." The same argument we find in Maimonides, Yad, Mada, H. Tschuba v.: 5. Dealing with the difficult problem of substantiating and squaring the moral freedom of man with the omniscience and prescience of God, he says: "Know that this question is very vast; difficult and many-sided. But thou must remember what I mentioned already before, viz: That the Holy One, blessed be His name, has no knowledge and ideas external of Himself, as men do who are different from their conceptions and ideas. As to the Supreme One, He and His knowledge are one and the same; something which human reason cannot fully grasp. Just as one cannot fully understand the divine essence, even so can we not His omniscience. But we see plainly that our deeds depend upon ourselves and that we are morally free, therefore are we responsible for our conduct." Here too we see that the theologian tries to conciliate faith with free thought, Mosaism with Aristotle and fact; and where he cannot succeed, he lets them stand side by side, declaring the incompatibility coming from human insufficiency, he remaining loyal to both. Thus he imitates Saadia, Philo and other thinkers, bridging over the difficulty with dialectics, or modestly saying: "I know not." His opponent and critic there, *Rabed,* sneers at his embarrassment and pointedly reminds: "What one cannot answer is best not to ask."

NEHEMIAH BRUELL, OF FRANKFURT, ON THAT.

More elaborate and untrammeled is the philosopher Maimonides, treating that theme in his "Guide of the Erring." I had on that a pointed correspondence with the great scholar and writer, the late Dr. Nehemiah Bruell, of Frankfurt, A. M.[1]

[1] Rev. Dr. N. Bruell may not be much known to the American reader and this note will be welcome: He was the late Chief Rabbi of the

The correspondence sets it forth and N. Bruell's letter is doubly interesting, by itself, and as it is, besides, his last scientific utterance on earth. The reader will not be sorry to find it here verbatim. I had inquired of him, as follows, on January 11th, 1891, concerning:

THE GOD-IDEA, BY ARISTOTLE AND MAIMONIDES.

"*Reverend Sir*—Allow me to call your attention to the following interesting passage in Maimonides' 'Guide of the Erring,' i.: 68: "It is well known that God is the thought, the thought of object, and the thinking subject.[1] . . . . God is the absolute thought, thinking Himself. . . . For the very essence of God is to think, viz: in actuality; never simply in potentiality. He thinks something, of which he bears the form (viz: the spiritual essence) within Himself, and this form is He Himself; for intellect is nothing else but the thing, the object thought about; . . . . that is, for instance, the form of yonder tree in abstract, and this is identical with the actually thinking agent. . . . . The potential thought and the potential conception or subject-matter, are two different things; but the moment the intellect becomes actual these three—thought, thinker and thought-of—are one thing."'[2]

Maimonides further elaborates his thesis, showing that these three, when in actuality, really are one and the same, claiming that this does not apply to God only, but is so with every intelligent being when really thinking, in actu. Thus far, *Maimonides.* Now, dialectically considered, that reasoning of Maimonides is correct. The thinking subject must think, think of some

historical, leading Hebrew Community of Frankfurt, A. M., one of the foremost scholars and thinkers of learned Germany. Great in Talmud, Philosophy, Theology and Philology, he was well qualified to play a great part in German Judaism if he had lived longer and in congenial times. The prevailing "blood and iron" policy of that period brought him to a premature grave, at 48 years of age. A few days only after this letter, I, amidst the entire community, mournfully bent over his hillock. A wreath to his memory and to blessing be his name!

1 הוא השכל והמשכיל והמושכל, ושאלו השלשה הם ענין אחד.

2 כי אין השכל דבר אלא הדבר המושכל. דבר המושכל הוא צורת האילן המופשטת. והוא השכל ההוה בפועל .... כל שכל בכח ומשכיל בכח הם שנים, וכשהגיע השכל בפועל יהיו השלשה ענינים אחד.

object—that means, conceive its form or spiritual essence. Hence are all three but one thing. So it is dialectically; but how is it logically, really and truly? The singer sings a song; the baritonist chants an air. Are here subject, object and action identical? Hardly! Somewhat clearer does our theme become when we refer to the original author of that doctrine—Aristotle. (Metaph., xii.: 7-9). He says: "God is the highest thought, thinking Himself. The divine thought is the object of His thought." [1]

Clearer yet do we find that theory in Aristotle's "De Animus," (ii.: 2), where we read: "The soul is the place of the forms (τοποσ αιδολων). It is never in contact with bodies. This active intellect (νουσ ροιητικὸοσ, not παθητικὸοσ) is the cause that every other intellect is really thinking, in actuality, that it is appropriating to itself the forms of things, identifying itself with them. Hence God, the active intellect in the highest potency, does not conceive the bodies, but only their innermost essence, the forms. God is just the highest form or essence of things, and the object of His idea is He Himself, *i. e.* the form of things. Hence, are in God thinker thought and thought-of, one and the same thing."—So far, Aristotle.

Now, this doctrine is pure Pantheism—Pantheism, nothing more nor less. Indeed, Aristotle's philosophy is Pantheism. But since this is not that of Maimonides; since, according to him, God is extra-mundane, creator of the material universe, made *ex nihilo,* since he is believing in and teaching that doctrine, not Aristotle's eternal matter; hence is Maimonides' claim that in God is thought, thinker and thought-of object one and the same thing, unsubstantiated, out of order and place. Exactly as that assertion is a fallacy in reality; for to know an object is to conceive a true image of its essence, to contemplate

---

1 "Αυτον αρα νοεῖ, ειπερ εστο το κρατιστον, και εστιν η νὸεσισ νοηεωσ νὸησισ." There too, he says even more explicitly: "Αυτον δε νοἒι ὁ νουσ κατα μεταλεψιν τοῦ νοητοὺ; νοητοσ γαρ γιγνεται θιγγανων κ̣αὶ νοῶν. ὡστε ταυτον νοῦσ και νοητον." The Intelligence comprehends itself in comprehending the intelligible; and it becomes the intelligible by that very act of comprehension . . . In that manner are the intelligence and the intelligible one and the same.—So reason, reasoner and reasoned are one and the same in God."

its correct reflex in our mind. Now, this reflex is neither identical with ourselves nor with the thing itself. Our ego and that image are and remain two things, the word "form" so indefinite and meaning vastly different things, once and now, is the cause of this confusion. (See "Religious Rites and Ideas," p. 56, on Maimonides and Spinoza). M. FLUEGEL.

N. Bruell replied: "*Esteemed Sir*—The chapter in Maimonides' Guide, whose contents you criticize in your kind letter, has caused much head-breaking to its commentators. According to Maimonides' theory, the intellect has no independent existence. It is the conception of something understood; so much so that subject and object are but one. Besides the intellect, there is, according to Maimonides, but a number of ideas arrived at by perception. Applied to the Godhead, it follows that there can be with God no question of any knowledge acquired by perception, the Deity being the absolute omniscience, in æterno. Hence, subject and object of conception cannot be separated in reference to God, they are necessarily identical in Him. This theory of Maimonides undoubtedly may lead, as you justly remark, to pantheism. Yet is pantheism not an absolute consequence thereof. The idea of the world was in God from all eternity. But God needs not on that account be in the idea of His creation. God realized the idea as His object. Nevertheless, He remains the active subject in whom the world ever was extant.

"The above is brought out only as the sense of Maimonides. I personally do not hold a theology basing on Aristotelian philosophems as a correct basis of Judaism, which as yet has no theology, in the close sense of the term, nor is such a theology recognized or desired by its adherents. Frankfurt, 14th January, 1891." N. BRUELL.

The forelast paragraph of Rabbi N. Bruell's letter might be questioned. He says: "The idea of the world was in God from all eternity, but God needs not on that acount be in the idea of His creation. God realized the idea as His object, etc." But Maimonides, after Aristotle, stated that with God is the act of thinking, the thinking subject and the thinking object identical; that God is thinking and that the divine thought is creation; that it is the divine essence to think, which thinking is creating, viz: emanating matter and mind. Hence was God thinking, viz: emanating the universe from all eternity! The better way of defending Maimonides against the reproach of Pantheism is perhaps the interpretation that with Maimonides, emanation means really creation; hence was the universe, materially, not in God, but externally as matter, a creation, extraneous to Himself, He being not the immanent Cause, but the supernatural, supra-mundane Creator, and that no doubt is not Pantheism, but is the biblical view.

MAIMONIDES, PLATO, NEO-PLATONISTS.

In this last quoted passage from the "Guide," Maimonides is more outspoken than in his religious compendium, the *Yad-Hahesaqa.* Here is the philosopher preponderant; and he is plain: God is the thought, the object thought about, and the thinking subject. He is the absolute thought; the ever active and eternally thinking, spiritual essence, thinking Himself. His very essence is thinking and His thinking essentially means, creating. The divine thought is creation. The universe is, ideally, in God's mind. He is the type of all existence. Now it is true that Maimonides advances the biblical creation of matter, extraneous of God. Aristotle, on the contrary, practically accépted matter to be uncreated and co-eternal with God. Nevertheless the argument of Aristotle and of Maimonides is essentially and really tending, yea leading downright to Pantheism. Plato placed all the reality of being in his Ideas, the types of things sensual, the Ideas alone are real and eternal. The single bodies and their classes are their clumsy moulds, their perishable and ephemeral habiliments, really non-existing. Yet in as far as they appear to be, they are co-eternal with the Ideas; with mind. What then is the cause and genesis of matter, unreal, yet apparent? He offers no solution. He cannot bridge over the chasm. But He inclines to monism and pantheism, against apparent dualism; though we see mind and matter, the first alone is real, the last is but appearance. As to the Neo-Platonists, they are even nearer to Pantheism. They were logicians and metaphysicians. They logically gave up the Platonic apparent dualism, the division of existence into mind and matter, both co-eternal; they accepted monism with the emanation doctrine. According to them, there existed from all eternity but one substance, mind, which evolved, emanated from its mysterious bosom, matter. Matter is but a gradual condensation of mind. The farther the emanated creatures are from their original, luminous source, the less ideal, pure and lustrous they become. Matter is simply the opposite pole of light, the other end in the scale of being. God is the mysterious essence and source of creation, and creation is its spreading wave and ocean, to use a Qabbalistical illustration. One luminous pole is mind, the opposite dark pole is matter. This is the logical reasoning and development of the Neo-Platonic emanation doctrine. This is too that of the ten Sephiroth doctrines, of Qabbala and Zohar. Even Plato's God, the highest Idea, with the descending scale of Ideas, types of the waning material beings, is really identical with the above. He postulated matter as eternal, yet giving pre-eminence to mind. He taught dualism practically, as a dark fact, as a preliminary hypothesis. His successors logically made the next step. The Neo-Platonists logically posited instead: Mind as the source of all and matter as its shadow and derivation. Does not that lead to Pantheism?

SPINOZA'S DOCTRINE.

Spinoza[1] spoke the last word: Mind and matter are no categories of existence. In God they are but one thing, for man's eye is everything and all being, as a broken ray, split in these two; really they are one. Man only sees things under these two aspects, as through differently colored eyeglasses. Mind and matter refer only to near-sighted man. He taught: Substance is that alone that exists by itself, by its inherent force, without any external assistance, nor cause; it is its own cause. Such a

[1] Amsterdam and Haag, 1632–1677, of Jewish, Portuguese parents, emigrated to Holland.

substance then can be but one, and this one must be God. It is not reason, will, creator, thought, extension, mind or matter! No! It is all that together and has innumerable attributes more; it is eternal and infinite, and so are its attributes. Human reason looks upon all being as mind or matter, but really the divine attributes are infinite. Mind and matter are human modes only of conceiving nature. Both are esentially the same substance, two parallels ever running alongside in the same substratum. Soul and body are thus identical, but looked upon from different standpoints or attributes; so bodily movement is mental thinking. All single beings, ideas or bodies, are but mere accidents, modes of the same substance. They are akin to the waves and the ocean; and even less than that: for the single beings have no reality whatsoever. The only real in all finite things is the Substance, God. God is not identical with the sum of all things or nature; these we, men, only imagine. No, God is to us the unknown reality of all existences. Nature is but the screen hiding the reality, and that hidden reality is God, the one, only and homogeneous Substance, the essence and substratum of the apparent, fallacious universe, which we men designate as matter and mind, extension and thought. As a man in a dark cave, with two windows painted, one blue, one green, sees all things blue and green, while in reality the things are of all colors. Thus Spinoza does not deny God. No, he denies the world. All is sunk into the abyss of the unknowable Substance, so constituted that the abyss of dualism, thought and extension is bridged over. They are identical, looked at with a different glass.—Maimonides and Zohar stopped yet in time not to fall into that abyss, that "lion's cave, where all steps lead into and none out," the boldest, yet most consistent philosophy. Pantheism is repugnant to the positive religionist, not so much on account of its theology, as for its ethics, viz: for its wrecked ethics. It leaves no room for freedom, willpower, effort, initiative, morality, virtue, human responsibility. The entire universe becomes thus a cast-iron machine. Stern necessity, crushing, infinite casuality governs man too; the Greek Fate, grins everywhere into our faces. All human strivings are scorned down. No free will, no choice, no use of efforts, no merit, no demerit, no good and no evil. The only rule of conduct is: Submit! for you *must!*[1]—Hence can no lawgiver, religionist, or moralist practically accept Spinoza's Pantheism. Nor could so Maimonides, nor Qabbala; both are eminently practical in their last reasonings and conclusions. Both sacrificed theoretical principle and logic to practical utility. Both accepted the premises, but stopped short of their ominous conclusions. Both started with monoism and emanation, but soon changed horses and rode smoothly emanation into creation. God, from immanent, became extra-mundane, supernatural. But thus they found a base for ethical teachings, free will, meritorious deeds, and got rid of grim Baal, iron necessity, fatalism.

Maimonides in good time accepted creation of matter. While the Zohar traveled further on the slippery road of neo-platonism and broke off midway. Without caring for logic or for consequences, it shows the practical human world as the offspring of emanation or creation, as you please, dropping metaphysics and going along with mysticism of the grossest kind. After having given a most sublime definition of the Supreme Principle and the universe, as Infinite, Unknowable and gradual light-radiation, the Qabbala stops short in the applied parts of the system and, by means of the personified Sephiroth and Adam Qadmon, it metaphorically depicts the Godhead as a monstrous man, following the gross anthropomorphism and anthropopathism of the most puerile and grotesque mysticism of antique times and of the middle ages, of the Brahmans and the *Shiur Qoma.* It followed no doubt the popular drift of its own times, to such an extent as to render the Supreme Ruler subservient to the miracle-worker and the Qabbalistic Saint, by means of combinations of letters and initials, of substitutions, numerical values, childish far-fetched exegesis and monstrous allegories. "Du sublime au ridicule il n'y a qu'un pas." This huge import of the Saints, as most of its leading theories, stands not isolated in the Qabbala. It is not of Vedánta, but of Brahmanic origin. There, too, are Manu and the Rishis stronger

1 Later we shall see, that is the view of the Vedanta philosophy. Yet it is independently arrived at and differently conceived by Spinoza.

than the gods. They assisted, it is claimed, in creation, and their prayers can even over-rule the Divine will. (See on that "Zend Avesta," etc., chapter Brahmanism). But even the Rabbis entertained like views. (Bably Sanhedrin 93 a). So said R. Johanan: "Great are the Saints, yea, even superior to the angels of the Divine Presence," (Malachai Hashareth), quoting in proof Daniel iii.: 25, where Chanania, Mishael and Asariah have the pre-eminence over Gabriel. The passage there continues: "The Holy One, blessed be He, desired to turn the universe into blood, when he looked at Chanania, Mishael and Asariah, and His ire cooled down."—While the Vedanta seems to award the price to the thinkers, not the Saints. I mention this to show that H. Graetz exaggerates when he says, that the Qabbala cannot connect with and refer to the Talmud as an authority to its statements. We shall later on enlarge upon these topics.

In the following pages and verbatim Zoharitic quotations we shall see that the above passages from Maimonides have been understood and used by mystic writers and Qabbalists after him, as really embodying the neo-platonic doctrine of emanation, and as offering the basis for the ten Sephiroth and the developed creation doctrines; that they followed that dangerous path to the very brink of Pantheism; in one word, that the Zoharic doctrine is pantheistic; that when fully in sight thereof, they, as Aeneas before Charybdis, abruptly left that dangerous sea and skipped over, by a bold salto-mortale, to mysticism, to the emanated God of the Sephiroth who, they claimed, led them back home to Mosaism and the Bible, of course, both rearranged in their own way by their exaggerated Philonian methods of artificial interpretation and allegoric exegesis.

We shall further see that Spinoza, though he has broken with the synagogue, had profited by his education there; that he must have been well acquainted with the rabbinical, the Maimonidian and the Qabbalistical literatures, bringing to him the pith and marrow of Talmudical and Alexandrine metaphysics and mysticism. Though passing in silence the Aggadas and scoffing at the mystics, he was familiar with both, themselves and their Greek predecessors. He profited by the metaphysical thoughts of Neo-Platonism, down to its latest developments, by way of Philo, Talmud, Gebirol, Maimonides and the Qabbalists. No doubt, he did not find there his theory fully elaborated and complete. Far from that; they never had the intention of building up a system antagonistic to the Bible. Never did they realize the fatal consequences of their accepted emanation premises. They went with these premises as far as pleased, and threw them to the winds when no longer utilitarian. Logic was not the strong point of the Qabbala. Spinoza followed out those premises to the last and bitter end. He brushed away their mystic cobwebs and systematized their metaphysics with all their sharp and desolate, logical consequences, not asking whether ethical, biblical, Judaic or not. Prometheus-like, he defied Olympos and arrived at his own stern *Ethics, the* philosophy without fear or favor. Spinoza was no plagiarist, he did not copy his system; he is its author; he is the boldest and most original thinker, the greatest iconoclast that ever lived. An Olympian thunderbolt, a logical aerolite struck his mind; he made it the cornerstone of his theory; he added to it block after block, from base to roof, taken from the quarries of his own thinking soul. He reared his "*Ethics;*" a colossus, a heaven-reaching pyramid, towering above all philosophy now over two centuries after his lifetime; an Egyptian sphinx, holding the thoughtful spellbound at the sad oracles it delivers, in answer to the riddle of the universe. Spinoza indeed constructed and reared that philosophical colossus; but as all other thinkers, he found the materials, in germ or distinct, among his predecessors. He had a long line of spiritual ancestors, the Qabbalists, the Hebrew mediæval philosophers, Maimonides, Gebirol, Saadia, Talmud up to Philo, Aristobul, the Alexandrian Neo-Platonists, Aristotle, Plato, Vedanta, Zoroaster; all offered him some elements to his later doctrines; all furnished him with some blocks to his heaven-storming system built up in his Ethics. Yea, its very foundation stones, the Infinite and Eternal Substance, with its innumerable attributes, mind and matter, thought and extension undifferentiated, inclusive, all may be retraced to germs scattered all along the philosophers' road from Manu and Zend-Avesta to Qabbala, from Brahman and Zrvana-Akarana down to the late Zoharitic Unknowable, Infinite Ain-Soph. Nevertheless there was enough left for Spinoza's originality. The cornerstone is not the full edifice. His predecessors gave the germ and impulse; he followed them up; he added thought to thought, old and new, borrowed and created; he made a whole, a solid structure, cemented with his own heart's blood, the philosophy of his own stern reason, careless of consequences. We shall see, finally, that though the Zohar is brimful of Trinitarian constructions and mystic metaphors, they are but formulæ and phrases, the result of its Neo-Platonic, Vedanta, etc., mystical ancestors; but that, as to the Zoharic metaphysics, rationally followed up, they are leading in a direct, logical line to pantheistic conclusions, an identification of Creator and creation, of God and universe. Of course it broke away from that line; as the Qabbalists, it stopped short; Spinoza did not; he went its full length as a philosopher, never looking to its practical consequences.

SPINOZA. W. WUNDT AND THE QABBALA.

It was in the winter of 1885-86 that I attended a course of lectures by the great scholar and metaphysician, Prof. W. Wundt, of the Leipsic University, on the genesis of Spinoza's philosophy. Discussing with him that subject in the Professor's room in the university, I called his attention to the fact that that Hollandish philosopher had undoubtedly and largely drawn from Jewish sources, too, which he, Prof. Wundt, had not mentioned. As such, I pointed out to him the Spanish Jewish mediæval literature and especially Maimonides' "Yad" and the "Guide." At his request I soon handed to him a literal translation of their corresponding passages, as reproduced above. Later on, in 1888, publishing, in America, a treatise on comparative religious doctrines,[1] I elaborated these parallels and sent him the printed little book. Previously in Leipsic, he had sent me the following letter in kind reply to my memorandum on Maimonides and Spinoza:

"*Honored Sir*—Best thanks for your transmission of passages from Maimonides, which I have read with great interest.

[1] Gedanken ueber Religioese Braeuche.

That they contain echoes of the doctrine of Spinoza, especially concerning the Intellectus Infinitivus, etc., appears to me also beyond any doubt. In many other respects, of course, Spinoza is original, as it cannot be otherwise expected of such a great thinker. Moreover here, too, as in all similar cases, it will be difficult to adduce the proof of direct influence. At any rate, I shall gladly utilize your remarks in my study on Spinoza.—

Leipsic, July 14, 1886." W. WUNDT.

When then in 1888 I sent him the treatise from America, embodying the remarks on Maimonides and Spinoza, etc., he was even more effusive and kind, declaring: "Your historical researches are calculated to vividly interest me," etc. Over a decade has passed since, and studying now this subject more elaborately, in connection with Qabbala, Gebirol, Maimonides and other Jewish mediæval writers, I am happy to find that my hint then was correct. For since Spinoza knew the Qabbala, the more he must have been familiar with Maimonides' "Yad" and "Guide," and must have had a glimpse at least of their predecessors, Gebirol, Saadia, the *Book of Creation*, etc., the expounders, then, of Jewish philosophical thought. Prof. Wundt, acknowledging readily that some of the very central ideas of Spinoza's system are in Maimonides, he opines that, as yet, it will be hard to prove that he actually had any knowledge of their writings, etc. Well, I am prepared to adduce such proofs in his own words and works; such words and ideas being identical with those of Maimonides, Gebirol and Qabbalists.

GEORGE WACHTER ON SPINOZA AND QABBALA.

Indeed, I believe to be enabled to show that, and even more. The familiarity of Spinoza with Jewish literature and the Qabbalists especially, was suspected long ago by the acute reasoner, George Wachter.[1] Of course Wachter shoots beyond the mark, he exaggerates greatly. He insinuates that the entire marble-block edifice of the *Ethics is a plagiarism* from the Qabbala, that Qabbala is but a compilation from preceding writers, and that both Spinozism and Qabbala "amounted to a deification

[1] Spinozism in Judaism, Amsterdam 1699.

of nature, without a living God."[1] Here is an exaggeration in every word and in each allegation. The *Ethics* are as much original as any scientific hypothesis ever was. Spinoza's pantheism is a thoroughly original and gigantic construction, of the most marvelous solidity, for any steel-cold reasoner. It belongs as fully to its Hebraico-Hollandish author as ever did any book or doctrine coming from a human brain. The claim that it belongs *entirely to* Qabbalistic, etc., models is preposterous and highly unjust. The books, properly termed Qabbala, and especially the Zohar, have in part, good metaphysical material, and even some grandly bold and original concepts. But they never formed a solid system, a logically constructed whole, a philosophy. They are philosophems; stray cosmologic, theologic, exegetic, mystic, theosophic, etc., ideas and sentences of a system but loosely connected. They are scattered views and hints of a spread-out series of ethical treatises, as a biblical commentary, a mystic midrash. Even the Talmudical Aggadas and Midrashim are of such a nature and origin. These latter ones are usually abrupt, sporadic, epigrammatic, accidentally and by the way, brought out and broken off ideas and hints, mentioned only to relieve the dry-as-dust discussions of the halacha. How, then, could the solid "Ethics" be a plagiarism from such uncouth originals? A treatise built with the marble squares of the sternest logic, written as a class-book of mathematics, in Cartesian method; without any other cement and ornamentation than the evident love of and search after truth; without fear, bias, pity or remorse! A plagiarism the *"Ethics"* are not! *They are Spinoza's soul,* stern and sharp as a dagger, sublime, clear and vast as the ether, deep and homogeneous as the ocean.

SCHLEIERMACHER ON SPINOZA.

Nobody else could have written them but Spinoza, in his peculiar circumstances: A man saved out of the debris of the ill-starred population of the Marranos; educated in Amsterdam, the stronghold, then, of sectarian dissidents, with all the pent-up passions of cruel wrong suffered and overcome; with a com-

[1] Franck Qabbala, p. 28—V. Cousin, Philosophie, 8th Lesson.

plex education of old Jewish and modern renaissance learning, familiar with Bible and Horace, with Talmud, Philo and Aristotle; with Plotin, Descartes and Zohar; wantonly rejected and cruelly persecuted by the petty tyrants, the hypocritical representatives, the "Parnassim" of the Synagogue; while yet bleeding from the wounds of the inquisition of the Church; misunderstood and overlooked by the masses; hated and feared by their leaders; proudly recognized by the noblest and best; relegated to a village, far away from kin and friend; without opportunity for giving or receiving sympathy; living there as a hermit on a pillar in the desert; deprived of all the amenities of existence, forgetting the world which had forgotten him; yet full of sympathy, love, worship; brimful of the sense of the divine and the sublime; absorbed in his own soul, world-vast and God-inspired; wrapt in the contemplation of nature and its reality behind, the All-God; alone He too, as Spinoza, absorbed in His own divine thought, in self-contemplation, meditating creation, God reflected in the soul of Spinoza, His finite mirror!—Only such a man could conceive the *Ethics,* the One God and only Substance, alone existing; the world and its troubles as but a wild dream, a fata-morgana, a wavelet, a bubble; God the only reality; and Spinoza, human reason, His miniature, mirror and reflex, striving after nothing but the knowledge of that All-God, the only virtue and beatitude worth aspiring at, a life of *Nirvana!* Such are the Ethics of Spinoza, and such only he could write.—Even so the brilliant and philosophic religionist, Schleiermacher (1768-1834 Breslau and Berlin) says: (Discourse on Religion): "Offer with me reverentially a lock of hair to the manes of the saintly, the repudiated Spinoza! He was brimful of the sublime World-Spirit. The Infinite was his begin and his end; the universe his only and eternal love. In holy innocence and profound humility, he mirrored himself in the eternal world and found out how he too was its amiable mirror. He was full of religion, full of the holy spirit. Hence he stands alone and unreached, master in his art, but sublime above the profane guild; without disciples and without rights of citizenship." The philosophy and the religious philosophy of Schleiermacher is strongly tinctured with the best gold of the *Ethics.* Others before and after him borrowed, consciously or not, from Qabbala and Spinoza. Schleiermacher magnanimously proclaimed and acknowledged it.

DESCARTES AND SPINOZA.

Others have claimed that Spinoza had his system entirely suggested by Descartes.[1] Let us examine: Descartes starts with the proposition: "I think, hence I am—Cogito ergo sum—hence, I am not a body but a thinking being, my real self, Ego, is spirit, mind, reason; thinking is my substance. . . . Examining its contents I find that this my thinking substance is harboring ideas which are innate and born with me; not educated, nor derived from my sensual experiences. Such are especially the ideas of God, of mind and of matter: God is the Supreme Being, the author of all existence. He is eternal, infinite, supremely wise, just, moral, veracious—perfect. Hence he must really exist. His existence is evident because it is the necessary complement of His divine perfection, for a being must exist to be perfect. Thus, I cannot doubt that my innate God-idea is correct. It cannot be an invention of my imagination, but must be implanted in my finite mind; in my limited, ethical constitution, by that infinite and eternal Supreme Being. Thus, safely feeling convinced that God exists, all He implanted in me must be true and no deception. For to God's perfection undoubtedly belongs veracity and goodness. Therefore all I clearly see or argue is true and accurate. Hence all my innate ideas about mind and matter are true as they too are self-evident. Mind and matter I clearly see to be the substratum and substance of all single beings I find in the universe. God alone is the absolute and true Substance. He alone is His own Cause. He alone needs not the assistance of any other being, is dependent upon none out of Himself. But He created those two

1 Descartes 1596, France and Holland—V. Cousin, Philosophie, p. 418, pointedly says: "Ne voir dans le Dieu de Descartes qu'un Dieu a la facon de Spinoza, depourvu d'attributs moraux, de volonte et de liberte, et d'ou tout derive par necessite, c'est se former un cartesianism a sa guise pour avoir le triste plaisir de le combattre."

other semi-Substances, mind and matter, as the substratum of the infinity of the single creatures. These two quasi-substances are in so far substances as they need for their existence only the assistance and causality of God. Mind and Matter, soul and body are opposites, ever separate, and held together only by the will of God. Their sole point of contact is in a certain gland of the brain, 'Zuerbel, (Pituitary'?) Their essence is thinking and extension or consciousness and sensual existence, the human Ego is the mind, and his body is matter. Their gap is never bridged over—except by the express and sustained will of God—a continued miraculous interference. Thus Descartes began with defining Substance as Spinoza did; but he abandoned it and allowed two other sub-Substances at the side of the absolute one. He assumes then spirit and body as innate ideas, or thinking and being, as irreconcilable contrasts, etc. . . . held together by the divine will[1] . . . ." What a gap there is between these two systems! Descartes is reverential, religious, full of piety. With all his claim of ever doubting everything and asking rational proof for every affirmation, he admits innate ideas, three substances, creation, liberty, human responsibility, divine Providence, the reality of phenomena—everything our mind and our senses suggest. His doctrine is fairly compatible with our social ethics and our churches. He believes to have proven all satisfactorily; while in reality, it is mostly faith, belief and assumption. Not a word of that is in Spinoza. There all is stern, pitiless, mathematical logic, without the least concession to our inherited views.

JACOB BOEHM. QABBALA AND SPINOZA.

We have seen that the Archilles heel of Spinozism is his ethics together with his sociology, his conception of human history. According to him, an infinite chain of causality connects and irrevocably necessitates all sequence of existences. This too

---

[1] Meditations (I T. p 279), A substance is a thing that exists by itself . . . is its own cause. (Principles I, 51, & T. III, 95) "Properly spoken, that is only God, no creature can be implied in that description. Nevertheless we discriminate between things needing but God's assistance and others dependent upon many created things besides."

is a Vedanta view, properly constructed. All is pre-ordained by Supreme inexorable Divine fate without will, reason, justice, pity or consciousness. The sun shines, the waves roar, the heart feels, the head thinks and the hand acts, all according to that fate. There is no freedom, spontaneity, responsibility in the universe, nor in human history. But Spinozism has another philosophical Archilles heel, no less fatal than the ethical one: Its overstrained monism. There is but one substance and that contains all. That is the sole reality of the universe and its endless varieties. What are then the innumerable things and forms which we behold on this planet and which exist in the entire host of the heavenly bodies? How could that one, homogeneous, Divine Substance become multiplied, presenting such infinite varieties? Spinozism answers: This infinity and variety of phenomena are but appearances, illlusions, deceptions of our senses, or of our imagination. Surely these phenomena are not such as they appear to us; or they do not exist at all; or they do not exist except in their last reality, in the all-absorbing Pan-Substance. But why do our senses, reason, experience charm up these phenomena, these phantoms? What for that deception? Why such persistent shadows? Spinozism offers no solution. It does not know how to bridge over the One Substance to the multiplicity of the phenomenal universe. Here Jacob Boehm steps in and gives us a hint; a rugged, hard-shelled hint, as rugged in sense as in expression, yet worth while pondering over. His theory seems to be: The infinite Divine Principle, as long as it remained one, integral, undifferentiated (before the creation of the universe), containing all in its chaotic bosom, it was impersonal, without consciousness, hence rather non-existing. Only after it disintegrated its oneness into plurality, after Self-distinction and differentiation, after emitting the universe, as different from and objective to Himself, as His emanation, yet His counterpart—only then the Infinite became self-conscious and God-revealed. For only by the contrary, by contrast, everything is clearly defined. Only by the negative, the affirmative becomes elucidated. The Living mind, God, became such, only when differentiated, when conceiving within Himself something different from Himself. And this was the cause of His creating or emanating the universe,[1] the single, multiple, various beings.

This seems to be the sense of the Teutonic mystic. Enigmatic as that appears, it is an attempt at answering the query: What induced the One Infinite Mind to create the multiple finite universe? The bold mystic replies: It is His desire to be revealed. God unknowable was and remained unknown. Only when He called forth finite beings, with reason and consciousness, He became God-manifested in and by the universe, to his rational creatures. It is vague enough, yet it is some sort of solution. Nearly every philosopher tried his ingenuity; but without success. Spinoza showed how all is but One, how the universe is really but the One Divine Substance. But he did not show how that Divine One brought out the multiplicity, the infinite variety of sensual beings, ephemeral and transient, yet staring into our senses and reason? How and why these phenomena? The stern logic of Spinoza offered no solution, no hypothesis. As a disciple of Descartes, he disdained any vague philosophems. That bold but vague reply of Jacob Boehm, the "Philosophus Teutonicus," ventured to propose: The God unknówable, non-existing, because undifferentiated, the divine arch-chaos, desired to be manifested to conscious, rational creatures and He differentiated Himself and emanated such beings.

The question is now, whence did Boehm get this bold theory? A man with hardly any learned education, without a trace of higher culture and any philosophical erudition, modern, Greek, Judaic, Oriental—where did he get such ideas? Who would imagine that the Trinitarian villager, a poor peasant, a herdsman by trade, later a cobbler, speaking and writing in a German

[1] Jacob Boehm (1575), Aurora: Alle Dinge bestehen in ja und nein . . . Das Eine als ja, ist Kraft und Leben, Wahrheit, Gott. Dieser waere in sich selbst unerkenntlich, ohne das Nein. Das Nein ist der Gegenwurf des Ja, auf dass dies Ja, die Wahrheit, offenbar und etwas sei. . . das Ewige Eine urstaendet also in sich, es wird sich selbst zu etwas. Es substanzialisirt sich dadurch dass es sich einfuehrt in die Zweiheit. . . Das Nichts hat ein Verlangen nach dem Etwas, es entwickelt den Gegensatz in sich und ist somit die Quelle des Creaturlichen (der Schoepfung).

jargon, would rise to such lofty bold heterodox speculations, construct such a new hypothesis, raise up mental wings like Giordano Bruno, Spinoza or Leibnitz! Could an illiterate man speculate: "on God in and out of nature," "undifferentiated," the "One Eternal One," the "Silent Non-Being," the "Nothing," the "unfathomable Will," "Emanation and reflection," the "One, as yes, as force and life," as the "Truth, Divine," as God. . . . The "Eternal One" becoming something upon entering on dualism; the "Divine Nothing" craving for something and becoming thus the source of creation; the creative germs of the Trinitarian Infinite, brooding in the depths of the womb of eternal Nature, divided into the scheme of seven categories, one emanated from the other, in orderly succession, forming the seven spiritual sources in which stands eternal Nature as the Arch-principle, (viz: unity, trinity and ten Sephiroth). All the creatures have their origin in the spiritual and divine Entity and become material after long deterioration and corrupting developments caused by sin . . . ." Boehm did away before Spinoza with the impassable gap of mind and matter, both finding their substratum, cause and origin in the one Deity, wherein "both are no longer contrasts, developed by the infinite causality of the same divine life and activity." (Aurora).—Where did Jacob Boehm find these ideas? Where even an impulse, a rudiment, a nucleus to them? Original and a genius, as he may have been, he needed some hint from without, some pre-existing impulse to lead him to his bold speculations! Well, the source of this theory, I think, can be no other but—the Qabbala, the Zohar and all the phalanx of forerunners inclusive of Gebirol, Maimonides, Neo-platonism and even the Upanishads, Vedanta and Talmud! No doubt Boehm could not read them, nor did he ever see them, but close to his humble quarters in Gœrlitz there surely lived some solid Jewish scholar and Qabbalist, as poor and unseemly as that Christian cobbler. Poverty and inquisitiveness made them fellow-students and companions by fate and taste. From that humble Rabbi, Boehm imbibed the doctrines of the Qabbala, Gebirol, etc., late heirs of Hindu speculations. There he heard of these bold investigations about universe and Deity and gradual development. There too he learned about the mystic Infinite and nature (Ain-Soph); God unknowable, hence Nothing (Aïn), who desired to reveal himself and emanated his other Self (Adam Qadmon). There he heard that Gebirol had taught the Divine Will; that Talmud and Maimonides designated Deity as *Absolute Truth;* the theories of emanation, of mind and matter identified in God; His differentiation in order to be revealed; the Ten irradiations or Sephiroth, etc. Boehm constructed these, to him, new ideas, in harmony with his native Christian ones, as the trinity and the seven divine categories, etc.; self-distinction or creation causing God-unknowable to become God-manifested. So the Rabbis also taught: "What for did God call forth creation? In order to be glorified," *i. e.* to be manifested in the consciousness of rational beings. This new light coming from the Qabbala, etc., Boehm received as his morning sun, a new dawn of thought, faith and initiation. As the leading Qabbalistic work, *Zohar, light,* he denominated his first revelations as "Aurora," the morning dawn with the desire of "there kindling up a flame for those who craved to learn."—This is too, in imitation of Maimonides' (More Nebuchim) "Guide for erring ones."

Thus I believe that Jacob Boehm's mysticism is to be logically derived from and genetically retraced to no other source, but the Vedanta, Qabbala and Zohar. I know not whether any one called attention to this fact, viz: that the "*Philosophus Teutonicus*" was really and substantially but a follower of Hebraic and Neo-platonian mysticism amalgamated with Christian Trinitarianism, as a graceful sugar-coat to a bitter heathen pill, Pantheism.

SCHELLING, VEDANTA AND QABBALA.

But not only Jacob Boehm drew from Upanishads, Vedanta and Qabbala. Another even more brilliant genius on the German philosophical horizon, also deeply drank from that mystic source. In his Nature-Philosophy, or rather, his stages, of philosophical developments, where the great eclectic gathered every honey drop he pleased, from every system, age and quarter he chose, passing it through the prism of his all-embracing and distilling brain, into his variegated, versatile, philosphical creations, there he also arrived at views apparently akin to those of Jacob Boehm and in last resort to the Vedanta and the Zohar. I am not prepared to say whether Franz Baader also is connected with that doctrine. In his "Philosophische Untersuchungen ueber das Wesen der Menschlichen Freiheit" (Landshut, 1809), Schelling gives utterance to such doctrines: "He distinguishes in God three moments:" I. The indifference as the arch-ground, Ungrund, Urgrund. II. The Differentiation into ground and existence—material and spiritual universe.—III. The identity or reconciliation of both. The arch-ground, the original abyss, primordeal nature, the indifference, wherein there was yet no personality, no Self-consciousness, is but the primeval point of the Divine Being, that *what* is in the Deity, not yet Himself. (The Zohar calls that, "Who," (מי), the inconceivable basis of the reality. . . . All natural beings have a mere existence in the "ground" (basis), in the desire not yet unified with intelligence. . . . Man alone is in God, and being in God is capable of freedom. . . . Man's freedom is derived from an intelligible, primordeal act by which he made himself what he is. . . . Empirical man is subject to necessity in all his doings. . . . To will is arch-being—Wollen ist Ursein—the union of the particular will with the universal will is the Good, their separation is the Evil. Man is a central being, and shall therefore remain in the center.—In him all things are created; just as only through him God assumes nature and unites with nature. Nature is the first stage. . . . Man is the higher development, the redeemer of nature. . . . Since he himself is united to God who, after the last differentiation even assumes nature and makes it one with himself. The careful reader of these pages will recognize here the theories of the Hindus and Qabbalists; Ain-Soph, Adam Qadmon, the world of Sephiroth and the developed material world all having their ground and source in the Absolute Unknowable.

In *Denkmal der Schrift Jacobis von den Goettlichen Dingen"* (Thuebingen, 1812), Schelling says: "God is to him both the first and the last, Alpha and Omega; that as *Deus implicitus,* impersonal indifference; this as *Deus explicitus,* God as personality, as subject or substratum of existence. A theism which does not recognize nature in God is empty and void." (Ueberweg, history of philosophy. Part iii.: 309). In his polemic against Jacobi (1812) Schelling says: "Naturalism thinks God as the ground of the world (immanent), theism as its cause transcendant. The truth is to unite both these definitions: God is both, the ground and cause of the universe. As long as no dualism is recognized in God, force and nature, the personal God-idea is not scientific."

Vedanta, Qabbala, Boehm and Schelling conceived veiled divinity as the infinite, indefinite, incomprehensible, unknowable Absolute; arch-ground, abyssmal and undifferentiated all-nature, which made itself by self-restraint, (Entzweiung, Corduero's צמצום), disintegration and differentiation, the finite ground and center of visible nature. "By such self-division and the friction of its severed, actualized properties, light was engendered, which forthwith illuminated and spiritualized all the forces of nature," poetically says Schwegler. The Absolute was indifference. The first moment in the divine Existence is indifference, identity of all qualities and all beings. This is the arch-ground. It is neither real nor ideal, neither matter nor spirit; it contains no contrasts. From this indifference, then, broke forth Dualism, the world of mind and the world of matter. By this disintegration and self-disunification, Selbstentweiung, the arch-ground became ground and existence, nature and life unified in love. God bears in Himself the cause of His existence, for there is nothing out of Himself. But to this cause as yet belongs neither intelligence nor will, but only the desire for creation. By this desire, He sees Himself in His image and likeness, the universe, creation. This is the *Verb,* the eternal Word of God, which appears as light, spirit or mind. This becomes the Will when united to matter. Mind brings light and order into chaotic matter—causing the creation of the universe. . . . At first nature attempted to create all things alone. But without intelligence they had no consistency and failed. Such were the creations found in the extinct species of animals and plants of prehistoric æras. Only gradually and slowly, nature yielded to mind, and each step was followed by a new superior creation of beings."—We have added these features of Schelling's mysticism, following Schwegler's, etc., History of Philosophy, in order to show that they are nearly all Hindu-Qabbalistic. Identical is the Zohar's definition of God, *Ain-Soph*. He was *Aïn*, non-existing as long as man, the representative of intelligence, was not created. *Ain-Soph* is all in all, matter and mind undifferentiated. Nature is part of himself. He is Being, uniting all qualities, in him identified and without any contrast. As such he is the arch-ground, the abyssmal all. In order to be revealed, his desire or will emanated the light, intelligence, Celestial man, Adam Qadmon, God's own image, the spiritual world or the Ten Sephiroth. The Celestial man containing all the germs, symbol of the spiritual creation, emanated the material universe, nature, the finite ground, God being both, the infinite ground and the Cause of the universe of mind and matter. Thus I believe to have shown that Boehm and Schelling have advanced and elaborated Hindu-Zoharitic theories. Both have amalgamated them with native Christian, trinitarian ideas. Boehm did it in uncouth, mystic language of the sixteenth century; Schelling as a scientific rationalist, yet a mystic of the nineteenth century. Both interwove Christianism with Vedanta and Qabbala to conform to their own Sabbath-schools and the views of their times, a task the more easy, as Upanishads and Zohar themselves are permeated with mystic trinitarian aspects. Further we find, but in Schelling more than in Boehm, elaborated ideas and strong reminiscences, not only from Zohar, but also from Philo and Neo-Platonism, the Logos or Sophia, as the mediator between God and creation. We find something also from Gebirol and Corduero, Gebirol's doctrine of the *Divine Will* as the creator of the universe, and Corduero's doctrine of divine Self-concentration (צמצום) by which the Infinite made Himself the substratum of finite nature, through

Adam Qadmon, his Alter-Ego. Even the Zohar's method of symbolical biblical interpretation, of amalgamating creed and free thought, of rationalizing faith, Schelling borrowed from the Qabbala, and, of course, he shares also in its vagueness, obscurity and arbitrariness.

Finally we have seen that apparently Jacob Boehm had no trace of a thought of the existence of the Hindu philosophy; that most probably he never heard of Vedas, Upanishads, Vedanta, etc. Hence his bold and mystic philosophems came to him from a neighboring humble rabbi, deeply imbued with Qabbalistic tendencies; hence the "Philosophus Teutonicus" was really an eclectic follower of Oriental mysticism. Not so was it with Schelling, Hegel and their schools of the past century. In the philosophical mysticism and rationalism of both, we find the paramount influence of those hoary eastern doctrines. But, since then, the Qabbala was already on the wane, while the Upanishads, Vedanta and generally Indian thought just received the impetus and began to be assiduously studied in the leading universities of Germany; therefore we feel rather inclined to assume Schelling and Hegel, as Schopenhauer expressly acknowledges it, as followers of the Vedanta philosophy, and, but in second instance, as disciples of the Qabbala. No doubt they knew it well as the philosophy of the Ghetto. But they studied far more zealously its predecessors, and especially its great Indian source, the bold speculations of the Vedanta, and that modified their entire mode of thinking, a mode so puzzling to the uninitiated. In the course of these pages we shall study and develop the grand outlines of the Vedas, Upanishads and Vedanta. There we shall see that both, their rationalism and their mysticism, were elaborated from materials first gathered by Hindu thinkers, entailed upon the Zoroastrians, then permeating Plato, Philo, Neo-Platonism, Yezirah, Gebirol, Qabbala, Spinoza, down to Schelling, Hegel and our own times.

HEGEL. VEDANTA AND QABBALA.

It is natural that those bold mystico-rationalistic elements of the Vedanta and Qabbala did not fail to greatly influence some of the German thinkers after Jacob Boehm. So we find them gradually developing and looming up in the versatile Schelling, and later in Hegel, first the junior and respectful follower, then the equal co-worker, and at last the independent and bold antagonist of Schelling. We have seen that a leading thought of Boehm was: "the disintegration, Selbstentzweiung, of the Absolute. The mysterious, ineffable Divine Being, the indefinable, infinite and unknowable, the unfathomable abyss, the arch-ground of substance, the Supreme Cause of all . . . . contracted itself into finitude, into the ground of nature, in whose dark laboratory the infinite variety of the original, inert and neutral properties were disintegrated and differentiated. In this universal, powerful shock arose and flamed up the lightning, which at once took hold, ruled and permeated the struggling forces of nature, as the spirit or light-principle. Thus the Deity struggling through the stage of the unknowable Arch-ground passed into the ground of nature and thence to the light of the spirit, there moving on in an eternal realm of beatitude." Similarly did Schelling describe in his earlier writings the Absolute as the indifference of all contrasts and the neutrality of all distinctions; as the Supreme, homogeneous being, bearing in its abyssmal bosom all the infinitude of later diversified existences. The Absolute is alienating its own being, and by that disintegration he rises to a higher unity with himself. His history represents the three stages of: God as indifference, the Absolute, as the Arch-ground; next God as the Ground or nature, disintegrated into the Real and the Ideal; lastly, the reconciliation of that differentiation and raising the original indifference into identity. The divine phases are thus: the arch-ground, nature, spirit.

A similar line of thought seems to have been followed by Hegel: "The Absolute is at first pure, immaterial thought. Second, it is differentiation, Anderssein, from pure thought; it is its distortion, dislocation, Verzerrung, through space and time—nature. Thirdly, it returns to itself from that self-alienation, it annuls that estrangement and differentiation of nature, and just by that it becomes real, self-conscious thought, Spirit."—Concerning his doctrine of being, Hegel says:

"The begin of science is the immediate, indefinite conception of being, "Sein." This conception is at first empty and void, amounting to a pure negation, the nothing. Both these conceptions are absolutely identical with and absolutely opposed to each other. Each fades at once into its opposite. This oscillation of both, constitutes rise and decay, growth and death—das "Werden." The result is existence, "Dasein." Existence is being, qualified, limited reality. .... This excludes things otherwise qualified. This reference to self and negation of others we term being-by-itself, "Fuer-sich-sein."—This constitutes repulsion; it is the *one*. By this very repulsion, the one posits many ones. But these many ones are not different from one another; one is the same as the other. The many are therefore one. But the one equals the many . . . . By these dialectics of attraction and repulsion the quality passes into quantity, etc. . . . The idea emanates nature from its bosom, breaking up into its opposite. Nature endeavors to regain its unity. Reaching that is the Spirit, as the object and end of nature . . . ." These ideas, abstruse and boundless, as the universe, vague, sublime and bold as the ethereal sky, attempting to describe what we hardly know, often coining terms and using words as indefinite and cloudy as the ideas they symbolize, all that goes in parallel lines with the vast, lofty and hazy Qabbalistic conceptions of God-all, as Ain-Soph and as Ain; as Adam Qadmon, as the Sephiroth-world, as nature, as the world-soul, etc.; the unique substance, the ineffable, the unknowable, the One, splitting and emanating the infinite variety of the ideal and the material universe, being one and many and again uniting into one, all hailing from the One Divine Bosom, passing from the supernatural All-Being into nature, and thence, after long purification and metempsychosis, again into the lap of the Supreme Unknowable One. Elsewhere Hegel says: "The contents of all religion are the reconciliation of the finite with the infinite. . . . All the religions aspire at the union of the divine and the human. The nature religions of the Orient do it roughly. . . . Higher is the God-idea expressed as the sublime subjectiveness full of power and wisdom in Judaism, the religion of the sublime; as a circle of plastic deities in the Greek religion, the religion of beauty; as the absolute object of the State, in the Roman religion, the religion of reason and utility. At the positive reconciliation of God and world attains the Christian religion, seeing in the person of Christ, the God-man, the realized unity of the divine and the human, God as the idea alienating itself, becoming man and coming back to itself from this self-differentiation, as the triune God. The intellectual contents of Christianity are thus identical with that of speculative philosophy."[1] Thus Christian trinity is but the formula and the symbol of Hegel's speculative philosophy! A devout Qabbalist would say just the same of the Zohar. In place of Christ put Adam Qadmon and the argument is identical. Thus I believe that Boehm, Schelling and Hegel wove their ratio-mystic speculations or dreams out of a nucleus found in the Vedanta and the Qabbala. Finally we see that the Qabbala is no isolated phenomenon in philosophy; that it is simply an important link in the unbroken chain of philosophic speculations; leading over from Brahmanic, Vedanta philosophy and Greek thinkers to Hebraic and Arabic ones, connecting the past with the present, the Orient with the Occident, Asia and Egypt with Europe; bridging over the abyss of the Middle Ages and leading the inquirer to the door of the very present time; showing the Oriental gulf stream in the philosophic ocean, in the reasonings of Jacob Boehm, Descartes, Spinoza, Schelling, Hegel, Schleiermacher, nay, even of Schoppenhauer's pessimism, Ulrici's optimism, deism and pantheism, and of others; however different their systems and views are, each has taken up some nugget or some pebble from the Hindu-Qabbalistic Reservoir, the Great Lakes of mystic and rationalistic philosophems.

WACHTER ON ZOHAR.

Nearer the truth than in his above quoted remarks, Wachter is in his claim that the Qabbala is but a compilation of centuries of Jewish and non-Jewish mystic doctrines. To a certain ex-

[1] Hegel, 1770-1831—Phoenomenologie; Encyclopædie, Religions Philosophie, etc.

tent this is true, but not to its full extent. The Zohar has taken up in its course most of the great and of the puerile but popular ideas on God, creation, man, soul, worship, aspirations, angels, demons, paradise, hell, etc., of former ages; from the Bible, Talmud, Midrashim, Apochryphae; from stray Greek, Chaldaic, Hindu, Persian, etc., philosophies. It brings many things good and noble, and many weak, clumsy, nay, abominable and execrable; mingled in grotesque and facetious juxtaposition; putting together the noblest, boldest and most abstract metaphysics and ethics, side by side with gross superstition, cunning and scheming to take hold of the fancy and overawe the ignorant and stupid. But with all that there is some system, some arrangement, some order in the Zohar, too, mingling great thoughts with exploded mystic notions. Its apparent object seems to have been the expounding of the Bible, a Commentary. But really it aimed at a mystic substantiation, a symbolical interpretation of Judaism, at giving its ceremonies and cult, a higher, diviner significance which the Rabbis never claimed. It was an attempt at spiritualizing religion and making it again the bearer of the world. But while this may have been the object of the book, it was further, really, an exposition of the boldest metaphysics of all times and climes, sifted through Jewish mind and having passed the prism of all the centuries and the brains of all the sages. Finally, it embodied all the mystic theories of by-gone and of contemporaneous ages, as current then among the people, Jewish and non-Jewish; yet elaborated and systematized, so as to appear new and striking, while it really was trite and well known. Here Prof. Graetz is perfectly correct in stating that the Zohar has hardly any really new ideas worth while thinking about. All good things there are compiled from preceding sources, Qabbalistic and philosophic.

IN ZOHAR NO ATHEISM.

Wachter exaggerates greatly when he says that the Qabbala and Spinoza are a deification of the Cosmos, leaving no room for divine guidance. Neither imputation is correct. True, the Qabbalistico-Neo-Platonic Sephiroth theory may lead to an identification of God and nature, since the emanations must have been originally in their Source. But, as we have argued above, the Qabbalists and the Zohar escaped that theological precipice by their Salto-mortale of the *Shiur Qoma*, mysticism, by skipping off their road and turning their backs upon that unavoidable, logical pantheism, resulting from their own Infinite emanating the universe. They took refuge in the safe harbor of the personal God of creation, providence, prophetism, revelation and bible. They simply tried their wings at independent thinking, as long as it went on, smoothly enough. But as soon as they saw the Scylla and Charybdis of atheism and blind, brute fate of pantheism, they turned their faces and galloped off into the warm, genial camp of the God of the patriarchs. They became as stoutly faithful and as little "Esprits-forts" and independent thinkers as ever pious Hassidai were. Ovid narrates of wrecked Phaeton when daring to guide Phœbus' Sun-Chariot. The Qabbalists boldly followed Philo and anticipated Spinoza. But they were neither so heroic nor so foolish as Phaeton. They jumped off the chariot and escaped his cruel fate. On their tombstone one could not engrave: "Hic situs est Phaeton, curus auriga paterni: Quem si non tenuit, magnis tamen excidit ausis." (Ovid Metam, ii.: 327). This prudent escape, this inconsequential reasoning of the Qabbalists, Wachter has overlooked. He saw the nonsense, not the good sense of it. Leaving the dangerous stallion of rationalism they turned their course to humble infantine, but safe, soft, anthropomorphic mysticism. Or as the child trying to look the sun into the face and finding it painful, turns the eyes away to green foliage and beauteous flowers, finding there relief and delight; even so the Qabbalists; from their dangerous scheme of inquiring into the nature of deity, cosmos, being, hereafter, etc., they turned for safety and comfort in their perplexities of metaphysics, to the "hanging gardens" of mysticism, *Shiur Qoma*, measuring God's height and width, his face, forehead, nose and lips, the length and width of his beard, by myriads of miles and millions of worlds—all to express His infinitude and hide their human ignorance. That was wayward, too; it led not to atheism, but to the opposite pole, idoltary and superstition. The cropping up of messiahs "Abulafia, *Caro,* Sabatai Zeby, etc., proved it; escaping Scylla, they fell a prey to Charybdis.—But the Zohar at any rate is not atheistic.

SPINOZA NO ATHEIST. GOD-WORLD.

Even so it is a gross exaggeration of Wachter to say that Spinoza's pantheism is tantamount to Atheism. No! With him pantheism is rather the contrary. Schleiermacher has well established it. Not that God is absorbed in the world of matter, but that matter and universe are absorbed in the God-substance. They are but bubbles, temporary appearances, wavelets on the surface of the ocean, shifting as sea-sands, as a straw in the current of the river. God alone, to him, is reality, permanent, absolute, not accidental and never changing. . . . All else is and will soon no longer be. God alone was, is and will forever remain. Spinoza was so much wrapped up in the grandeur and majesty of the Deity that he overlooked the universe of fleeting creations. The world lost its interest for him. God alone engrossed it. All was sunk in the ocean of Deity. Its surface wavelets lost their importance for him. He saw everywhere the divine, and his system fails to give any account of this material, shifting, busy world, all-absorbed as he was by his God-idea. "We see the traces into the lion's cave (of his godhead), not the steps out of it." Spinoza was an extreme monotheist, not an atheist. To his grand, theoretical mind all was God and the world but a bubble. Everywhere he saw but God, the world was but His shadow. And as he was no atheist, just as little was he a pantheist, in the popular sense of the term. He did not assume that the sum of beings makes out the God-head, or that nature and God are identical. Far from that. To him all the individual beings were shadows and bubbles. But their reality, the substance behind their appearance, was the one Divine Substance. Nature is but the screen, the shadow of the reality, which man designates as mind and matter, and that reality is the deity. Thus Spinoza denied the world and affirmed the Deity as the only reality. He was thus neither an atheist nor a pantheist. He was the most rigorous monotheist, a monist. Thus I believe to have shown that Wachter, having correctly guessed the influence of the Qabbala upon Spinoza, exaggerated it enormously. Prof. W. Wundt, though less acquainted with the special features of the theme, has intuitively and correctly stated their exact mutual relation, viz: Some of the leading ideas, the premises, are nearly identical. Yet on the whole, was Spinoza original and creative in his Ethics. Maimonides and Qabbala, both gave up in time rationalism and free-thinking, each in his own way. Spinoza followed up the track and created the "Ethics." He created a new, original pantheism, not an automatic universe, not a soulless matter-and-force machine. No, these dwindled into insignificance and mere shadows. *God was the reality.* The grand figure in the world's tableau was the Godhead behind the curtain of nature; and Spinoza, or man, was the high priest absorbed in worship and contemplation. "The holy Spinoza!" I say with Schleiermacher, in due vindication and rehabilitation of a great and good man long misconstrued.

SPINOZA REFERS TO ANCIENT HEBREW THINKERS.

Spinoza in Epist. xxi., says: "Affirming that everything exists in God and moves in Him, I affirm this with Paul, and, perhaps, even with all the old philosophers, though expressed in other modes; nay, I dare say even with all *the ancient Hebrews,* as far *as it is allowed to conjecture* of them from certain traditions, however much these are variously adulterated."[1] This is plain; Spinoza here affirms that his leading idea: God, the One Substance of the universe, in whom the latter exists, is a derivation from ancient systems, affiliated with, if not derived from, ancient thinkers, Jewish and non-Jewish. Let us remember that Talmud and Aggada designate the Deity by the epithet, "Maqom," מקום, place of the universe. So opines Male-

---

1 Omnia inquam in Deo esse, et in Deo moveri, cum Paulo affirmo, et forte etiam cum omnibus antiquis philosophis, licet alio modo, et auderem etiam dicere, cum antiquis omnibus Hebraeis, quantum ex quibusdam traditionibus, tametsi multis modis adulteratis conjicere licet. (Spinoza Epist. XXI.)

branche (1638 P. Ch.): "Mind and matter are contrasts; how do I arrive at the cognition of the external objects, their bodies and ideas or images? He answers: My mind perceives the things alone in God, who is superior to that contrast (of mind and matter). He, the absolute Substance, contains all, ideally. In Him spirits and bodies are identical; no longer opposing each other. He is the universe intellectually. In Him we see all the things. He may be thus termed: the *place of all the ideas or* spirits, of all the images and types of the things."—Malebranche combines here the views of Plato, Descartes, and in some sense of Spinoza, too. Now Prof. Franck,[1] who by all means is bent upon overestimating the importance of the Zohar and the Qabbala, claims that Spinoza alludes exclusively to these latter ones. But I feel strongly that Spinoza was here much more sweeping and general; he really meant: first, all the old philosophers, as Philo, Plato, Aristotle, the Neo-Platonists, etc., who, though yet speaking of mind and matter, nevertheless "saw, as through a veil," the unity of both; the latter being the emanation of the former. Next, he alludes to the ancient Jewish thinkers, as mentioned in Talmud, Aggada, Apochryphæ, expounders and commentators, whose kindred ideas are vaguely hinted at there, much stinted, truncated and curtailed, in order not to give offense; and, lastly, he implies the Qabbalistic metaphysicians of the centuries preceding him. He alludes thus to the Alexandrine school, especially Philo, Aristobul, etc. He alludes to the echoes from the Essenian, Therapeutic and Gnostic doctrines, which, too, claimed God to be unknowable, and the Messiah or Demiurgos, etc., to be his emanation and originator of the universe. He alludes to the mediæval Jewish philosophers whom he knew, directly or indirectly, as to Saadia, Hai and Sherira Gaon; Gebirol, Yehuda Halevi, and above all to Maimonides, whom he quotes verbatim, as if his "Yad" and "Guide" were lying spread out before him. In conclusion he alludes to the Qabbala and Zohar also, which he spares not with his sarcasms, as we shall see soon, on account of the extravagance and want of logic so salient in their pages, side by side with the poetic exposition of the grand, metaphysical ideas of past centuries. . . .

---

1 Franck, Qabbala, p. 26.

I have the intuitive conviction that Spinoza's words: "With all the old Hebrews, though adulterated in many ways" (Cum antiquis omnibus Hebraeis, tametsi, multis modis adulteratis), refer to Talmudical and Aggadic teachers, who have held such heterodox opinions alluded to there, who intentionally veiled their views in order not to offend the ear of believers. I shall spread here before the reader such Rabbinical, etc., passages. We need not search long; they are myriad, but usually misunderstood and misinterpreted, gratuitously assumed as supernatural, while really they are but veiled and mutilated unorthodox opinions cautiously expressed.

TALMUD ON MIRKABA AND CREATION.

I shall quote from Bably, Hagigah, xi. a,[1] already familiar to our readers: "It is not allowed to expound on sexual matters in the presence of three persons; nor to speculate on creation before two persons; and not on the Mirkaba (metaphysics) before one; except if that one is a scholar and an earnest truth-seeker." Whosoever speculates on what is above and below, before and after (whether the world is endless or not, created or eternal, whether time and space are limited or boundless), etc. "Who is not respectful in speaking of the Deity, it were better for him, he were not born." What means that? It is identical with Kant's honest declaration that all such speculations and meditations are beyond the human ken and transcendental. Divine Essence, creation, boundless time and space, etc., are ideas to which we can neither say yes nor no; hence is their discussion futile. When a young scoffer asked Luther: "What did God do before he created the world? he answered: He was in the woods cutting sticks to whip bad boys asking foolish questions."

The Guemara expounds in many long pages that *Mishna. It* discusses there physics, metaphysics, astronomy, history, theology, etc., of the most obstruse and various nature, but all in metaphors, by hints, respectfully, intelligible only to the initiated, to the wise, learned and sincere truth-seekers, leaving

---

1 אין דורשין בעריות בשלשה ולא במעשה בראשית בשנים. ולא במרכבה באחד.

no room for scandal and frivolous scoffing. Let me give a sample of how the Talmudists discussed metaphysics, with all the earnestness becoming the subject:[1] "It happened that R. Johanan b. Sakkai was riding on the road and R. Eleasar b. Aroch behind him, who said: Rabbi, teach me something on the *Mirkaba* (divine science). B. Sakkai gave no reply. B. Aroch resumed: Shall I discuss what thou hast taught me concerning that? B. Sakkai at once giving him permission, stepped down from his beast, veiled himself in his sacred scarf, and sat down to listen, under a tree.—B. Aroch asked: Rabbi, why didst thou descend from thy riding ass? The Rabbi answered: Shouldst thou expound the Mirkaba, the Shekhina being present, and the angels of the Service around us, and I remain sitting on my riding beast! B. Aroch thereupon began his lesson—when fire came down from heaven and illumined the scene, and the trees began chanting in chorus."—Now this is not a wizard's trick. It means, be careful when discussing such abstruse themes; be not frivolous and fashionably bold, but wary and cautious; for the peace and order of the world depend upon respecting its moral basis! The Jews are the boldest thinkers and conservative withal.

There you will find discussed all the questions involved and treated in these pages. I have no doubt that the weighty themes about the Logos, Verb, Sophia, Adam Qadmon, Mithra or Metatron, Plato's Ideas, the Neo-Platonic Ten emanations and dualism, pantheism, the later Qabbalistic Sephiroth, etc., are alluded to there, and were familiar to the Talmudic teachers: "R. Eliazar says: In the beginning, Adam, the first, was from earth to heaven; when he sinned God made him small."[2] Rab says: "Adam was from the begin to the end of the world; when he sinned he shriveled under God's hands."—(Here may be the origin of the Qabbalistic Adam Qadmon, etc., in allegorical language). "Rabbi Jehudah says: Ten things were created during the first creative day: Heaven, earth, chaos, light, darkness, air, water, day and night. . . . The divine spirit brooding over the waters. . . . God was enclosed in Chaos. . . . . He created light on the first day . . . . by which one could see from one end of the world to the other end. God then

[1] Hagiga, 14 b. [2] Ib., 12 a.

withdrew it, reserving it for future days of brighter virtues, and created on the fourth day a smaller light instead. . . . He created the universe with ten words . . . (Here is the analogy of the Logos, Sophia, Verb, the ten Emanations, Sephiroth, etc.) . . The Shamaites say: First were the heavens (universe) created, and then came the earth. The Hillelites say: The contrary[1] took place. (This involves the question: is the earth the center or but a dependency of the universe . . . Follow speculations on its elements and its parts . . . . whether sudden creation or gradual development took place." It is written: God created the heaven and earth; that means that heaven and earth are creatures of God—not that Zrvana-Akarana or *Ouranos* is Creator,[2] alluding to Greek and Parsee views. Then follow long discussions on physics and metaphysics, the *Mirkaba* of Ezekiel[3] with speculations on deity, world, matter, soul, creation, etc. . . "Every word God spoke became an angel."[4] Here is the Verb of the Gospel and Gnostics[5] . . "His garment white as snow and his locks black as a raven . . .[6] the first in council, the other in war" . . . Here is the Aggadic anthropomorphism, later in *Shiur Qoma* and the Zohar, etc. . . . . "His throne is flaming fire, then we hear of two thrones?[7] to which answers R. Akiba, one is for God, and one is for David."[8] Here is the king messiah, the heavenly redeemer and the "Crown" of Christian and Jewish mysticism. R. Yose, the Galilean, objects: Akiba, how long wilt thou blaspheme the Godhead! That verse alludes to the two divine attributes: "Justice and Grace." The mystics imagined the deity under two aspects, that of justice and of grace, or love. Personifying these attributes, they then spoke of God Supreme and of his Son, God of Love. These became current views among the Gnostics and the incipient Christian Sects. Even so later popularly: the God of Israel was imagined as rigid justice, and the Christian messiah as the God of Love, a phrase current yet today. These two were originally but phases in the one deity, later personified as deities. "Four men entered Paradise,[9] viz: B.

[1] Ib. 12 a. [2] Ib. 12 a and b. [3] Ezekial 1. [4] Hagiga 14 a. [5] John I, 1. [6] Daniel 7—Song of Songs, 5. [7] Daniel 7. [8] Hagiga 14 a. [9] Ibid. 14 b, Paradise, means metaphysical studies.

Azai, B. Zoma, Ahar and R. Akiba. Said R. Akiba: "When you reach the clean marble stones, do not shout, water! water! It is written:[1] "The liar will not prosper!" That may allude to the Greek, Thales' hypothesis that water is eternal and the world's origin.—B. Azai looked and died. . . . (that may mean that he became an infidel) . . . B. Zoma looked and was hurt, as written: when thou findest honey eat moderately thereof, or thou wilt be surfeited.[2] "*Aher* lopped off the plantations," viz: ruined the young disciples by his bold, heterodox opinions. So was Spinoza, fifteen hundred years later, reproached by the Amsterdam Rabbinate. Some surmise that Spinoza was the *Aher* of our modern times. Pity that we know not more of the Talmudical *Aher* to prove the parallel. The evil reports of him in the passages alluded to, are popular exaggerations. Closely seen, they harbor a hidden nucleus that reveals an unflinching character with independence of thought and great self-sacrifice. Pythagoras or a Qabbalist would say that Aher's soul breathed in Spinoza's *Ethics.* Of course the Synagogue had to condemn all three in its own defense and in self-preservation.—"R. Akiba alone went out in peace," viz: he was not alienated from his religion; but he became an ardent mystic, kindled a disastrous war against Rome, believed in the supernatural messiah, practically indorsed and assisted the leader, Bar Kokhba, as such, and thus brought untold misfortune upon his country and people in Hadrian's times (120 P. C.) by his patriotic supernaturalism.

AHER.—B. ABUYAH.

Of this *Aher,* viz: Elisha b. Abuyah, with his full name, the Talmud narrates a great deal of wonderful things.[3] He was the infidel of Talmudic literature, was execrated by and ousted from the synagogue. All bad things were told of him. Smoke came up from his grave after he had died. It is hinted at in Talmud Jerusalem and Babli that he believed in two divine principles;[4] hence his name, *Aher, Ahriman,* the "other" principle, besides God. He was an incarnation of sin and the evil passions. Else-

---

1 Ps 101. 2 Prov. 25. 3 Hagiga 15 a.

4 שתי רשויות. Parsee dualism, the good and the bad principle.

where we have identified him with the Persian *Ahriman*. But Aher, the "other" one, the contrary principle, the opponent of the Good one, was also a Platonian term and assumption. Plato taught the Good, or Ideal universe, and that of the senses or matter, the principle of Evil, the opponent of and ever rebellious to the Good; the Evil was termed the "Other" one. At the bottom of Plato's sensual world, the antagonist of his world of Ideas, as well as of the Rabbinical *Aher*-conception, of which Elisha b. Abuyah was the incarnation, is the said Persian Ahriman, the opponent of Ormazd, the *Good* principle. The real *Aher* was the Spinoza of his time; he was simply a free-thinker, heterodox—the Guemara there devotes to him whole, long pages about his heresies, his evil conduct, his discussions with R. Mayer, *his disciple,* his fate, death and punishment, ... horrible things! He is the bug-bear of the Midrashim. But curious, all is narrated in hints, curtailed phrases and broken sentences, as if the Talmud intentionally avoided to repeat plainly his bold and deep-cutting opinions. If we literally accept all that is said in that mysterious report, then he repudiated all, Judaic, metaphysical doctrines, morality, worship and ritualistic laws. Nevertheless was the great R. Mayer anxious to learn of him, and followed him many miles on foot—Aher riding—on the Sabbath to receive his instructions! Even when dead he was held in awe on account of his great learning. The fact is the Talmud is not a book, but an encyclopædia. It contains the utmost variety of thoughts and doctrines. In its every treatise we meet with such discussions, reported shortly, enigmatically, mysteriously as *"Mirkaba"* and *"Genesis,"* as mysticism, but really as a discreet exchange of free opinions on all the branches of human knowledge. Had the Talmudists reported on Spinoza, they would have done it in the same mode. Thus free thoughts and bold doctrines, not in consonance with orthodox Judaism, were known to Talmudic teachers and their literature. To such frequent Rabbinical passages does Spinoza refer in his quoted allusion: "I believe to be in accord with many old Hebrew thinkers" concerning his own concepts about God, creation, mind, matter, etc. Prof. Franck[1] says: "Evi-

[1] Franck, Qabbala, 26.

dently there can be here none other meant but the traditions of the Qabbala, for those that the Jews have collected in the Talmud are but tales and ceremonial laws, Aggada and halacha."—I beg to differ. The Talmud contains innumerable passages treating of other things than tales and ceremonial laws. There are plenty of discussions on all important matters known to the ancient world, all expressed in their depths, and with the greatest freedom of thought, reported only under a veil, discreetly, so as not to give offense to the old, nor create a stumbling block for the young and the ignorant. The examples quoted are but an infinitesimal part of what the Rabbinical literature actually contains of that kind. Therefore, concerning our theme in discussion, I beg to say that Spinoza claiming "to be at one with certain ancient Hebrew thinkers," alludes not necessarily to the "Book of Creation," the Qabbala and the Zohar. No, he hints at those metaphysical and cosmological utterances,[1] to the "*mystics,*" as the Mishna quoted, denominates such speculations, treated by ancient Jewish and non-Jewish thinkers and boldly reflected in the Talmud and Midrashim, as those just mentioned, whose subjects and reports are truly legion. Spinoza may allude for instance to b. Zoma, b. Azai, Aher, etc. He may further allude to Philo and the Alexandrines, to the Gnostics, the Neo-Platonicians and their successors; to Paul, who is, according to him, too, an ancient Hebrew, to all who took as their point of departure the emanation doctrines, and logically could not help arriving at the identity of mind and matter, to one Substance in whom all moves and centres.

SPINOZA QUOTES FROM MAIMONIDES AND QABBALA.

But Spinoza does not simply allude to ancient Hebrews: he quotes their ideas and opinions as reflected in Maimonides and Qabbalists. Speaking of his doctrine of the one Substance, essence of all existence, mind and extension inclusive, with myriads of diverse attributes, he says: "This is even that what some of the Hebrews appear to have dimly seen, as through a nebulæ, when namely, they state: that God, His thought and the

---

1 מעשה מרכבה ומעשה בראשית.

object of His thought are one and the same" (Ethics, part ii.: Prop. 7 Schol.)[1] Curious enough; Prof. Franck, in his eagerness to prominently bring forward the Qabbala and the Zohar, gratuitously assumes that passage as by all means referring to them, he showing a similar theory to be found in the Zohar's Commentator, Moise Corduero, Pardes Rimonim, p. 55: 1. No doubt it is there *also,* but before there it is to be found in older and more original sources, long before Moses de Leon and Moise Corduero: It is Moses Maimonides who had said that; and as seen above, Aristotle and, to all appearance, Plato (and Vedanta too) have said that. For if even these two latter masters have taught and accepted mind and matter as primordeal, nevertheless as logically developed by their successors, the Neo-Platonists, that was on the basis and tacit supposition of the emanation doctrine, of unity of substance, as one protoplasm of all existences, viz: that in the Divine Mind lived all forms and types, primordeally; Divine Mind is ever thinking, and God's thinking is creation, emanation, irradiation of beings, which beings the further they are distanced from their original, sacred Source, the more they condense, become less luminous, less spiritual and pure, until at last they become our own dark sensual material world. This is the emanation theory taught distinctly (and tacitly postulated by Brahman and Parsee), from Plotin and Philo to Gebirol and the Zohar. Thus I say: Spinoza's quotation just mentioned is to be found *also* in Moses Corducro. But before him, who lived in the fourteenth century, it is literally and verbatim in Maimonides of the twelfth century. It is as seen above in his "Yad," "Mada," "foundation of the law," ii.: 9, and also there in "Repentance," v.: 5. Corduero has simply copied that passage from Maimonides word for word, and Prof. Franck has overlooked that. That theory, that in God is thinking, thinker and object of thought identical, appears to have been a well-known "Shibboleth," and the universal property of the educated. It was among the dialectical current ideas, a kind of truism hailing from Aristotle, and probably,

---

[1] Hoc quidam Hebraeorum quasi per nebulam vidissi videntur, qui scilicit statuunt Deum, Dei intellectum, resque ab ipso intellectas unum et idem esse.

too, from Plato. Let us now bring here the leading traits of that Academic philosopher, which bear, too, upon our theme, viz: "In God is thinking, thinker and object of thought identical."

PLATO'S METAPHYSICS.

Pupil of Socrates, Plato elaborated his beloved master's practical virtue-doctrine into a philosophical world-system, embracing dialectics, physics and ethics. Plato (429 B. C.) assumes that the single sensual bodies of the universe are perhaps but phenomena, appearances, uncertain what they really are. Real in them is but their type, their *"form,"* their ideal. Each genus or species of sensual beings, has such a single spiritual archtype. The type alone is real and of that type the genus is but a multiplied re-impression of copies, and that only one real type of its species, Plato calls *Idea.* The idea is real and eternal; the genus and its infinite specimens are but phenomena and evanescent. Ideas are the eternal substances alone true, in the stream and flow of single existences. These latter ones are, perhaps, but an illusion, shadows of their type. The bodily universe is modeled after the ideal-universe. It is its dark clay and shadow, ephemeral and passing, as the waves in the ocean. The world of Ideas is an articulate organism, from lower to higher, a scale, a spiritual hierarchy, the higher containing the lower type, and the highest containing all of them. This highest Idea is God. He is the highest Good. He is the intellectual, the ideal universe, the prototype of the sensual one, of whom the latter is the doubtful shadow. Plato further assumed two principles in the phenomenal universe: "Supreme, self-existent reason, intellect or mind, called God, the Principle and Source of all good, of all the moral and intellectual excellencies perceptible in the universe. He is *the Good.* The human soul is derived from that divine Source; it is a spark, an atom, an emanation from him, a god in miniature, uniting as God does, but on a small scale, all the perfections possessed by man. Side by side with that mind-principle, there appears to exist another one, matter; it is the proptoplasm of the bodies of the universe. It is passive, chaotic, plastic, instinctively resisting the volition of the active mind-principle. It appears independent and co-existent with that, eternally and forcibly, receiving its impressions or forms from Mind. Mind is the active force and form of nature, as Matter is the passive force, the body thereof. God is the supreme type, the highest Idea of the universe. He comprehends in infinitude all the inferior types or Ideas which are gradually impressed upon the plastic apparent bodies of the universe. The Ideas are the forms or souls of those bodies, the governing intellectual principles permeating them, representing the life, the reason and real being thereof. The human soul is, as its Origin, God, immortal and does not participate in the decomposition and decay of the body. It is a single, elementary force containing all the mental, moral, spiritual, ethical, etc., capacities of man. God is thus the ideal universe and the universe is a kind of material copy of the Deity. Between both stands the Universal Soul, intermediate between Mind and body. The Qabbala utilized this in its conceptions of Adam Qadmon, the Sephiroth-world, the material world, the human soul, etc.

The Ethics of Plato are naturally the outcome of his metaphysics. The human soul, being divine and immortal, passes through many evolutionary stages, transmigrations, and reaches at last its heavenly origin. It attains there only by wisdom and goodness. Virtue is her goal, to become good as God is! a Mosaic ideal.[1] Virtue and wisdom are one and the same thing. Virtue is wisdom practiced, and wisdom is virtue in theory; both are the inevitable result of correct thinking. Thus virtue is a science; to become good, one must necessarily be well educated.[2] A solid reasoner cannot help being virtuous, good and wise, since all three are but one thing looked upon from different standpoints. They are really one in the divine human soul, as they are identical in its source, the Supreme Intelligence. We shall see that these platonic metaphysics and ethics were not lost to the Neo-Platonists, and that in part they reappear in the Qabbala. Their origin is the philosophy of Socrates.

---

1 Levit. 19, 1, "Ye shall be holy as I am your God." 2 So in Abboth: "An ignoramus is not pious." ולא עם הארץ חסיד

Thus to Plato is God the highest Idea, containing the entire scale of Ideas or types of the universe, which are infinite as God is. Now these Ideas and types of all the classes of beings are really their essence, and they are all contained in the highest Idea. Hence is the Highest Idea really the essence of all existence. Therefore, with Plato as with Aristotle and their spiritual descendants, the Neo-Platonists, Gebirol, Maimonides and Corduero is: "Thought, thinking subject and thought-of-object in God, one and the same thing." Consequently there is but one substance and one essence of all existence, the view of Spinoza! Of course, neither Plato nor Aristotle so boldly and plainly stated as the latter one that: "Mind and matter are opposite things when seen by human eyes, but that in God they are one, two attributes among myriads of such." With Plato and Aristotle, mind and matter are two things yet and co-eternal opposites, contraries, the one acting upon the other and but temporarily and forcibly united. That the two are really and essentially one, this plain statement belongs to the Ethics of Spinoza. But it is involved in the theories of his predecessors mentioned. He but developed what was silently implied in their premises. The Persian dualism, too, hinged upon that, and Spinoza boldly cut the Gordian knot. That view is further elaborated and enlarged upon in Maimonides' "Guide of the Erring" (i.: 68) cited above, in connection with Aristotle and Bruell. Indeed, here is its Jewish source; here it is worked out fully and rationally by the thinker, Maimonides, without any hesitation or backthought. While in his "Yad" he is reticent, yet conscious of its difficulties and logical discrepancies with Mosaic ethics and world-conception, Weltanschauung. But before proceeding let us first survey the views of Aristotle, Plato's successor.

ARISTOTLE'S PHILOSOPHY.

Aristotle (384 B. C.) strongly modified Plato's philosophy. He taught: *God is the first Cause of all,* mind and matter, both eternal. The Platonic Ideas are but abstractions, never independently existent. The idea or type exists but in its body, as concrete. It is repeated in its species. The Idea is immanent in the body. The class is the multiplication of its single copies, body and type, or Idea. The Idea is the common or general of the single things repeated in the class.

Matter is the eternal substratum of all that is, the potentiality actualized by the immanent Idea or form. Nature represents the eternal flow of growth and decay of matter becoming form, of the chaotic brute substratum becoming organized beings of body and form, ever rising to higher organizations, as earth, root, tree, forest, building material, house; so that each is the form of its predecessor, and in turn the body or substratum of its following higher type; *God is the eternal, purest form* of the eternal, brute matter. Thus form is the development of matter by gradual organizations ever rising in the scale. Nature works on unconsciously, instinctively. It is a living organism, ever elaborating matter into form. Absolute form is spirit. *Man is the highest within a body.* The universe is a globe, a sphere in circular motion. The earth is its centre; then come the planets; Heaven is the periphery. The stars are eternal. The five Planets, Sun and Moon are all in eternal motion.

Human reason is a purely intellectual, independent, immortal being, as God is in nature. Man is a social animal. Virtue is not identical with knowledge. It is first instinctively, then consciously followed. Practice and habit render virtuous, not mere knowledge. Beatitude is the highest good. Not pleasure and luxuriance, but unimpeded energy, satisfactory activity, that is the highest pleasure and true beatitude. Virtue is the readiness of the soul to act morally. It is the *juste-milieu* between two extreme vices. The state is the sphere of virtue. The individual and the family are its important features; no communism in goods or women. Thus Aristotle searches the Ideal in the concrete. He is more empiric than ideal. His method is Induction, proceeding from the special and empiric to the general and the abstract. Thus Aristotle is more avowedly dualist, while Plato and his successors, Greek and Judaic, anxiously cling yet to monism, to identify all phenomena. Let us now come back to our preceding theme.

Indeed, the only way of absolving Corduero of plagiarism, is to assume that that doctrine was in his time universal property, a philosophical truism belonging to the circle of Plato-Aristotelian philosophy, from whence Maimonides, too, has drawn it. A fact it is that the passage quoted by Ad. Franck as belonging to Corduero, is literally taken from Maimonides' *"Yad"* quoted above. In his *"Guide"* (i.: 68) the doctrine is expressed more elaborately: "It is long ago known what philosophers (Aristotle, Plato, Plotin, Proclus, Philo, etc., the philosophical masters of the middle ages) have said concerning the Deity, viz.: that He is the intellectus, the thinker and the thought-of-object, and that these three are identical in Him, there being no plurality in Him. . . . For He being one, there can be no addition to His being, as we have explained concerning all attributes which must be discarded from the Godhead."[1] This theory he expounds fully in some of his most abstruse, metaphysical chapters.

Above we have quoted that fine passage, practically reproduced as an epitome in the *"Yad," Mada Foundation* of the Law ii.: 9. We shall adduce now the same chapter at more length, as rendered by Corduero in "Pardes Rimonim" (55:1): "The science of the Creator is not like that of the creature. In the creature is the knowledge distinguished from the subject possessing the knowledge, and is exercised upon objects distinguished from the subject. This is expressed by these three terms: 'Thinking, thinker and thought-of thing.' On the contrary, the Creator is Himself all in one—the knowledge, the known subject and the known object. Indeed, His manner to know does not consist in applying His thought to objects that are out of Himself. It is by knowing Himself that He knows and perceives all that is. Nothing exists that is not unified in Him, and that He does not find in His own substance. He is the type of all being and all things exist in Him in their purest and most perfect form; to such an extent that the perfection of the creatures con-

---

[1] אמרו הפילוסופים בשם יתעלה, שהוא השכל והמשכיל והמושכל....בו יתעלה הם אחד . . היותו אחד לא יצורף אליו דבר אחר. ר"ל שאין דבר קדמון זולתו.

sists just in that existence by which they are united with the Source of their being. The more they depart and move away from that source, the more they deteriorate and fall short of that perfect and sublime condition."—This passage of Corduero's Pardes is absolutely identical with that of Maimonides', phrase after phrase, as in the latter's "Yad," and in substance with the "Guide," too. But it transcends the premises of Spinoza, at least as far as he refers to it. I acknowledge that the pantheistic idea is in Corduero much more fully expressed than in Maimonides. This latter one is more wary and cautious in his expressions, because he is more conscious of its clashing with the Judaic views. It is remarkable, indeed, that Prof. Franck did not notice the pantheism of Corduero's doctrine announced with hardly any mitigation.[1] But he justly coincides with Wachter's later opinion concerning the Hollandish philosopher, that closely seen, his, Spinoza's, pantheism is not atheism, but it is rather an exaggerated Theism; not a world-machine without a machinist, but a universe permeated and entirely absorbed by the All-deity; as the wave is by the ocean. That is really a monotheism pushed to its extreme. The cosmos is but an accident, a mere appearance, a shadow of the divine Reality. Behind the screen of nature hovers that Reality, God Supreme, the biblical Ihvh One, the Qabbalistic *Ain-Soph,* the Neo-Platonic and Hegelian Unknowable, the Platonic Highest Idea, the Zoroastrian Zrvana-Akarana, the Hindu Brahman, etc.

MOSE DE LEON, COMPILER. IMPORT OF ZOHAR.

I coincide with Prof. Franck in his affirmation that that grand theistic pantheism, the theory of the Supreme one, absorbing the universe and alone occupying the thought of sage and cherubim, the philosophy half-way developed in the Zohar, too, is not derived from the brains of the mediocre penurious and shifting Mose de Leon, of the thirteenth century. He is at the utmost one of its compilers. His claim to the possession of a book by R. Simon ben Jochai was fictitious, too. He wrote that book, but he only compiled its doctrines, old as human intellect,

---

[1] Franck's Qabbala p. 29.

developed from hoary times, slowly growing, expanding and broadening in the laboratory of the many thinkers of the past; alternately amended, corrupted, improved, adulterated, purified, never completed and never finished, because impossible, because beyond the grasp of the human faculties. "No man can see me and live," says Scripture. No one can say anything positive concerning such transcendental matters, says Kant, and Mose de Leon can least of all. In the Zohar he compiled with a grand apparatus of poetry and grandiloquence some of the best and some of the worst things ever said about such themes. He simply united the metaphysics of olden times with the gross superstitions of his own and other ages. He fused noble metaphysics with gross anthropomorphism; the great thoughts of the past he united to the children's fancies of magiism, mythology and Spanish-Judæn *hassidaic* dreams; things most heterogeneous and absurd, but well calculated to catch the fancy of the masses. By these heterogeneous elements, Mose de Leon succeeded in creating his curious, poetical Zohar, half philosophy and half fancy. With all its faults, monstrosities and its many baleful, practical results, this work is an important and integral part of the history of religion, metaphysics and philosophy, and must be studied as such. It is not sectarian, not Jewish, Spanish, mediæval, but cosmopolitan. It is necessary for the perfect understanding of the history and the development of human thought. It is a link in the chain of metaphysics of mysticism, of history, of religion, of cult. It holds the key to Christian Trinitarianism, to the sociologic Messiah-Ideal, to the many actual religious upheavals that made their appearance in the Christian, Mohammedan and Jewish world. It is especially interesting for the study of human thought, of philosophy; without it modern metaphysics and philosophy would not be understood. It is the hanging bridge between Zoroaster and Comte, between Plato and Philo on one hand, Spinoza, Kant, Hegel and Schelling on the other. It immediately connects with Spinoza.

INFLUENCE OF QABBALA ON SPINOZA.

Spinoza connected through the Zohar and the Qabbala with Maimonides, Gebirol and their predecessors, the Neo-Platonists,

Philo, Aristobul, the countless talmudical, midrashic and mystic utterances, reaching back to the doctrines of Plato, Zoroaster and the Vedas. All have contributed their share to Spinoza's pantheism. Consciously or not, they were stored up in his mind; he knew them, directly or indirectly; he teemed with their germs, unconsiously, as every scion is the product of all its ancestors and predecessors. In his youth he had imbibed their teachings. Gradually he developed and fructified them, shaped and harmonized them, eliminated the crudities and the grandiloquent poetry of Mose de Leon and the vagueness and vacillations of acute Corduero; he corrected the indefiniteness of Gebirol and Saadia, the timidity and inconsistencies of Maimonides and Philo, the dualistic incompleteness of Plato and Aristotle, and the haziness of the Avesta and its Hindu predecessors. He sifted out all the solid, metaphysical ideas of the entire past, selecting the most rational from the brainy stock of all the sages and creeds, Jewish, Greek, Parsee, Indians, old and new, of others and of his own. He threw all these many diverse elements into the crucible, the laboratory of his own vast mind. There they were elaborated and distilled. The heterogeneous was eliminated, the homogeneous, fitted, polished, harmonized and fused into a system, solid and lucid as adamant, his own modern, bold, monistic pantheism. The universe is but an accident, an appearance, the shifting, visible, shadowy frame of God, who is the real grand tableau absorbing all; the Reality, the Absolute, Infinite and Eternal, the Hebraic, native Ihvh, the One-All, יהוה אחד ever present, hid behind the thin, transparent veil of nature. Was Spinoza a rank plagiarist, or all original? He was neither. He was the legitimate heir to the past, and he, in his way, improved that past. His patrimony multiplied by his honest, grand, self-sacrificing industry. He collected the materials from all the four corners of history and created his own *Ethics*. His Monism or Pantheism, is his. He was original as much as man ever was and ever can be. All well considered, I think some of the hugest marble blocks of the *Ethics*, perhaps their very vital ideas, the grand all-god doctrine, the universe as but the splendid robe, the ever-shifting, veiling manifestation of the Deity, all creation but effulgence and emanation, permeated by the immanent Godhead, absorbed in the divine lap, as the wave in the ocean—all such ideas are the entail from the past, from Upanishads and Avesta to Zohar and Corduero, but originally reshaped and co-ordinated into a bold logical system by himself, by his own genius.

It is thus evidently proven that Spinoza did know, both the Jewish rationalists and the mystics, the Maimonides, etc., and the Qabbalists. Indeed, a descendant of a Spanish refugee, a student in Amsterdam could not help knowing them. He knew their strong and their weak sides. The question of Prof. W. Wundt, whether this can be shown, is thus decidedly answered. Spinoza says expressly, in Tract. theol., polit., ix.: "I have read especially certain new nugatory Qabbalists, at whose madness I could not wonder enough."[1] Thus he knew the Qabbala. But he knew its weak points too. Indeed, side by side with the highest, most logical and abstruse metaphysical ideas on divinity, universe, ethics, soul, etc. there, the larger part of the Zohar is occupied with measuring the several visages and phases in or of the Godhead, the nose, eyebrows and eyelashes and the dimensions of the divine beard! The absurd and revolting metaphors and loose images are claimed to express the relation of the visible to the invisible worlds in the universe. After long and abstruse studies and meditations concerning the Supreme Universal Essence, which is the sober and sublime part of the Zohar, treating of the Incomprehensible, Unknowable, Infinite, Non-existing for human experience, called: Ain-Soph and Aïn—the Zohar leaves off abruptly that bold flight of speculation, and as if to hide that, resorts to puerile anthropomorphism, of a diametrically opposite school, of the book *Shiur-Qoma,* dragging down the Deity into the low sphere of the senses and describing the Supreme One with the dimensions of a Hindu idol, the mythologic "Briareus," or the Avestean "Mithra with his ten thousand eyes," thus aiming at satisfying the thinking and the unthinking ones. To this refers Spinoza, "sneering" at the madness of certain "nugatory Qabbalists!" He had, indeed, no easy task to sift out the grain from the husk, the solid, metaphysical ideas and

---

[1] Legi etiam et insuper novi nugatores aliquos kabbalisticas quorum insaniam nunquam mirari satis potui.—Tract. Theol. Polit. IX.

vistas from the entangling and overgrown weeds of ancient and mediæval, exploded superstitions and vanquished notions. It was a Herculean task to clean that "Augean stable" containing the dead remnants of by-gone metaphysics, mysticism and common priestcraft. But he was rewarded for his labors with noble finds, the costliest gems of pure metaphysical thought and the sad yet sublime ethics imbedded at the bottom of the ocean of the Qabbala and all its predecessors, hailing from all creeds, all countries and all ages. Bound to no doctrine, no creed, no race, nor country, he devoted his services to what he thought to be the truth. He waved as G. E. Lessing, the absolute truth offered him, ready-made, by supernaturalism, and grasped after the possible truth to be reached by human reason. "Truth is the seal of God." To the search of that divine seal, he devoted his energies and his life, and what he believed to be truths, he deposited in his *Ethics*. The religionist cannot accept them as the final divine truths, nor can the philanthropist, nor the sociologist. As Heine says: "Lampe needs a personal God," a father and providence. But Spinoza had not devoted to either creed, church, philanthropy or political economy. His only love, his cult, was the truth as found by his own reason, and that was his *Ethics*. His is a philosophy, desolate and arid as the eternal granite rocks; cold and unproductive as the Alpine snows; but solid and irremovable as granite; pure, chaste and sublime as those everlasting snows. Whether we like and accept those *Ethics* or not, we would by no means miss them, and the nearest stepping stone to these *Ethics* was, indeed, the Qabbala and the Zohar. Many important elements are original. So especially did he remove the everlasting philosophical stumbling block of original dualism. Nearly all the preceding systems stumbled over it. He bridged over smoothly that yawning gap between mind and matter. His bold genius showed how these may be but human forms of vision, while to the Infinite Source of Existence they may be identical, the same thing under different aspects or attributes, attributes which really are infinite in the infinite Godhead. Contemplate to what subterfuges all the preceding systems resorted to bridge over that abyss, from the Vedas and Plato to Zohar, Malebranche and Geulinx. The Neo-Platonic Emanation doctrine does not solve it. If thought and extension, or mind and matter are opposing, irreconcilable principles, how can the Infinite Mind emanate or create the other, its own contrary? Spinoza alone satisfactorily solved the difficulty. His hypothesis of their relative difference, but real and absolute identity in the Supreme Infinite, is strongly probable, the fact of their simultaneous existence and constant harmony proves that they are not irreconcilable, but phases in the Supreme Essence, split alone by the prismatic short-sightedness of human vision. Gebirol came very near that view. He says: "The form is never without matter, and matter never without form. They are held together by the divine Will . . . . and stand to each other in the relation of writer, writing and writing material." (See later on Gebirol.) He failed only to show that mind and matter are but human forms of viewing separately what in reality is but one Substance. This Spinoza did, as many other leading features. Hence is he the author of the system, because he collected all its rays into one focus, and shaped all into one logical body of doctrines. As a whole, as a system, the Ethics are undoubtedly original. Spinoza was one of the most independent and self-reliant thinkers that ever lived. As the builders of the pyramids, his work will stand forth as the product of a single man of genius; nevertheless he owed the materials to his predecessors, the Zohar inclusive.

PROFS. FRANCK AND WUNDT ON THAT.

We conclude this discussion concerning the affinities between Spinoza and the Qabbala, generally coinciding on this point with Prof. Franck, that the import of the Qabbala for the modern student is not its mysticism, nor its allegorical Bible interpretations, nor its practical miracle working, nor its claims to be a tradition from yonder fabulous Mishna teacher, prophet or patriarch. The real interest in the Qabbala is purely scientific. It is its rational, metaphysical theories supplementing a link in the history of human thinking. It offers an epitome and abstract of the metaphysical and ethical thoughts of nearly all the preceding ages and thinkers from Zoroaster, Thales, Pythagoras and Plato down to its own times, all are roughly worked up into a sort of harmonious system, showing one fundamental line of reasoning, ever unfolding and developing, until comparatively modern times, and connecting the past philosophic thought to the present one. It holds the keynote also to the theosophy, the philosophy and ethics of the Jewish people. It offers its own reply to the great humanitarian and sociological questions as developed further in these pages, concerning the destiny of man and the final aims of history, according to the genius of the Hebrew people. Especially it shows:[1] "That the philosophy which at first produced so much surprise and indignation, viz: the idea of God as unique Substance, the immanent Cause and the real nature of all that exists"—that idea is not entirely new. It proves that long before, some of the leading minds of all the nations and zones have speculated and meditated, if not entirely and identically in the same way, but at least inclining towards and parallel to that line of thought. This is for the modern truth-seeker very important, and this is his real interest in the Qabbala, and the Zohar in particular. It further adduces the proof that the antecedents and predecessors of Spinoza's *Ethics* were, no doubt, Plato, Aristotle, Philo and the Neo-Platonists as long ago surmised; but they were also much earlier, as early as Zoroaster's doctrines as emphasized by Prof. Franck and as more fully elaborated in my Zend-Avesta studies, followed up by Vedanta studies. On the other hand, Philo and his Alexandrian school, Mishna, Guemara and Aggada, Book of Creation, down to Maimonides, Gebirol, the Qabbala and the Zohar, with its commentators, all of them deposited their germs, fructified Spinoza's mind and rendered it capable of logically constructing and producing his *Ethics* with their grand, metaphysical doctrines. And this is no derogation to the creative genius of the Hollandish thinker. For since philosophy assumes that even God creates, not ex-nihilo, but by emanation, and that every effect must have its adequate cause or precedent, it is not belittling Spinoza when assuming that he brought out in his system, ideas latent in him and in their germ existing in his mind, derived from his predecessors and more fully elaborated, harmonized and completed by his own constructive genius. When,

[1] Franck Qabbala, 30.

therefore, Professor W. Wundt, of the Leipsic University, more than fifteen years ago remarked to me that, "Admitting the great analogy between Maimonidean doctrines and those of Spinoza, remains yet the difficulty of proving their direct influence upon him,"—this proof has been adduced here, and the direct influence demonstrated, since he himself quotes them in his *Tractatus, Theol. Polit.*, in his *Letters* and in his *Ethics.* He not only quotes them, nay, he appeals to their opinions as coinciding and corroborating his, not on minor points, but on the very leading ideas of his system, those involving a theistic pantheism as a logical congruency. While he at the same time repudiates and smiles at the extravagances of the Qabbalists. I trust that these lines will find yet Prof. W. Wundt hearty, hale and sound, and will be kindly received by him as a message of genial greetings from a former pupil and reverent friend beyond the Atlantic.

CHAPTER III.

PHILO'S PHILOSOPHY.

Among the many known thinkers of ancient times who have made a deep mark in the literatures come down to us from olden times, who have moulded human thought and turned it into channels not yet dried up today, who greatly influenced Judaism, Christianity and Islamism, who have simply stood godfather to the very leading doctrines of the present official, reigning churches, who have created both rationalism and mysticism, metaphysics and thaumaturgy, religion and superstition in Synagogue and Church, who connect the doctrines of Bactria and Chaldea, of Plato and Aristotle, of Plotin and the Zohar, to those of Descartes and Spinoza—is Philo, the Judaean of Alexandria, contemporaneous with the birth of the Christian founder and the Teachers of the Mishna. Frequently having the opportunity in these pages to mention that philosophy and that voluminous writer, Philo, whose doctrines are, indeed, pervading in a modified or accurate manner the metaphysics and the mysticism of the Talmud, Midrashim, the *Book of Creation,* etc., down to the Qabbalists and the Zohar, let us have here a survey of that personality and his philosophy. Philo flourished at the dawn of the present era in Alexandria. He had all the science of his age, united to Jewish lore as far as cultivated in that Egyptian-Greek metropolis, a center of wealth, refinement and learning. He made great efforts to combine the methods and views of Greek science with those of Judaean religion and thought. In that attempt he hardly succeeded, because they really and widely differ. He was a follower of Plato, and believed to be a Platonist. But really he loomed away from him and most essentially modified his system. He was, in fact, a Neo-Platonist. He accepted, but strongly modified the platonic theory. He taught: There exist from all eternity two substances—luminous mind and chaotic matter. God is Supreme mind and the highest Idea. He holds all the prototypes or

Ideas in his being; an infinity of Ideas; they are the types and powers of all individual existences impressed into inert matter. But soon he abandoned that view for biblical "creation," then again for the emanation theory; approaching soon Monotheism, and soon Pantheism, matter being but the last condensation of *mind.*[1] "God is all."—Let us elucidate:

PHILO ON GOD.

Philo's philosophy teaches: "God, per sĕ, in His essence, cannot be conceived by our senses, nor defined in our thought, nor described by our language. He is without attributes and without name. All we can say of Him is but in a negative way; He is not limited in time nor in space, nor by any other being; His existence is not dependent on anything, nor accidental. He is not in time, He holding eternity in his bosom. He is the Being, the Essence. He is, He is who ever will be, as He ever was. The Sacred Writ expresses that by Ihvh.[2] He is the ineffable unchangeable, alone uncreated and uncomposed, the only reality. He is the arch-type of all perfection, the Absolute, the Only One; higher than goodness, virtue, science, beauty (God-Ideals of Socrates and Plato). He is the Intellectus Activus of the universe. He is omniscient, omnipresent, ever creative, the Space[3] holding the universe. He is unlimited since He is one and is all. He is the Arch-light, eradiating innumerable rays, (emanating creations), the Source of light, the Sun of the sun."[4] Thus we see here Philo following biblical views on God and creation.

ECLECTICISM OF PHILO.

But Philo is an eclectic; soon he resorts to emanation ideas, anticipating later Neo-Platonists, then, too, Avestian views: God is light, "Ahura." He says: "Evil does not come from God,"[5] a saliently Zoroastrian view, later largely and profusely borrowed and used by the Zohar to express such Parsee and Neo-Platonic philosophems. All this Philo affirms as inductions from the manifestations of the Deity in the world. Thus he

---

1 Posterit. Caini, 239 M. 2 אהיה אשר אהיה 3 ὁ τόπος, מקום. 4 Vita Mosis I, M, 92—De Somn I, 648, etc. 5 De Posterit. Caini, 286.

says: "God exists; it cannot be otherwise since there is a universe. The effect must have a cause, and this cause must be adequate to the effect. Since there are beings, there must be a Supreme Being, of whom sensual existence is but a reflex. He is above the universe, time and space."[1] "The universe is such a wonderful work, hence must its architect be most perfect and excellent."[2] This is all Jewish thought. Again elsewhere he follows Greek models: God is not the author of the universe, but the Logos is,[3] the Sophia, is . . . .

SACRED WRIT. TALMUD.

The sacred scriptures of the Hebrew Canon are to him the product of divine inspiration,[4] and he believes to prove and substantiate that with arguments. He makes efforts to conciliate his platonic theories with those of Mosaism. The anthropomorphic expressions of the Bible, those ascribing to God, limbs, affects, changing moods, etc., he explains as does the Talmud, as accommodations to man's limited understanding. "The Thora speaks in human language."—Again he expounds i. M. i.: 27: "God created man in His image," not meaning God's image, but that of the Logos, the middler between God and the world.[5] The Talmudists and Targums follow often his interpretations in their desire to discard all anthropomorphic notions from the Deity. In Philo's eclecticism we often find expressions re-echoing pantheistic theories. The Talmud reproduces but modifies such views usually. So Philo designates "God as the Place of the universe," (the Persian "Zrvana-Akarana"), or "God and the universe are one and the same," or "God is called the *Place*, since He is the being that embraces all."[6] All such sentences are strongly modified in the Aggada. The Rabbis frequently use *"Place," Maqom,* as a metaphor and standing epithet for the Deity. So R. Jose b. Chalaptha (of the II cent.)

---

1 De confus. ling. 425, M.—De Mundi Offic. 8, 5. 2 Philo De proem. et poen. 414 M., etc. 3 Vita Mosis, M. 155. 4 Vita Mosis, III, 165, M.

5 De Opif. M. 23, I, 16, Not *ὲικόνα θεοῦ*, but Κατ' *εικόνα θεου*. 6 Philo de confus. ling., 339, etc. *ο των ὃλων τοποσ.*—Philo de confus. ling. I, 425, M: *Εισ και το παν, αυτοσ εστιν.—Αυτοσ ὁ θεὸσ καλειται τοποσ το παρεχειν μὲν τα ὅλα.* Philo de Somn, I, 227.

says: "We know not whether God is the Place of the world or the world is the Place of God." While R. Isaak says: "It is written 'the residence of the God of old' . . God is the residence of the world, not the world the residence of God."[1] That means: God is not limited by anything. Such utterings of Philo's philosophems, modified by the Rabbis, we hear often, even from Maimonides,[2] all being anxious to ward off pantheism.

PHILO ON MAN AND LOGOS. MANU AND BRAHMAN.

We read (i. M.: 3.22): "Behold Adam is like one of us to distinguish between good and evil."—Conform to his preceding view, Philo interprets this as saying: "Adam is like the Logos, the mediator between God and the world." Philo follows here an old oriental view that the first man was a semi-divinity, who assisted the Supreme Being in the development of the universe. So in the Vedas is Brahman the first divine manifestation, and Manu, the lawgiver, is among the first creations and assistants in the further production of the world. In nearly all mythologies the first man is divinized and made a partner in creation. Brahman and Manu, both signifying intelligence, were identified by Philo in his conception of the *Logos;* and in the Qabbala they were sublimized into that of *Adam Qadmon.* Manu is remembered in the Talmud as the "first Man, *Adam Harishon,*" and fabulously magnified. That lies, too, in part, at the bottom of the later messiah ideal, and shows strikingly the growth of mythological conceptions turned into philosophems. Pappus, a Talmudical teacher, expounds in that same sense, in presence of R. Akiba, mitigating a little and saying: "Adam is as one of the angels."—"Nevermore," interrupts R. Akiba. The real import of the verse is to say that man is free, as God is, to choose between good and evil. "Behold, man is the only one earthly creature that, by his own free will, can distinguish and choose between good and evil."[3] That view is decidedly rational and soundly biblical. Nevertheless we have seen above, quoting

---

[1] אין אנו יודעין אם הקב"ה מקומו של עולם, או אם העולם מקומו, דכתיב, הנה מקום אתי. Midrash Rabba I, M, 68.

[2] Nore Nebuchim, I, 70.

[3] כאחד ממלאכי השרת—דייך פפוס—שנתן לו הקב"ה שני דרכים. Midrash Rabba, I, M, 21.

from Talm. Hagiga,[1] that R. Akiba had a belief in a halfway supernatural Davidian Messiah, who occupied even a throne nearby the Deity Himself! He could, therefore, afford to let pass Pappus' exegesis. His own "Davidian with the second throne" is just the Talmudical and Zoharitic *Metatron*, viz: a second throne, beneath that of the Supreme Deity. The rebuke he gave to Pappus he got back with interest from R. Jose, who expounded the two thrones (of Daniel VII.) as belonging to the two divine aspects, "love and justice." Such were Gnostic views too, of a Philonian type. But the Qabbalists, and the Zohar especially, made the greatest use and abuse of Philo's Logos and the Hindu Manu. He became the Alter-Ego, the first Sephira, the All-powerful "Adam Qadmon," the viceroy, the *"Crown"* of all; he became the great universal type, the real creator, the Celestial Man, fully corresponding to the Hindu II. Brahman and *Manu*, and occupying even a higher position in the Qabbalistic mythology than Manu is in the Vedas. He is the Celestial Man, and the earthly man was his copy and image. He is the model of the trinitarian Messiah. The Rabbinical *Adam Harishon* and Metatron are kindred exemplars of the same prototype, the fabulous *Adam Harishon*, of the Talmud, and the mythologic *Adam Qadmon*, of the Qabbala, are simply the Adam of Genesis i. 26: "Let us form a *man of earth* in our image and likeness to rule over . . ." Him Oriental and Occidental mysticism raised to divine Vice-royalty, "Metatron," near the throne.

PRIMORDEAL MATTER.

Philo thought with Plato that the material universe is coeternal with God. It existed primordeally as the original inert mass, the Greek *Chaos*, the Biblical *Tohu-Wabohu*, and the crea-

---

[1] Hagiga 14, a: It is written in Daniel vii, 9: "Two thrones were placed,... His throne was fire-flames?"—R. Akiba expounds: "One for the Ancient of Days, and one for David." R. Jose rebukes him: "How long will you desecrate the Shekhina!" It means one throne for "Justice" and one for "Mercy," "Middath Haddin and Middath Harahamim" divine attributes, mystical expressions, denoting the two phases of justice and of mercy in the Deity; later developed into the "God of Justice" and the "God of Love," and claimed as characteristic of the Deity in the Old Testament and that in the New Testament.

tion of Gen. I. was really but a formation of organisms out of pre-existing materials. This work God did not perform Himself, but through His Logos, His *first-born Son,* and creation he describes as God's second-born Son. God began this creation by the formation of the ideal, the intelligible world of ideas; he emanated spiritual types and models of the individual existences." Philo says: "When God was about to create the world he recognized that without a finished model no fine image could be produced, that every work must have its spiritual arch-type. Thus he formed first the intelligible world of *ideas.*[1] But these typical ideas are not only models; they are also forces and efficient causes; they worked on the rough mass of primæval matter, and really made it what it is." We shall further on see that the Zohar copied this theory ad literam in putting into the mouth of its pretended author, R. Shimeon B. Jochai, the mysterious words that God began creating worlds by Himself and directly, which worlds collapsed! Until he emanated the first Sephira, Adam Qadmon, then only by the assistance of this latter one He succeeded in calling forth the world as it is. This primæval Adam is the ideal universe, its prototype, the spiritual pattern after which the sensual one is modulated. This is a Philonian theory, followed by others, and also by the Qabbalists. This theory we find also in the *Vedas,* as alluded to above; the first man, *Manu,* was the first type and the arch-father of mankind, though a creature, he assisted the Self-Existent, the Supreme God, in the creation. The Brahmanic role of Manu was thus taken up and further elaborated by Philo, the Talmud and most of later mystico-philosophical systems, and finally it came out in the Qabbala, greatly exaggerated and sublimized, as Adam Qadmon, the real Creator of the universe. Thus I believe to find here the cue to the curious fact that mystics and philosophers claimed to place a human mediator between the Deity and the universe. Manu, Deucalion, Buddha, Zarathustra, Adam, Logos, Messiah, Demiurgos, Adam Qadmon, etc., were stages in that concept, all derived from born-Brahman.

Great initiators begin as men, live as martyrs and finish as gods. They link heaven to earth, showing to their struggling

---

1 Philo de Mundi Opif, 4, 7 and 50 M.

fellow-men the avenues to more goodness, intelligence and happiness. As a reward, they are apotheosized by posterity. Pity only that usually the apotheosis takes its way by the cross; this latter one being, alas, the necessary stepping stone to the former. Happy for mankind that there are some enthusiasts who are not deterred even by that. The vulgar sneers at them; they equanimously pray: "Father pardon thy children! They know not what they are doing," and rise from the martyr's block to the heavenly crown of thorns.

PHILO ON CREATION, EMANATION.

In that way Philo believed to have steered clear through the difficulty of choosing between the biblical "creation from nothing"[1] and Plato's "co-eternal matter," by the compromise of the chaotic informal mass—the "Tohu Wabohu," mentioned, too, in Gen. i. 2—which only the divine ideas or types fully organized. But this can logically and really be understood only in the light of the doctrine of emanation. God emanated the Ideas which alone made chaos a real substance. An aboriginal primæval matter in the sense of Plato and Aristotle, Philo could not accept, though claiming to follow them. Nor did he accept the biblical view that God created the world out of nothing, because as a philosopher he affirmed that every effect must have its adequate cause, and that something cannot come from nothing; that since, according to Gen. i. 1, God created matter, then matter must be inherent in God—which again he could not accept, that being anti-Judaic. Originally claiming to follow Plato, his biblical instinct felt repelled. Desiring to follow Genesis I. and creation, his philosophical instinct was not satisfied. He then believed that he could reconcile Mosaism and Plato by the doctrine of his ideal *types,* or divine ideas impressed by God into dim chaos, which ideas alone made matter what it is. This was the compromise between his religious and his scientific conscience, and really whenever he is not hampered by the shadow of Plato, he inclines toward emanation, soon fully and frankly taught by his successors, the Neo-Platonists. Those arch-types

---

[1] בריאת יש מאין

or ideas are parts of the Deity Himself, rays from His original arch-light, eradiations from His being.[1]

Have these ideas any independence, any existence for themselves? Or are they but reflexes from the great mysterious Light? Philo answers this diversely on different occasions. They are often divine servants and representatives like the biblical angels and the mythical gods. Their number is six and more even. That reminds one of the Zoroastrian Ameshas Spentas, varying from six to thirty-two and more. Two of those emanations, Philo calls "Goodness and Power!"[2] These two we find also in Talmud. So Hagiga 14 a, R. Jose says: The two thrones (of Daniel VII.) refer to the attributes of "Mercy and Justice," as quoted before. Philo says: The first, Goodness, created all; the other, Power, governs all. . . . Both are combined and united by a third agent, that is the Logos.[3] We see here the genesis of all such speculations, the later ten emanations of Neo-Platonism, of the Talmudical ten words, the Maimonidean ten classes of angels, and the Qabbalistical ten Sephiroth. Originally they were but abstractions of divine attributes, the deity viewed from different standpoints by the human contemplator. Gradually they became beings, metaphorically; at last from love of the mystic, they were accepted as realities, as divine genii and independent powers influencing the world and men for good and for bad, whose ire was to be deprecated, and whose favor was to be gained by worship and offerings. This is the evolution of the mythological gods, the mystic angels and the Zoharitic Sephiroth.

ZOROASTER, PLATO, PHILO AND ZOHAR.

Let us not overlook this interesting feature, viz: the Platonic God-mind, the highest Idea, etc., and its opposite, the primæval matter, rebellious to God and harbinger of evil and sin, strongly reminds us of the Zoroastrian God of Light and his opponent, God of Darkness. As the original matter is naturally instinct with evil, even so is the Zoroastrian God of Evil. Both appear to be but one and the same philosophical view, differently expressed; or a further development from some common origin, or

---

1 Philo De Somn. 652. 2 Philo De Cherub. 143. 3 Ibidem.

the same doctrine differently interpreted. The Platonic God-mind and highest Idea is the Zoroastrian Ahura Mazda, God of light; and the rebellious, inert, chaotic matter of the first is the Agro Mainyu, head of the wicked dævas of Parseeism. Plato only called the two by their real names, Mind and Matter. The Avesta spiritualized and personified both as the highest genii of existence, God and Daeva, Ahura and Agro Mainyu, the good and the bad spirits, as according to Avestean mythology, the god represented the patron, and also the thing patronized, which again is Platonic, too. Each being had its heavenly type in the ideal world. Philo followed the same system to a certain extent. He, too, placed the crude, dark, eternal matter at the other end of the scale of beings, inert and impregnated with evil and sin, rebellious to the God of light and virtue. There, too, we recognize the Parsee *Ahura,* and his opponent, wicked Ahriman, both with their hosts of genii and dævas. The Qabbalists and the Zohar following Philo and unconsciously also Parseeism, converted the rebellious matter into their evil spirit, *Ashmedai* with his *Kliphoth,* shells, spiritless matter, lifeless and lightless. Thus we find Zoroaster, Plato, Philo and Zohar enunciating the same theories, identical in reality, different but in words, and this is another illustration of the identity of leading doctrines in the ethical domain of human thought, the view often followed up in our series of publications all along. Here we find a striking instance of the parallelism. Parsee Zoroaster, Greek Plato, Judaean Philo and Rabbinical Qabbala all offer, closely seen in different words and forms, really but one and the same substance of thought.

PHILO'S LOGOS.

Philo, a born Jew, even a patriotic Jew, but educated an Alexandrian, a platonic philosopher, labored hard to conciliate both these heterogeneous ethic and cosmic systems of Moses and of Plato. In all his very numerous writings we find this struggle apparent. Sometimes this system and at other times the other one preponderated in his mind. Then again both were fused together, and not always very happily and logically. This is especially apparent in his definition of the Logos. We have seen his theory: The Deity eradiated from His own spiritual essence two original forces: goodness and power, and those two are united by a third one, the Logos. What the Logos is, Philo indicates only by poetical figures and tropes. The Logos is [1] the arch-type of the universe; he is the universe spiritually, the model after which the material one was formed. But he is not only the model, he is also the creative and conservative original power; God created and maintains the world through the instrumentality of the Logos. It is not easy to understand how he can be a created power and at the same time the original power? He can be but a borrowed power and reflex, God Himself being the original power, source of all. Here Philo is in opposition to himself. Most interesting! This contradiction, this hesitation and vacillation is going on to this day. Philo's Logos became the rabbinical Metatron, the "first-born Son" of Christology and the Adam Qadmon of the Qabbala. The uncertainty of Philo's definition clings to its evolutions to this day. Are they divine phases and attributes, or creatures, or co-equals? If they are created, they cannot be original powers, God alone being the origin of all.

According to Philo (Ibidem): "The Logos is declared to be the efficient divine wisdom, 'the highest Idea' of Plato, encompassing all other Ideas; or the supreme, divine Power, comprising all other powers; or again the sum total of the intelligible, supernatural world." That means: Dividing all existence into the philosophical triad: God the Infinite and Unknowable All, the spiritual forces containing the efficient types, and finally the realized universe, modulated after these types—the Logos represents the mediating link between God and the created world; he is the sum total of the efficient, spiritual forces between God and World. "Logos is the spiritual house of God, as the world in his material house. Or he is simply being, the essence of all things created."[2] Here is, then, the protoplasm, the eternal matter at the side of the God of Plato! Again, "Logos is also the Book of God; he is His metropolis, the middler between God and men; the Vice-gerent of the universe; the ambassador or the high priest; the herald and the prophet of God; the arch-

[1] Leg. alleg. III, 106 M. [2] Hence corresponding to Ihvh.

angel and the advocate of the world; who brings pardon and conciliation to men."[1] All that was well utilized by the church in her Christological doctrines. Philo serving many gods and wishing to conciliate many philosophies, Greek, Egyptian, Zoroastrian, and last, not least, his own dear Judaism and Bible, pays court to each of these systems in turn—except to logic and consistency. He does this to a marvelous extent: "The Logos is neither created (as other beings are) nor is he uncreated as God is."[2] "He is the combining link of the goodness and the power of God." "He is higher than they." "He is but a metaphor and attribute identical with the divine wisdom."[3] Again "he is a reality, the second Divine Being, extraneous to God! The image of God! the shadow of God! He is everything, poetically, but we know not what he is really." Sometimes again Logos is but a created being, but the first and highest creature, the first-born son of God. "The Logos is the elder, the world the younger son of God," which is but a metaphor and a poetical form of speech to express the relation between the Supreme Source and its emanations. Soon he calls the Supreme One, ὁ Θεοσ and the Logos, Θεοσ without the article, or δευτεροσ Θεοσ, the second God in order to discriminate between them.[4] And with all that he believes to be a Jew and a consistent monotheist. He holds the Bible to be inspired, the revelation of that very Logos about whom he spends such a vast amount of—poetry to express and define what nobody, inclusive of himself, is fairly able to understand—something beyond all human ingenuity. So Goethe says, just there where the ideas are lacking, words are most welcome to fill the gap. Dr. J. Hamburger, in his Real Encyclopædia, Part II., gives an excellent account of our theme, adducing all the necessary passages from the numerous works of the Alexandrine philosopher.

Philo finds, with the same facility and ingenuity, his Greek pantheism in the Sacred Writ. By means of his allegorical interpretations he makes every biblical person, story and commandment embody and illustrate his own theories. In such a way he finds his many-fold Logos also in Pentateuch and Bible. Of

---

[1] De profug. 20. [2] Qu. rer. divin. haer. 501 M. [3] Leg. alleg. I, 56 M.
[4] Philo de Somn. I, 655 M.

course, the Church utilized these exegetical and allegorical interpretations to the utmost of her powers and ingenuity for her own purposes. The Talmud and Aggada have from him their Metatron. And the Zohar utilized exactly the same reasonings for its vastly developed Sephiroth theories, especially its own gorgeous logos version, the Adam Qadmon, all of which we shall see, are but a logical and natural development of Philonian metaphysics and mystics. This is the reason why we are sketching here the system of the father of Alexandrine Neo-Platonism. Without its knowledge, the Zohar and the Qabbala would be riddles. They would be considered revealed wonders by the credulous, and rank nonsense by the logically thinking. They would be deemed at any rate original, but, in fact, they are none of these three. They are a historical development of Philo's philosophy and system, with a Hebrew-Chaldee nomenclature.

Before proceeding let us condense what we have seen concerning that Alexandrine system. It teaches: the origin of the universe, God, the first Cause, is unknowable, beyond the conception, beyond the senses and the reason of man. God did not create the world; its creator is the Logos. The mystics and apocryphæ denominated that the Wisdom or Sophia. The Qabbala and Zohar made of that the Adam Qadmon. This Logos is metaphorically the first-born son of God. The Logos emanated six great powers and many subordinate ones, and these by further emanations and developments called forth the universe, the younger Son of God. This is our universe of matter, a late and far-off condensation of its original Source; the further therefrom the less luminous and spiritual it is. God, Logos and emanated world are the triad of Philo's system.

The intelligent reader will see that Philo here has entirely abandoned Plato's and Aristotle's dualism, and that he has rather elaborated Avestian theories with some slight biblical coloring. In Parseeism we find Infinite Space and Time calling forth Ahura Mazda and his oppponent Agro Mainyu, the six Ameshas Spentas, the subordinate genii, etc. Later Philo's philosophy gave to Christianity the Christ Son of God, etc. It gave to the Qabbala its Adam Qadmon, Sephiroth, emanated universe, etc. These are all Philonian conceptions, with new names.

PHILO IN THE TALMUD. EVIL. APOCHRYPHÆ.

There is no doubt that these Parsee-Hellenic doctrines of Philo are unbiblical, and were recognized and accentuated as non-Jewish in the Talmud. So in Hagiga 14 a R. Akiba argues, with his philosophizing colleagues concerning such extraneous theories as the acceptance of an original matter, non-created and co-eternal with the Infinite. He alludes maybe to Thales, who claimed that the original, eternal matter was water. R. Akiba there says in his metaphorical and mysterious way: "When ye arrive at the pure marbles, viz.: the typical matter, do not shout 'water! water!' (as the original chaotic matter)." So, too, the Evangelist (ii. Petri, 3-5) reads: "Earth was made by water." In Jerus. Hagiga xi. a, we read: "B. Soma says: I looked at the water above and below, and saw there is but a hand's breadth between both (going to show that the original matter of the universe was water). For it is written: 'And the spirit of God hovered over the water.'" This doctrine is there declared as anti-Judaic. Such Hellenic allusions are to be found by the scores in the Talmud, and usually rejected as anti-biblic by the disputants. Even so are mentioned and refuted as non-Jewish the theory of the Logos and Philo's other powers as being concerned with the deity in the creation, as middlers between the Infinite and the creation. The large majority of Talmudical teachers do not recognize any such mediators. But the Platonic theory of typical ideas as spiritual models, not original co-eternal forces and sub-divinities, only as simple types, created ideal patterns, after which the material world was fashioned, found its rabbinical advocates. So in Pesachim 54: "Seven things were created before the creation of the world: Law, repentance, hereafter, the divine throne, the temple and the name of the messiah." Most characteristically is this theory expressed in a Jewish garb: "As the architect builds his palace to conform to his plan previously made, even so God looked into the Thora and created the world."[1] So, too: "With ten words creation was

[1] Midrash Rabboth I, M. first chap.

effected: Wisdom, intelligence, science, power, energy, justice, right, love and mercy."[1] These philosophems were elaborated and extended by Qabbalists and Zohar with slightly altered names, but with that salient and radical difference that there they were not simply ideals, types or divine attributes, but real entities, personal forces, living creative powers, mediators between God and world, just as in Christianity, as in Philo's and Zoroaster's schemes. Nevertheless, are many passages extant in Talmud and Aggada, where the Philonic doctrines of emanation, or mediating, divine powers, found their unqualified expression; especially do we find this in the Apochryphæ, Wisdom of Solomon, etc. The biblical passages adduced by Philo as teaching a second deity, the Logos, are often discussed by the Talmudists and Philo's heresies are warded off and discarded.

According to Philo is this our sensual world, a material image of its intellectual prototype,[2] modulated after that primordeal pattern. That intellectual world alone is the divine residence, *οικοσ θεου.* But our material cosmos is also perfect and everlasting. This view is not Judaic, nor do I believe biblical. The Bible to all appearance teaches creation out of nothing, and not the eternity of matter, nor even emanations; the world, as all creatures, is perishable. Above we saw that Philo assumes that from God is derived but the good, while evil is the result of the material world; it is innate in the original matter, rebellious to the deity. This, too, is non-Judaic. More realistic is the theory of the Rabbis: "Not in the world, but in man is the seat of evil, as the result of his moral freedom. Being free, he chooses the wrong side sometimes, and hence comes his own harm. Evil is the result of the human evil-doers."[3]

PHILO ON THE SOUL.

Philo says: "The verse, and He (God) breathed into his nostrils a breath of life, (Gen. ii. 7), means to say that part of the divine nature irradiated into this sublunar world."[4] Again:

---

1 Hagigah 12, a. 2 "Κοσμοσ νοητοσ" Philo De Opif. mundi 4.
3 Midr. Rabboth 5 M, Portion ראה. "See I place before thee life and good, or death and sin, choose." 4 De Mundi Opif. I, 92.

"The spirit of man is a part of God."[1] He thus believes in the pre-existence of the soul. The Aggada sometimes follows that view, though it is not Jewish, nor biblical. But Qabbala and Zohar adhere to it and elaborate it. They gloat over it. There is a treasure of pre-existing souls, all divine emanations, gradually joining their bodies in this world, transmigrating in several bodies, and when purified, rejoining the Deity.[2] That is Philo's theory. He says: "How could the human soul, such a diminutive thing, with its brain or heart comprehend the vast universe, if it were not a part of the soul of God! It is its radiation ever remaining in connection with it.[3] Correctly remarks here Dr. J. Hamburger[4] that this is decidedly Greek pantheism, thinking the Deity immanent in the universe, not extra-mundane. Of course the Talmudical teachers repudiate such views. Philo is inconsistent herein as generally in his versatile utterances. Elsewhere he questions whether the soul outlives the body.[5] Maybe he means there the animal soul, *Nephesh,* not the higher one, *Ruach*. For the Qabbala, too, distinguishes three sorts of souls in the one and same body—the highest alone being divine. Another result of Philo's doctrine of the eternal, rebellious, sinful matter and of the co-divinity of the soul, is that he assumes the soul is but with repugnance and against its will, united to the body. The body is the hot-bed of sin, a burden to its divine *psyche,* a prison.[6] The soul feels liberated after the body's death. In Pentateuch and Bible the opinions on that subject are diverse. "God blessed the first couple." (Gen. i. 28). Later he expelled them from the Garden of Eden (Gen. iii, 23). "For the inclination of man's heart is but evil every day" (Gen. iv. 5). Even so in Talmud and Aggada, sometimes assuming the body to be the temple of God, and sometimes the incarceration of the soul. Qabbala and Zohar are consistently of the Philonian opinion that the body is radically bad. Nature and matter are the husks and offals,[7] as the eternal sinful matter of Philo. When about to enter the body, the soul

---

1 De Somnis I, 18, Pf. αποσμασα θεῶν 2 There also he follows earlier models, Brahmanism, etc. 3 Ibid, Pf. II, 202. 4 Real Encyclopædia on Philo. 5 De Somn. V. 16. 6 Leg. alleg. II, 19—III, 22—III, M. 95, etc. 7 Zohar I, 27 and Supplem. to Zohar 8.

weeps: 'Lord, I am happy here in heaven. I wish no other world. Slavery and contamination await me there."[1]

GOD AND ANGELS.

Philo accepts the mythological divinities and daemonia of the ancient world as real entities, divine emanations, spiritual potencies, the logoi and mediating spirits between the Supreme and the world.[2] The Bible mentions created spiritual angels, servants and messengers of God, executing His orders, creatures as all other created beings. Philo conceived them as emanated deities; they are part of the Supreme. The Pagan deities, he assumes to be identical with the angels of the Bible. The Jewish mystics are not far from that view. Their Metatron is a semi-god bearing even the sacred name *Ihvh*. Occasionally we find sentences in the Pentateuch that seem to admit of the reality of such heathen gods as patrons of the nations, corresponding to the Zoroastrian national genii and the rabbinical celestial lords of their respective peoples.[3] So Deuteronomy iv. 19: "Lest thou shouldst lift up thine eyes towards heaven and see the sun and moon, the stars and all the celestial hosts . . . . which *Ihvh*, thy *Elohim*, has allotted to the other nations . . . . but thee He has selected for Himself to be His own people" . . . .

As the creation of the material world formed from the original matter is not the work of God, but of the primordeal forces, the logoi, even so is the government and providence of the world their work, not that of the Supreme One. He says: "The universe is preserved by the invisible forces which take care that it should not collapse. For these forces are the indissoluble ties of the world.[4] These forces are omnipresent as God, everywhere active and creative.[5] God fills and encompasses the entire all. God and the All are one."[6] That clashes with the Jewish view of God being extra-mundane. He concludes: "God is the only Cause of all things, the Source of all that is, sole King and Ruler."[7]

---

1 Zohar II, 76. 2 De Somnis M. I, 22. De Gigant II, M. 263. 3 The Persian "Fravashis." 4 De Migratione Abr. 332. 5 Id. De Monarch. begin. 6 Leg. alleg. I, 14. 7 Leg. alleg. III, 3.

SINAI AND REVELATION.

Concerning the revelation on Sinai, he says: "When we read that God spoke to men, one must not believe that a voice was sensually audible in the air, but that the listening soul was filled with the purest divine light. Only in that way the divine word reaches the human ear. When the law was promulgated on Sinai, it is not said: the voice was heard, but it was seen by the entire people."[1] This is mostly constrained and inaccurate. The philosopher Philo wishes to conciliate here Philo, the Jew, and he spoils it with both. He wishes to interpret revelation as a psychic process, a subjective feeling, a vision: the divine word was rather a spiritual, inward experience, an intuition. Hence his claim that the divine voice was not heard, but seen, viz.: conceived. Now innumerable passages prove that the sacred writer accentuated the very contrary, viz.: that the voice was heard and no vision seen. Because to him was a vision, a figure, etc., more repugnant and anthropomorphic than the hearing of a voice. So we read in Gen. iii. 8: "And they heard the voice of Ihvh Elohim."—Deuter iv. 10: "And I caused them to hear my words" . .—Ibid. iv. 12: "And God spoke to you . . you heard the sound of the words, no vision or figure did you see, only a voice" . . Ibid. iv. 15: "Take well heed . . . you saw no manner of image when God spoke to you." More such sentences follow. The sacred writer deprecated images as most idolatrous. While the Alexandrine philosopher, his age having passed that coarser idolatrous phase, thought that hearing a divine voice also is humanizing the deity, and interpreted it by an intuitive vision, discarding thus the idea of God being seen or heard. Another time he conceives revelation more literally, and yet with a mystic interpretation,[2] following closer the expression of the Bible. While he at first, as a Greek rationalist, assumed that God speaks to man only by works, that only nature manifests the divine will, he again on other occasions, urged by the plain expression of the Sacred Writ, assents to the belief that man can receive revelations and divine commands directly by intuition, or by other, supernatural

[1] De Migr. Abr. [2] Vita Mosis I. 38.

means. Such suggestions are in the Talmud: "Ben Soma says: The voice of God to Moses was that of Metatron."[1] Even so in the New Testament:[2] "The law was delivered by angels, or through angelic mediation." R. Akiba says against that: When it is said: "God spoke to Moses" that means just that He spoke to *Moses,* not to an angel.[3]

ON PROPHETISM. VIRGIL.

On this theme Philo teaches: "One must despise the external forms, as one must despise the body and senses, in order to grasp the naked truth by intelligence and intuition. When God says to Abraham: 'Leave thy family, thy house and thy country,' this is to say that he should give up all externalities of body and senses, and pay attention only to the inwardness of things, for our body is but part of the earth on which to dwell the soul is compelled."[4] This is the consequence of Plato's "matter rebellious to God and seat of sin." The earth and the earthly body of man is but the husk, if not the prison of the soul, hence an obstacle to any higher intellectuality, and must be expelled as Hagar was by Abraham . . . . Priests and prophets renounce this world, rising above all sensuality to the realms of the Spirit . . . .[5] If thou wilt participate in the divine, thou must leave thy own self, leave the body and all sensual perceptions and receive the prophetic inspiration in a kind of excited, corybantic madness . . . .[6] When the divine frenzy of prophetic enthusiasm is to come over man he must become unconscious; the human merges into the divine. Ecstasy is the essential form of prophecy . . . . Then the prophet speaks not his own; the divine spirit dwells in him; he is moved involuntarily by that as by the strings of a musical instrument.[7]

Philo thus assumes prophecy to be a mystical, supernatural force, working unconsciously and involuntarily on man, he being but the vehicle and tool of divine inspiration. It is a divine ecstasy in the highest sense. Whatever we find in

1 Midr. Rabboth I, M. 5. 2 Heb. II, 2, and Acts VII, 53. 3 Midr. Rabboth 4, Moses 14. 4 De Cherubim I. 5 De gigant. 62. 6 Quis rer. divin. haer. M. 482. 7 De Migrat. Abr. M. 441, etc.

Hebrew and classic literature on that theme, seems to indicate that this was, too, the gentile and the Jewish view of prophecy.

Virgil describes a prophetess in the following verses (Æneis lib. vi. v. 42): "In the vast and enormous sides of the Eubean rocks, a profound cavern is cut out; a hundred avenues lead to its as many gates from where issue the responses of the Sibyl. Æneis scarcely entering there, she exclaims: "Here, here is the god, inquire into His oracles!" At once her features and color are changed. Her hair stands on end; panting, distracted, heavily breathing, her bosom swells and heaves, possessed by a divine madness. Her stature appears to grow taller; her voice has nothing mortal. It is the god that takes possession of and inspires her . . . . The Trojans are shaking with religious terror . . . . Æneis prays fervently to the present deity. The prophetess, yet wrestling with the God possessing her, is trembling with fury in her cavern striving to conquer her feelings. But the more she struggles the more the god overpowers her. Her fierce soul is overcome, her mouth is foaming, she is enslaved, body and mind, to her inspiration. In that manner delivers the sybil of Cume her oracles, and announces her redoubted mysteries, truths enveloped in profound darkness."[1] . . . . Here we have a sample of prophecy and prophets exactly answering the description of Philo. Whenever the Sacred Writ introduces a heathen prophet, he is depicted with

[1] Virgil Æneis, liber. VI, v. 42:

Excisum Euboicae latus ingens rupis in antrum,
Quo lati ducunt aditus centum, ostia centum,
Unde ruunt totidem voces, responsae Sibyllae
Ventum erat ad limen. quum virgo: "Pascere fata
Tempus, ait: Deus, ecce Deus . . .
"Subito non vultus, non color unus,
Non comptae mansere comae; sed pectus anhelum, . .
Nec mortale sonans, aflata est numine quando
Jam propiore Dei . . .
Tremor gelidus concurrit per ossa dura Teucris,
Rexque fundit preces . . .
At Phoebi nomdum patiens, immanis in antro
Bacchatur vates, magnum si pectore possit
Excussisse Deum: tanto magis ille fatigat
Os rabidum, fera corda domans fingitque premendo. . .

these Philonian colors of enthusiasm and excitement. So for instance is Balaam, etc., prostrate and closed-eyed, having ecstatic visions, apparently, in a high degree of excitement uttering but the words of an external, mysterious agent, claiming to be unconscious of their value, pretending to speak the very contrary of what he is asked and hired for.[1] "Come curse for me that people, so strong, that I may conquer it." Balaam refuses the offer: "For this house full of gold and silver I could not change the decrees of God . . . . How can I curse whom God has not cursed . . . . Who can count the dust of Jacob, and who measure the camps of Israel . . . . may I end as he . . . . ." Hosea ix. 7, mentions the prophet as foolish and mad. The grand Isaiah speaks with the impetuosity of a mountain torrent, burning the dross of sin and hypocrisy with his fiery tongue. He seems to be impressed with the truth of his mission, carried away by his desire to improve his hearers: "Hear, O heavens, listen, O earth, for God speaks. Children I have reared and made them great, but they have rebelled."[2] Similar is Jeremiah as a clear crystal reflecting the divine word, the burden of his message. So does the Bible describe the Jewish prophet as a conscious tool of the Deity, as an agent acting without frenzy, madness, or jugglery. He prophesies an unpleasant but an imperious duty, the sad divine duty of enlightening and improving mankind.

BIBLE PROPHETS. TALMUD ON IT.

The leading biblical prophets, as Moses, Elijah, Isaiah, etc., are fully conscious of their burden and deliver it spontaneously. The compulsion is but ethical, spiritual, the feeling of duty! They are far-seeing, strong, bold, mental giants, heaven-reaching. They feel it is most unpleasant to rebuke the wicked, to unmask the hypocrites, and to chastise the insolent. It is unpleasant and dangerous to wrestle and fight with the tigers and wolves of human society. But they feel they are called upon to do it; they are "appointed from their mothers' womb" to that honorable and onerous, dangerous and grand duty, to act on

---

1 IV, M. 22, etc. 2 Is. I. 2.

earth the part of providence, to assume the divine office of improving and enlightening, of forcing the tigers to spare the lambs, and the shepherd not to flay the sheep. There is here both compulsion and liberty, free agency and blind instrumentality. The self-sacrificing scientist, the true philanthropist, the patriotic statesman, etc., are such modern prophets, conscious and tool, free and involuntary, acting spontaneously because it is his duty, because God bids it! In most cases biblical prophets speak thus consciously, voluntarily, though truthfully claiming to deliver superior mandates, the echoes of their times, pointing to the hand on the disc of history.

The Talmud declares: "The Shekhina reveals herself only to the sage, the strong and the rich (ethically ?) and all three were united in Moses.[1] The Shekhina inspires not the despondent, the indolent, the pleasure-seeker and the frivolous, but those who are happy when doing good."[2] This is a magnificent paragraph, most rational and deeply psychological. The strong-minded, the magnanimous, the courageous and hopeful, those wholly engrossed by and busy with the great problems of human destiny, and with the ardent desire to do good, the truly great, philanthropists, statesmen, sages, to these the Deity imparts revelations. They alone are the worthy receptacles of the divine inspirations. Comparing the grand, luxuriant visions of Isaiah I. and II. to the clumsy ways of Ezekiel's *Chariot* and airy journeys, the Rabbis wittily say: All the first saw did the latter see too, but the one saw as a cosmopolitan, the other as a villager.[3]

MAIMONIDES ON THAT. MOSES. THE LAW.

Maimonides says: "Prophecy is entailed only upon the wise, the great in learning, the morally strong one, superior to his passions, broadly liberal[4] and firm in his convictions. Such an ethically constituted man of a healthy body, occupying his mind with metaphysical ideas and other great abstruse matters; who

---

1 אין השכינה שורה אלא על חכם גבור ועשיר. —Nedarim 38.

2 אין השכינה שורה לא מתוך עצבית ולא מתוך עצלות שחוק וקלות ראש.
אלא מתוך שמחה של מצוה—Pesachim 117 and Sabbath 30.

3 Hagigah 3.

4 בעל דעה רחבה נכונה מאוד ,Yad Mada. found. of Law 7.

has the firm will to conceive and grasp his studies correctly; who consecrates himself to holy things and abandons the ways of the vulgar and the worldly; who inures and diligently accustoms his mind not to have to do with any of the frivolities and vulgar aspirations; whose thoughts are constantly open to and engrossed by higher interests connected with the divine; who is ever contemplating the celestial beings[1] and the wisdom of the Holy One from the highest to the lowest forms and types, and learns by them the grandeur of God, viz: who devotes his thoughts to the constant contemplation of God and nature, the study of the universe and its forces,—upon such a man the holy spirit rests without fail.—Now comes Maimonides' mystic opinion of prophecy, after the rational one: "At once the holy Spirit rests upon him, his soul is identified with that category of the angels called Ishim[2] (*man-angels?*) he becomes another man and he understands that he is no longer what he had been, but that he has risen above the usual level of wise men. . . . There are many degrees of prophets, just as the wise are not all alike. All have their revelation in a nocturnal vision, in a dream. When they prophesy, they all tremble and shake in all their limbs, and feel their bodily forces failing and their senses dulled; but their intellectuality remains closely intent upon the vision. With all that the revelations to the prophet are but in riddles and metaphors, and the trance over, he has to find out their meaning, as had the 'ladder of Jacob with angels ascending and descending it (Gen. 28, 12)' The prophets do not prophesy at will, but they prepare themselves for it by a proper serene mood, by isolation, quiet contemplation and musical recreation . . . "

Moses alone prophesied at will, at any time, clearly and soberly in a wakeful state of mind. All other prophets were inspired in a dream or trance by an angel. Moses alone was so by the Holy One, in full consciousness and serene quietude. He saw things without a metaphor or veil in their reality . . . with his full intellectual powers, without trembling or faintheartedness. And when returning to his tent after the revelation, he con-

1 צורות הגדולות. 2 אישים.

tinued to be the same exalted and holy man, ever ready for, and ever worthy of the divine presence."—Thus we see that the higher God-idea gave the biblical writers a higher and nobler man-ideal, hence a higher idea of divine inspiration. Moses', Samuel's, Jerem.'s, Isaiah's prophetism amounted to something like a mental, intuitive, clear vision of the truth gained by their unremitting efforts for goodness, purity and higher intellectuality. But as to the usual prophet and the common conception of prophecy, we find with Philo, in the Bible and Talmud, in Virgil, Homer, Maimonides, however different in cult, country, speech, station and century, they were pretty nearly of the same opinion, the same mystic appreciation. All explain prophecy in almost identical terms. Proof again of the similarity and tenacity of religious ideas with their shadows, biases and superstitions. All agree that the prophet is in a mental alienation, unconscious of himself, possessed by a superior, external power, a spirit, a god, the involuntary mouthpiece of supernatural oracles. The rationalistically inclined Philo and Maimonides, as well as Bible, Talmud, Greek and Roman classics, all agree on this one point, that frenzy and supernaturalism were at the bottom of prophetism.

Philo says: "There are people that take the written law of the Thora as symbolizing doctrines. They then study the doctrines as alone essential and neglect the laws. That is wrong. It is correct to seek after the hidden sense of the Law, but that law must be practically observed, too. Such men live as if they were in a wilderness, or as if they were without a body, as if they were purely soul, so they care only for the ideas, not for the body, the practical law. They ask only for the naked truth—without the adequate, symbolizing form.—The hidden sense of the Sabbath is the idea that God alone is activity, while the creation is passive. Nevertheless, we must practically observe the Sabbath rest. The holidays symbolize human happiness and gratefulness to God. But we must also keep them sacred practically. Circumcision means suppression of the passions and of lascivity. But we must practically observe it. The knowledge of the ideas does not dispense us from observing the rites."[1]—We have reproduced here but a few examples of Philo's legal aspects.

CRITICISM.

Most of his mentioned interpretations of the Mosaic laws are weak, but the leading argument is correct, viz: that the trial of finding out the hidden object of a religious statute or social institution, is no excuse for neglecting its practical observance. For we may be mistaken in our interpretation and the real object of the lawgiver will then be frivolously frustrated. Or certain objects may be of little importance today, but most important in the future. He speaks excellent common sense in reminding that as the soul needs a body, even so the spirit of the law must have a form, a symbol, a rite. The followers then may differ in their interpretations, but as long as they agree in the performance, the body religious, social or political, will remain intact and thriving. While as soon as each member has his own practice, the body is broken in fragments, and the organization is undone. While there is here uncommon good sense, showing the Alexandrine sage as having looked deeply into the complicated organism of society, State and church, his given reasons of the laws are rather weak, as if he had not looked deep enough into those grand problems which are most intricate and complex, usually at once ethical, physiological, economical, political, social, and hence, in their highest sense, religious. So is the object of the Sabbath of an immense import, real and practical, in the above-mentioned complex sense, embracing body and mind, the individual and the society politic. It is not simply as he claims—a symbol of a metaphysical doctrine. It is the most far-reaching and realistic doctrine of Mosaism. It is at once sanitary, ethical, political and social. It is unsectarian. All the great lawgivers have some equivalent for it. It is older than Mosaism. It has been adopted by Christian, Moslem and freethinker. It is a vital institution to this day. It will ever remain the exponent of civilization and freedom.

In his interpretations of the holidays, Philo has overlooked, too, their natural, their historical, their agrarian and their

1 De Migrat. Abr. M. I, 450.

social import. Concerning circumcision also, he has not touched upon the historical and symbolical background thereof. Nevertheless, the thinking religionist must be thankful to him for having attempted at solving such problems. Later thinkers, standing upon his shoulders, may see farther and clearer, just because he built their pedestal. He began the work, they continue to and get farther than he.[1] Nevertheless, to him belongs the honor of the initiative and priority, and that honor shall not be begrudged to him.

DIETARY LAWS.

Most pertinently he insists:"He alone may neglect the ceremonial laws who is without a body, who has done away with all earthly concerns and lives as a pure spirit. While as long as we do not live in a wilderness, nor without a body, we are bound to earthly forms, and cannot hold the truth without its garb.[2] According to him, the Moriah Temple's *Sacrificial Service* was the symbolical representation of the idea that the sinner has deserved death.[3] "God needs not the sacrifice, but man does."[4] "Who admires not the yearly fastday (Atonement), its abstinence and edification, its devotion, prayers and conciliation . . ."[5] "The law allows only such animals to be used for food that are cloven-footed and ruminants, viz: chewing twice their cud.[6] That symbolizes that man should remember and discriminate between good and evil."[7] That, too, may be challenged, that vast discrimination between clean and unclean by Mosaism, with most accurate criteria of allowed and forbidden quadrupeds, birds and fishes, must be more than a farfetched symbol of differentiation between good and evil. Philo may possibly allude here to Zoroastrian notions, with the two-fold world of good and evil, and that the alimentary discrimination reminds that the clean animals were assumed to belong to the God of good, and the forbidden ones to the genius of evil. That may be at the bottom of Philo's reasoning. But that bottom is not

---

[1] See on these topics, also Fluegel's Spirit of Biblical Legislation.
[2] De Cherubim M. I, 540. [3] Vita Mosis 156. [4] Ibid. 151. [5] Ibid. 138.
[6] III, M. 11. [7] De Agricult. 57.

deep enough. Such a discrimination we find has been made by all the great religious legislators of the past, and it can be no vulgar superstition, nor a petty symbolism. Just recently, Physiologists have shown evidently that such dietary discriminations are mostly hygienic, and have not been overlooked by the laws of China, Hindustan and Egypt, and that the Mosaic categories of healthy quadrupeds, birds and fishes are generally to be recommended by a wise physician. The Mosaic, Chinese, Hindu, Parsee, Egyptian, etc., dietary laws were really public hygiene, while the mystico-spectral reasons assigned were but a scare-crow for the ignorant. (See my Mosaic Diet and Hygiene on that. See Nossig, Sozialhygiene d. Juden).

Philo continues: "The prohibition of killing the young before the eighth day after its birth, or of killing the mother and young together, or of boiling the kid in its mother's milk, means to implant the ideas of sympathy into the heart."[1]—That prohibition has rather other objects in view, of an agricultural, economical, etc., nature.[2] The Mosaic legislator was no sentimentalist. His aim was the preservation of the species, not of the individual. Yet as a by-thought, the feeling may have had some share in such a legislative enactment.

In the year of release and jubilee, Philo sees the intention to give the soil time to recuperate, the slave to obtain his liberty, and the poor his alienated property; it is an institution for the poor.[3] Much farther-reaching are the institutions of the years of Release and Jubilee. They are of an immense economical and agrarian import, the greatest one is of a political and sociological bearing. They are the very foundation stones of the Mosaic democracy. Equality before the law and inalienable freedom must have a strong economical basis. Plutocracy and pauperism will wreck them. The Release and Jubilee years are the remedy proposed by Mosaism.[4] "Again, the law ordains that the strangers, non-Israelites, observing the moral law, and inhabitants of Judaea, should enjoy all the advantages of fellow-

---

1 Philantrop II. 2 See Maimond. "Guide" and Michaelis "Mos. Legisl." on that. 3 Ibid. 1 to 2 M. 23.

4 See Mosaic Legislation. Whenever the author refers to his own works, he does not mention his name.

citizens (Ibid)."—In Vita Mosis, iii., Philo declares: "The intention of the entire law is that man should ever strive to imitate the Godhead, and not neglect any opportunity to reach that ideal of human existence." The Talmud teachers adopted that view of the Alexandrine philosopher: "The aim of the law is to make man godlike." Philo again says: "The aim of Moses in his entire legislation is that peace, amity and purity of morals should prevail in order that the family, the State and entire mankind should reach the brightest happiness."[1] Here Philo is perfectly at the height of the law.

PHILO'S BIBLICAL ENTHUSIASM.

He says: "The Thora contains the law as revealed in nature. It teaches how to live according to nature. The law-abiding man shall emulate the example of nature and arrange his life, conform to the order of the world."[2] .... "The Thora will never be annulled .... All nations will gradually accept it. .... Only the laws of Moses have remained intact, unshaken, indestructible; as if marked with the seal of nature, uninterrupted since the day of their promulgation to our own times .... No doubt they will continue and exist forever, and be immortal as long as there will be sun and moon, heaven and earth.[3] .... I believe mankind will discontinue their own usages, the rites of their fathers, and do homage to these laws, for with the improved conditions of the people (Israel) these laws, too, will appear to better advantage; they will become more illustrious and will throw into the shade all other laws, just as the rising sun does the stars."[4]

Eighteen hundred years ago this passage must have appeared as a prophecy, as if Philo had been illuminated by a ray of future history; as if the Alexandrine sage had been permitted by providence to raise the curtain of coming events and look into the divine laboratory of mankind's destinies. Just at the time when he wrote down that proud phrase that the "Sun of the Law is to overshadow all the stars," arose on the horizon of the Roman world John the Baptist, Jesus of Nazareth, Peter,

[1] Ibid. I. [2] Vita Mosis I. 141. [3] Vita Mosis II. 136. [4] Ibid.

etc., shouting into the world: "From Zion issues the law, and the word of God from Jerusalem." They set on foot their revolutionary movement; the gods of Olympos began to tremble, the gods and laws of Greece and Rome, of Alexandria and Antiochia began to pale, recede and flee to their rural retreats, to "paganism," and the law of Moses found recognition in all its ethical, social, God, purity and duty-teaching portions. Rome and Athens resounded with the message: "From Zion comes the law, and the divine word from Jerusalem."—Philo Judaeus suffered as all sages and prophets do of far-sightedness.[1] What he believed imminent and nearby, is coming, yet taking centuries and milleniums to be fully realized. During his own lifetime he found in Alexandria but few Jews eager to practice the law in its ceremonious parts. Nascent Christianity, as yet but a sect in Judaism, accentuated the import of the Thora: "Rather shall heaven and earth pass, but not a tittle of the law shall remain unfulfilled." But soon by the intervention and change of front of Paul, that law was disestablished, abolished and practically dispensed with. Reasons of state, of utility, of necessity, were invoked by his party in favor of that dispensation. There came then the Gnostic Christianity, the Catholic, Arian, Reformation, and now the humanitarian Christianity. It will yet take a while before it becomes a fact. Yet that vision of Philo is gradually gaining substantially in its great leading features: "Nations are discontinuing their own mythologies and do homage to the Mosaic institutions" of an ethical, political and sociological character.

---

1 See Messiah Ideal II. 5.

CHAPTER IV.

YEZIRAH, BOOK OF CREATION.

The Qabbalists, in general, as also the Zohar in special, often refer to a mysterious book, claimed as very ancient and called the *"Book of the Creation," "Sepher-Yezirah."*[1] The earnest thinker and great rabbinical authority, head and Gaon, of the Academy of Sora, Saadia,[2] wrote a commentary to that book, and spoke of it with the utmost respect. It is a starting point and important source of that phase of Hebrew thought, properly termed Qabbala. It combines both the sides of rabbinical theosophy, the rational metaphysics and the poetical anthropomorphism. It reasons on divinity and on nature, on the "divine Chariot and the Genesis." It stands half way between the mystic booklets called "The Mystery of the Divine Hight," etc., describing the godhead as mythology did, and the philosophical Qabbalistico-Zoharic School, representing a kind of poetical metaphysics, a combination of rationalism, theosophy and mysticism. It claims a fabulous antiquity, handed down by an ancient Mishna Teacher, derived from Moses or Abraham, as its authors cannot be too old and venerable for some of its enthusiastic adherents. It is given out as tradition, Qabbala proper, dictated by a supernatural authority, not by human reason. It is mysticism, dogmatically producing doctrines, some of a rationalistic and others of a supernatural character; as also miracle-workings by the computations and speculations on interchange, shape, combination, etc., of the numerical letters,[2] the words, the divine names, the notaricon or initial letters, etc., starting that method, later abundantly used and abused by the Qabbalistic school and the Zohar in particular. It is a com-

[1] ספר יצירה [2] 892–942, P. C. [3] סוד שיעור קומה and אותיות ד״ר עקיבא See further on, a mystic book, post Talmudical, measuring the Deity hyperbolically by myriads of distances.

[2] In Hebrew the letters have, as in Greek, a numerical value.

pound method, rationalism and authority; bold, reasoned metaphysics and most unreasonable mysticism. The Yezirah-book to the later Qabbala stands in the same relation as the Mishna does to the Gemara. It contains in the same ratio nearly all the elements, rational and irrational, bold and acute, as also their very reverse, of the Qabbala and the Zohar. There can hardly be any doubt entertained that these latter ones are but the development of the earlier several booklets called Yezirah, Shiur Qoma, Letters of Akiba, etc. A rabbinical proverb says wittily: "All depends upon luck, even the Thora-scroll in the holy ark." Indeed, while the Qabbala and the Zohar especially, have been so boldly confronted, yea, repudiated, the Yezirah has been so tenderly and respectfully treated. To my humble opinion, the entire Qabbala is but the fruit developed from the germ and egg of our Creation book. All are a growth, links of the chain of human thought, acuteness and fallacies, all deserve the same sifting, selecting the wheat from the chaff.—Yezirah-book is composed not in the Chaldee, nor in the Judaeo-Aramean idiom, as the Zohar is, but in Hebrew; not, indeed, the Hebrew of the Pentateuch, Prophets or Hagiographs, but half way between that and the rabbinical Hebrew. A fabulously antique origin—Abraham—is assumed in its pages; but its very late Hebrew, and especially the philosophical ideas and mystical practices it advances, show that it is a product of the epoch long after the Mohammedan hegira, 622 P. C. A fact it is that in the tenth century, Saadia Gaon commented upon and treated it with great veneration, as a book coming down from ages gone by. Its precise date cannot be given, but apparently it is post-talmudical, of the period of the *Saboreans* or *Gaonim*.

YEZIRAH-BOOK IN TALMUD.

A book of that name, "*Sepher-Yezirah*," is mentioned in the Talmud of Babylon and of Jerusalem. The first says:[1] "Every eve of Sabbath, R. Chanina and Oshayah were studying the

[1] ר״ חנינא ור״ אושעיא הוי יתכי כל מעלי שבתא ועסקי בספר יצירה ומיברו להו ענלא תלתא ואכלי ליה.

'Book of Creation,' and were fed in a miraculous way." The Talmud of Jerusalem narrates of another teacher who performed similar miracles by means of the same book.[1] The mystic tone of these passages and the miracles connected with the tales may be taken as fair proof that they refer to a book of a character similar to the book now extant. But it is a fact that Saadia Gaon is the first one to speak of it historically. Prof. Franck, wishing to give to the Zohar an antique background in this work, argues that it can be but identical with the Sepher Yezirah of the Talmud. But could it not be a new book with an old revered name? Such pious fictions are often met with.

IS IT IDENTICAL?

Such are the canonical books of Job and of Daniel. Could not a later author borrow the name? Prof. Franck pleads that the style of its Hebrew[2] places it at the very dawn of the Mishna. That does not convince me fully. He uses the very same argument to prove the antiquity of the Zohar! The argument is weak in both these pleadings. The Zohar is not the product of Simon b. Jochai; nor is the Creation-book older than the Christian era, yea, probably than Islam. Many of the later Rabbis wrote a superior Hebrew to that in the latter book, and a superior Arameo-Chaldaic than that in the other. One will find in Russia and Poland even today rabbinical scholars doing either. The same it was during the centuries of the dispersion, after the close of both the Talmuds. The Hebrew and the Chaldaic remained the literary tongues of Jewish Talmudists and thinkers. The exceptions only wrote in Arabic, Latin, or in a modern tongue. Hence as little as I can believe that the Zohar is the work of R. Shimeon b. Jochai, as little can I accept that our book

---

1 אמר ר׳ יהושע בן חנניה יכול אנא על ידי ספר יצירה נתיב קתיין ואכטוחין ועביד לון איליין טכין.

The reader will remember that there are extant two versions of the Talmud, that of Jerusalem and of Babylon.

2 "La langue dans laquelle il est écrit nous atteste qui 'l ne peut appartenir qú à l' époch où vivaint les premiers docteurs de la Mishna. (Franck Qabbala, 80).—Fluegel's Philosophy and Qabbala.

in discussion dates from pre-Mishnaitic times. At the utmost the mentioning of such a book by the Talmuds may prove that a separate treatise of metaphysico-mystical contents may have existed in those early rabbinical ages. I need not much argumentation for such an assumption. As treatise *Aboth* on Ethics, as the Talmud, Aggadas, Midrashim, etc., abound in metaphysical and naturalistic sayings and theories enlarged upon and discussed, even so the Yezirah-book. It was a collection of little tractates devoted to such *materia*. It could hardly be otherwise. As Jews discussed such themes from the times of the Essenians down to modern ages, they needed some depositary for their thoughts on "*Mirkaba and Bereshith*," God, creation and nature. Hence there may, most naturally, have been such a treatise, dozens of treatises even, as there had been dozens of holy Writs, Gospels, Korans, etc. But the question here is: Whether the "*Book of Creation*," now extant, is identical with the one mentioned in the Talmuds? This proof Prof. Franck has not produced. Nay, that very fact that Saadia Gaon first brought it to light and commented thereupon, suggests that it is of a later age than the Talmud, and this is the most probable assumption, until something more positive can be ascertained.

ITS DOCTRINE. PHILO.

The *Book of Creation*, as now extant, may be rightly considered as a *Zohar* in miniature. It treats generally and briefly of the same themes, and in nearly the same methods as the later Qabbalists do, viz: God, being, emanation, creation, man, worship, their mutual relations, influence, powers, etc., discussing the elements of the *Zohar's* metaphysics, physics, ethics, even its "*practical Qabbala*," or miracle working. It teaches that God has irradiated the universe by means of 32 marvelous ways of His Wisdom,[1] Sophia, *Hokhma*. These thirty-two marvelous ways are: The first ten numbers or principles of all existence, a reminiscence of Pythagoras' ten numbers of the universe; an echo of the ten "He said," the ten times repeated: "God said let there be"—of Gen. i.;[2] combined with the twenty-two letters

---

1 י״ה בחכמה יסד ארץ. 2 ויאמר אלהים.

of the Hebrew Alphabet: "God irradiated existence by means of His Wisdom." This is the Logos of Neo-Platonism and Philo, the Alexandrian school. "The Divine Wisdom" had its ways: "The Ten Numbers or the principles," "the forces" of Philo, the "ten emanations" of Neo-Platonism, the Ten "Sephiroth" of the Qabbala. The Ten Numbers of the *Yezira-book,* emanations of the Divine Wisdom, exactly correspond to the "Crown" emanating the Ten Zoharistic Sephiroth. While the twenty-two other ways answer to Philo's and Plotin's spiritual universe and its forces. Each system had its Triad; God, Infinite and Unknowable; God manifested or Logos, and at last the material world. This is a development of Plotin's trinity: Nous, Intelligence and World-Soul. The *Sepher-Yezira* had its ten categories, called *ten Sephiroth.* Already, with Philo, it is not quite clear whether the six, etc., Powers of the Logos are divine attributes, or independent divine *beings, subordinate, but real deities.* Just the same is the case in the *Yezira-book,* with its ten Sephiroth; at first they are but categories, the proportions of the world, simply showing the abstract relation of things, Sephiroth of purely Hebrew etymology and derivation, simply meaning *numbers.* But soon they are assumed to be divine beings, intermediate between the invisible God and the material world, of Greek derivation, Sphaira or Saphir, efflux. These ten numbers, principles, emanations, *Sephiroths,* were combined with the twenty-two letters of the Hebrew alphabet, and together made up the "thirty-two *marvelous ways* of Divine Wisdom." That appears to mean the creation called forth by the ten Principles. The twenty-two letters symbolize the Biblical fiat, Word, Verb or Spirit of God. The twenty-two letters form the alphabet in the Hebrew language; the divine tongue being Hebrew, according to ancient belief. Here are God, Wisdom and Verb. Here is the later Qabbalistic triad: Crown, Wisdom and Intelligence; or God unknowable, Adam Qadmon or Zoharitic "Crown," with the Ten Sephiroth and the universe emanated. This seems to be identical with Aristotle's doctrine that "in God is thought, thinking, subject and thought-of-object united," mentioned above and reiterated by Yezirah-book, Maimonides, Corduero, etc.

NUMBERS ONE, TWO, THREE, FOUR, TEN.

The furtive hint mysteriously thrown out in the *Book of Creation* concerning the cosmic import of the number *Ten*, suggests some more symbolism. The number ten is the total of its subdivisions—1, 2, 3, 4—all together making the total of Ten. Now these numbers have, in the metaphorical speculations of the Qabbalists, their special significance. *One* is the symbol of God-One. Two is the dualistic conception of divinity. So is in Zoroasterism the one Zrvana-Atarana split into Ahura Mazda and Agro Mainyu. The Greek Plato and Aristotle, as also man's sensual experiences, divide all existence into two classes, mind and matter, thought and extension. Three is the Trinitarian conception of the Divine Being. Such it is with Brahmanic, Assyrian, Egyptian and Greek triads. So is philosophy, too, in God being thinking, thought and its object one and the same. The Essenian mystics imagined God under three aspects—God unknowable, Messiah, his first creation, and the holy Spirit, or communion of the invisible with the material world. So, at last, the Christian Trinity follows the same drift of thought. This Triad of the *Book of Creation* was followed up by all the Qabbalists and by the Zohar in particular. The first three Sephiroth represent the manifestation of the unknowable Infinite; that means that God, unknowable, is manifested to man under three aspects.

NUMBER FOUR, MAIMONIDES. THIRTY-TWO, AVESTA.

The number 4, I hesitatingly venture to say, may have its importance in *our Creation-book* on account of the four dimensions of space—East, West, North and South; but more so on account of the *four elements* believed in ancient cosmology to make up the sum total of this earth and the sublunar world. It was the opinion of the ancients that all the bodies of this earthly globe are a composite of four original elements. So it was among Gentile and Jewish thinkers, and the mystics could not help attaching a great value to that; hence the great import of the number 4 with them. Maimonides is a fair exponent of this view of ancient physicists. He says:[1] God created

---

[1] האל ברא למטה מגלגל הירח גולם אחר . . . וברא ארבע צורית לגולם זה . . צורת האש רוח מים ארץ.—Yad Mada foundation of Thora III, 10

beneath the sphere of the moon one body, otherwise than the other spheres. There he created four forms or types, other than the types of the other spheres; each type he sank into a part of that earthly sphere. The first type is that of fire, which, combining with part of its sphere, became the body of fire. The second type is that of air, which combining with its spheric part, became the air-body. The third is the form of water, and the fourth is the earth-form, each combining with its respective sublunar matter, became respectively the body of water and that of earth. Thus are under the firmament (Rakia) four different bodies, one above the other, enveloping the lower one as its sphere, viz: fire, air, water and earth, without allowing any vacuum between them. Each of these four bodies is lifeless, dead matter, unconscious; each has a particular patron and guide, obeying his commands."—Now these numbers 1, 2, 3, 4 combined make out number *Ten*. The Thora in Gen i. gives ten divine fiats as the creative Verbs. Pythagoras had ten numbers, as the underlying principles of the universe. The Neo-Platonists counted ten emanations. The Talmud had its ten creative words. Parseeism had its triads and Ameshas Spentas, etc., making ten. Even so the Book of Creation has its ten numbers or ways of the divine Wisdom to effect the creation. These ten ways, numbers, Sephiroth, in time, grew and expanded hugely to the Ten Sephiroth of the Qabbalists and the Zohar in particular. So we read in Aboth v. 1: With ten fiats, מאמרות, the world was created; Bably Haggigah 12 a, with ten words, the world was created: With wisdom, intelligence, knowledge, force, command, all-power, goodness, justice, mercy and love. Ostensibly here they are attributes of the Deity, the Qabbalists imperceptibly personified them, and made of them Divine beings, emanated from the unknowable Infinite, and mediating between Him and the visible universe.

That the *Sepher-Yezirah* counted ten, and the additional number of twenty-two to make up its thirty-two ways, may be a parallel to or a development from Zoroasterism, which also had thirty-two leading genii, viz: Zrvana Akarana, Ahura Mazda and Agro Mainyu, the six Ameshas Spentas and Mithra, making in all ten leading genii. Then came some twenty-two more divine beings, good angels, making altogether thirty or thirty-two,[1] corresponding, perhaps, to the solar, monthly days, each of the 30-32 gods having his own appropriate monthly day of worship. Some such analogous ideas may be the underlying reason for the *thirty-two ways* of divine Wisdom in our book under consideration. Next, there may be a doctrinal and symbolical meaning attached to that: God created all by means of the ten ways of His Sophia. These were the first ten irradiations or emanations of the Infinite. They represent the thought of God. Now came the Word or the scripture of God. This was done, borrowing a human figure of speech, by the twenty-two letters of the Hebrew alphabet. That means to say that God, His thought and the object of His thought, viz: the universe, all are but one. It is the above much-quoted philosophical formula, seen in Aristotle, Maimonides and Corduero. This formula we find, also as we shall directly show, in the *Yezira-book*. That compresses into a single pregnant sentence, the whole theory of ancient metaphysics combined with cosmology, viz: that in God is the intellectus activus or real thinking, its subject and its object, all united in one.

FROM ARISTOTLE TO SPINOZA.

This corroborates our line of thought repeatedly argued on this most important point, viz: It shows that from Aristotle to Zohar, Spinoza, Hegel, a rigorous monotheism, to the extreme of pantheism, ever reigned; that creation meant emanation. Whatever their metaphysical and cosmological formulæ may have been, the bottom of their theories, the kernel of their systems, was that God is the essence of all existence, the Source whence all flows; that from Him all emanates and to Him all returns; that He is the substratum of the phenomena of thought and extension, of mind and matter. Aristotle, as Plato, accepted two original substances. Philo, as Aristobulos, logically and correctly elucidated their real intent as monism. He let matter be irradiated from the Logos and his forces. Plotin

1 See my Zend Avesta II, Daily Shirozas.

and Proclus openly taught emanation, the divine unity containing all, just as Philo had taught; God is all, and nothing is besides Him. Maimonides, Sepher Yezira, Qabbala and Zohar follow suit in their reasoned expositions, and Spinoza but drew the last conclusion; he formulated their rigorously logical result, without fear, favor or scruple; he could truly say that "ancient philosophers and Hebrew philosophers, too, were at one with him on this point." They stopped half way. He went the full length.

The thirty-two Avestæan gods, or daily genii, were altogether too cumbersome. Later thinkers knew nothing about Zoroaster's calendar. Perhaps the Christian calendar, an imitation of the Parsee one, rather frightened them away with its daily patron-saints. The symbolized idea was also far-fetched. They dropped, therefore, the "twenty-two additional ways of wisdom," and were satisfied with the ten intellectual ones, attributes of real emanations. Thus they spoke but of the Ten Numbers, of the divine Logos, and hence come the *Ten Sephiroth* of the picturesque Zohar, meaning number, sphere and light irradiation, sapphire.

THE TRIADS IN YEZIRAH-BOOK.

The following will make the above surmise about the twenty-two letters more clear and plausible. After the *Creation-book* had posited its leading doctrine that "God has created the universe by the thirty-two ways of His Wisdom," it represents this number again by the known Qabbalistic formula of the *triad*, viz: The numerator, the object enumerated and the very act of enumeration. Or it may mean: God created His world with book, writing and theme; or by writing, writer and theme, which reading may just as well answer the purpose.[1] R. Jehuda Ha-Levi[2] comments thereupon to mean: "The thought, the word and the scripture of God, which in Him are but one and identical, while in man they are three distinct things." Abraham b. David[3] expatiates here on many pages, is very mystical, and at

---

[1] אלהים ברא עולמו ב״ג ספרים. כספר וספר וסופר. I, i. Mishna Ed. Warshau, 1884, p. 13, a.

[2] Kosari IV, 25.

[3] הם כנגד השכל והמשכיל והמושכל, *or* הדעת, היודע והידוע. In his Yezirah Commentary, 17, a.

last appears to reduce that to our well-known proposition often repeated, viz: "The three terms of the Yezirah-book refer to the subject thinking, the object thought of and the very act of thinking, being all one in God."

THE TWENTY-TWO LETTERS. JEHUDA HALEVI. TRIAD.

Thus the twenty-two letters mean the scripture of God, viz: the object thought about, the universe created or emanated. Creator, creation and created objects are thus comprised in and symbolized by the thirty-two ways of the Divine Wisdom. Now, the reader will remember that we have closely discussed that theme in our preceding pages, and shown it to be the metaphysical theory of Aristotle, Philo, Neo-Platonism, Maimonides, Qabbalists and Zohar; and this is to be found intact in the *Yezirah-book,* too! This book is thus distinctly built upon late Neo-Platonic, and later rabbinic theories and formulæ; hence it is idle to claim for it a fabulous antiquity or any independent existence; it is a link in the chain of the world's philosophies.

Elucidating the ten numbers of the ways of Divine Wisdom, the ten principles of the universe, the first principle is declared to be the "Spirit of the living God," or as in another version expounded; voice and word and spirit,[1] and that is the holy spirit. This triad confirms the above-mentioned one of the Divine Wisdom, the ten numbers and the twenty-two letters. It corresponds to the first triad of the Zohar: "Crown, Wisdom and Intelligence," the first three of the ten Sephiroth. It follows the line of thought and the numerical symbolism of that Aristotelian philosophy as taught in the middle ages, and is again a proof of the late origin of our *Book of Creation.*

ITS AGE.

Moise Botril, in his Commentary to that book, says: "It is Abraham, our patriarch, who wrote this work to demonstrate the Unity of God; at least Gaon-Saadia says so. He narrates that the Chaldean sages attacked Abraham in

[1] אחת רוח אלהים חיים.—Mishna, 9, Chapter I—קול ורוח ודבור, וזהו רוח הקודש.—Ed. Warshau, 29 b. Ed. Mantua, 40.

his faith. Some of them believed in the two principles (of Parseeism). Some assumed three principles (of Brahmanism?) And some accepted the sun as the leading force."—The authorship of Abraham was probably assumed on account of the book showing no other one, and because it closes with the following passage: "When Abraham, our father, had well examined into and investigated all those things of the creation, the Lord of the universe revealed Himself to him, kissed him, called him his friend and made with him an eternal covenant, which was accounted to him a great merit. He made a covenant with him between the Ten fingers of his hands, viz: the covenant of the tongue, and between the Ten toes of his feet, viz: the covenant of circumcision; he fastened the twenty-two letters of the Thora to his tongue, and revealed to him His mysteries in water, fire, air, Eden, Gehenne, etc.,[1] and the skies or Zodiac." This passage concluding the Yezirah-book is simply a midrash, expounding the biblical chapters on that patriarch, especially Gen. xv. 6: "He believed in God, and this was accounted to him as a merit."—This homily was put at the end of our mystic book and taken as history; hence it was accepted by Saadia and Moise Botril as a proof that Abraham was its author. The Hebrew Chronicler Shalsheleth haqabbala (fol. 20) claims that its author was R. Akiba (120 P. C.), and that there exists besides another book by Abraham, commented by Moise b. Nachman (thirteenth saeculum). All that is unhistoric and cannot stand the test of criticism. Graetz and Franck, with many others, decidedly opine that neither the age nor the author of that mystical book can be found out. But since it contains Aristotelian, Neo-Platonic and Talmudical views as the very base of its doctrines; and since it is, closely seen, but a rough outline, an incipient attempt at the later Qabbala and its leading book, the Zohar; since it teaches God unknowable, His creating Wisdom with the Ten Sephiroth as the creative powers, the triads in different versions and formulæ—all that may be accepted as fairly proving that the *Book of Creation* is of a late date, not older than the first part of the Middle Ages, the epoch

---

1 גילה לו את סודו. משכן במים . באש . ברוח . מזלות—Ibid. VI, Mish. 7

of the Saburæans and the Gaonim. Again, since Saadia, commentating on it in the tenth century, treats of it with profound respect, and believes it to have come down from Abraham, it must have been assumed as very old during his time. Hence I should take it as a composition between the close of the Talmud and Saadia; yea, rather after the rise of the Spanish Arabian literature; hence between the seventh and the ninth century. It was the first attempt at systematizing the scattered elements of philosophic mysticism of the Talmud and Midrashim, of their metaphysical, religious and anthropomorphic views, denominated *"Mirkaba and Genesis"* inclusive of the Aristotelian scholasticism of the mediæval ages. That book became then in its later turn the nucleus and starting point for Jewish thinkers, who gradually developed the Qabbala, until it found its full expression in Mose de Leon's Zohar.

EPITOME OF YEZIRAH-BOOK.

After this general outline, let us introduce the *Book of Creation,* with the remark of R. Jehuda Halevi:[1] "The Book teaches the existence of One God, showing us unity and harmony in the midst of variety and diversity." As already quoted, the very first proposition thereof is:[2] "The ten fundamental Sephiroth with the twenty-two letters of the alphabet are the thirty-two wonderful ways of Wisdom, with which the Eternal the Master of the universe, has established His name.—These thirty-two ways are then reduced to a triad,[3] representing the formula of Aristotle, viz: thought, thought-of-object and thinking subject, all being one in God!" The universe is the thought of God. God's thinking is creating, hence are He, His thinking and His creation identical. The ten numbers are the origin of the well-known ten Qabbalistic Sephiroth; Sephiroth in the Hebrew sense yet, *number,* not in the Greek one σφαιρα, nor sapphire, irradiations, splendor. In the Zohar, speaking of these Sephiroth, each of these meanings is alternately implied. Orig-

---

1 Cusari Discourse 4. 2 I. Chapter, I. Mishna. 3 Ibid. בספר וספר וספור or numerator, numeration, objects enumerated; or writer, writing, things written.

inally it simply meant number or category; then it meant also sphere; and at last radiated light. The ten Sephiroth are the abstract ten categories of the universe, emanated from the Unknowable.[1] Ten is the fundamental number underlying the proportions of the universe. So, too, taught Pythagoras. We have above hypothetically offered some speculations concerning that number ten and its ingredients, 1, 2, 3, 4, of whose value the reader may judge for himself. Ibid. i. 3: The ten Sephiroth of the Blima correspond to the Ten fingers (of the hands of creation). It continues (Ibid. i. 4): "There are Ten Sephiroth, irradiations from the Unknowable; ten, not nine; ten, not eleven. Make an effort to properly understand them. Seek closely and deeply, search and speculate.[2] Place things upon their foundation and establish the Creator upon His base." They are the ten attributes, emanations, manifestations, particular aspects of the one and same divine Unity, developed from Pythagoras, Philo, Mishna, Talmud, etc. It continues (i. 5): "These Ten Sephiroth are Ten, but each is infinite. Deep is their beginning and deep their end; deep for good and deep for bad; deep for height and for depth; deep for East and West, North and South; one master rules them all from His holy sublimity." Says thereunto *Rabed*: "Though limited by the Number Ten, nevertheless each direction in itself is infinite and illimitable." It is so in the future or in the past; for good, for bad; in the height or depth, etc.—The Ten Sephiroth represent the diverse attributes of the invisible Supreme in the infinitude of space and time. The Ten Sephiroth are as the ten fingers of the hands. (Ibid. i. 3.), all-growing out from one unity, viz: they are the tools and mediators between the Creator and His creation. (Ibid. i. 6): They have the appearance of the thunderbolt; their limit is out of sight; they are commanded in going and coming; at the (divine) fiat they hasten as the whirlwind, bowing to His throne. (Ibid. i. 7): The Ten have their end connected with their beginning, and the begin

[1] עשר ספירות בלימה I. 2, *Blima* corresponds to the later Qabbalistic Ain. Nachmanides there explains: The Ten Sephiroth are the door of *Ain-Soph*. Since He is unknowable, He is not existing—*Blima*, for man.

[2] הכן בחכמה וחכם בבינה.

with their end; as the flame is bound up with the burning coal .... (Ibid i. 8): Concerning these Sephiroth stop thy mouth from speaking and thy thought from brooding .... The first of these Sephiroth is the Spirit of the living God, the blessed and Eternal One (i. 9, etc). The voice, the Spirit and the verb, that is the holy Spirit.—The second is the breath emanating from the Spirit. In that are sculptured the twenty-two letters, which form but one breath. The third is the water coming from the air. In the air God merged chaos, darkness and void, earth and clay, spread out as a tapestry, built them up as a wall and covered them with a roof.—The fourth is fire coming from water, wherein He sculptured the throne of His glory, (alluding to the heavens, in Hebrew termed, *Shamaim Aish Umain,* fire and water), the celestial Ophanim, Hayoth, Seraphim and the administering angels.—The other six Sephiroth represent the ends of the world, its four cardinal points, its height and depth. These extremities have also their reference to the letters in "*Ihvh,*"—III. 2, 5, 6, etc., remembers also the male and female sides of the Sephiroth just as the Qabbalists do. "The last and all of the Sephiroth are connected with their Supreme Principle, as the flame is with the burning material beneath it, for God is one. There is nothing besides Him. In presence of the One what are the Sephiroth! (Ibid. i. 8). Close your mouth and speak not, think not; do not stir!"—That means that all existence has been emanated from the unknown Deity, and in His holy presence everything dwindles into insignificance. Creation is emanation. This appears to be pretty much identical with the doctrine of Spinoza. Creation is irradiation from the Divine Light, emanation, reducing all being, the universe, to one Substance. "The second Sephira is the air coming from the Spirit. In that breath are engraven the twenty two letters (letters being breath, modulated to speech,) which united letters form but one Divine breath .... With the twenty-two letters giving them sound, form and figure, and combining them in diverse ways (as names or symbols for each being of the universe), God has formed the souls of all that exists.[1] Upon the same letters, the holy One has established his ineffable name.[2]" Here is the boldest and most uncompromising monism ever expressed, fully intelligible to the thoughtful, though veiled and picturesquely formulated. The twenty-two letters of the (Hebrew) alphabet are simply human speech, symbolize the universe and contain it in thought. These twenty-two letters also are the composite name of the All-Holy-One, for He, the universe, and its conception, the thought, or language, the symbol thereof, are all one and the same Substance; or "God, His thought and the object of His thought are really identical and one." They are torn asunder and assumed as diverse, solely by the prisma of our human subjectivity . . . Spinoza, Bruno or Hegel never were so concise and peremptory in their statements as some of these Qabbalists, so bold in substance, and so weird in form. The twenty-two letters are divided into groups of 3, 7 and 12.[3] Such numbers are to be found everywhere in the world, intellectual, moral and material. They are the holy numbers of all nations and ages. A grand display of symbolism is made with these numbers in all the domains of human thought, time, space, the physical and the moral universe, etc.—"All these Sephiroth form one unity. One is above three; three above seven; seven above twelve."

Chapter II. treats of the twenty-two letters of the alphabet. They symbolize the principles of the material and of the ethical worlds. They are subdivided into three mother letters, seven double and twelve simple ones. The three mothers אמש are, *ethically*, the scales of merit and of guilt, and the tongue of Law holds the equilibrium.—Chapter III. From them issued also the elements, fire and water, the sexes as male and female; the three patriarchs, too, are born of them. The same אמש represent air, water and fire. The heavens come from fire, אש ומים; the earth is no element, and comes from water. The air holds the equilibrium. Hence are derived cold and

---

[1] צרפן ויצר בהן נפש כל היציר והעתיד לצור.—Ib. II. 2

[2] אלו כב אותיות שבהם יסד הקבה שמו מרום וקדוש.—Ib. II. 2

[3] כב אותיות וסוד שלוש שבע ושתים עשרה.—Ib. II, 1

heat. A triad is vindicated to the animal bodies and the same to the souls.—The letter aleph, א, combined with the breath, banded it with the crown, inclosed therein the air of the world, the plenty of the year, the body of the soul, with the male and female sexes. Similar combinations entered the other two letters and produced the many creations of body and mind, all male and female.—Chapter IV. Such combination also entered the seven double letters, בגד כפרת, (viz: those capable of a daggesh forte. That the ר, too, is included should prove the venerable page of the Yezirah-book). They are the base of life, peace, wisdom, wealth, grace, posterity, dominion, etc., as also of their opposites. The starry world, too, is the result of such combinations. So are the different dimensions; so the holy Temple, the seven planets, and many other sacred Numbers Seven. Hence comes the sacredness of Number Seven. Chapter V. treats of the twelve remaining plain letters. They are at the bottom of the senses, the affections, the distances, the Zodiacal stars, the yearly revolutions, the months, etc.—Chapter VI. emphasizes the triads in the twenty-two letters, consisting of groups of three, opposed by another triad, with the link combining them. Such are in the starry world, in the sublunar one, in the human body, in the affections of the soul. God One is their unit and root. Abraham recognized all this, "whom God took to his bosom, kissed him tenderly, declared him his friend and made a covenant with him." . . . Such is the epitome of the far-famed *Book of Creation,* which collected early in the Middle Ages the rational and the mystical materials, religious, physical and metaphysical, from gray antiquity, and piously handed them over to the Qabbalists and their Bible, the Zohar. We have here given an outline, mostly literally, closely following the text. Of course, the reader must use his own good judgment in deciphering the sense. We gave intentionally a verbal rendition in order not to prejudice the reader, but to leave him to his own acumen, for even the host of commentators differ from one another. The whole treatise seems to impart the doctrine: that God is unknowable to human reason; that He is dimly reflected in the sensual and in the intelligible creation. This creation he permeates and upholds by His inherent Presence. It is His light-habiliment. It is His visible garb. All He created, or rather emanated indirectly, by the mediation of the ten Sephiroth, which are likened to the ten fingers of man, through which he performs his work. After the ten Sephiroth, come, as agents, the twenty-two letters, as the forces, the tools, the skeleton, the principles of the universe. Creation is compared to a "book, its writer and its contents." The ten Sephiroth are the fingers and the twenty-two letters are the tools of the Divine architect. They are also the types and leading principles, forces and bodies of the intelligible and the material worlds. On the whole, the booklet is a sort of metaphysical, physical and theological treatise, expressing its views enigmatically, cautiously, only by hints, allegories, poetic tropes and quaint figures of speech, gradually merging into supra-naturalism, mysticism, obscurity, vagueness, whereupon every commentator has ventured to put his own construction and interpretation. Even so may the reader try his own Pegasus wings and fathom the heights and depths of the unknowable. Such was the Oriental method of discussing metaphysics. Such are the Hindu *Upanishads,* allegory, mystery, parable, obscure language of mystic ideas; "a father may tell that doctrine of Brahman to his worthy son or pupil, not to anybody else." (F. Max Mueller Upanishad I. 44). Read there: it is a riddle, not nonsense. It is aimed at secrecy from the masses.

PROFESSOR FRANCK ON THAT.

Professor Franck says:[1] "The last word of this system is the substitution of Unity to any kind of dualism. The pagan philosophical dualism postulated that the eternal matter was ever rebellious to the Divine will." So also did the biblical dualism: "God and the world are absolutely diverse substances." Let us explain: Greek philosophy opined that two supreme principles are in the universe—mind and matter. God, or mind, is the original active, spiritual substance, and side by side with this was primordially a dark, gross, inert second substance,

[1] Kabbala, 159, by Ad. Franck.

matter. They were described as the universal Intelligence, and the universal mass of body, the *intellectus universalis* and the *materia universalis.* Both were united in different degrees and made up the universe. But this union was a forced one, incongenial, constantly tending toward disruption, the spirit ever felt as incarcerated in the body and the eternal matter was always inclined to rebel and throw off the yoke of Mind or God.

Zoroasterism expressed the same view by its two antagonistic principles of Ormazd and Ahriman, or Light and Darkness. The Qabbala following the same train of thought expressed it by "the empire of the good Sephiroth and its antipode, that of Hell." That was the other extreme of the scale of creation, the kingdom of impurity, sin and suffering; of evil spirits, the Qliphoth, the shells, the disspirited, darkened shadows of *Gehenna.* Now Franck says: "In the Sepher-Yezirah is God regarded as the infinite and indefinable Being in the entire extension of His power and existence. He is more sublime, but not out of the Sephiroth and the letters; viz: He is not out of the principles and the laws which we recognize in the universe. Each element has its source in a higher element, and all have their common origin in the Verb, the Holy Spirit. . . . This Verb, the first Sephira, the sublimest of all things which we can define, what else is it, if not the sublimest and the most absolute of all the manifestations of God, viz: thought, the Supreme Intelligence? Thus is God in the highest sense, the matter and the mind of the universe. Nothing can exist out of Himself; His substance is at the base of all beings; all bear His impress; all are the symbols of His intelligence." This theory so bold, so strange, Professor Franck affirms, is at the bottom of the doctrine taught in our *Book of Creation,* and, as we shall soon see, it is in its later derivations and developments in the Qabbala and its bible, the Zohar.

THE SHIUR QOMA. שיעור קומה.

But the Sepher-Yezirah has besides such rationalistic, metaphysical ideas, also others which likewise were entailed upon its offspring, the Qabbala. These we find expatiated upon and elaborated in another little book entitled: *"Shiur Qoma,"* the measurement of the divine dimensions. It is mysticism, symbolism, anthropomorphism, depicting the deity, not in thoughts, attributes and activities, but in fabulous dimensions and magnitudes, measuring the height, width and extension of the divine body and limbs, his head, face, nose, eyes, hair, arms, etc., by myriads of Persian parasangs, expressing by such enormities the infinitude of the Deity. We offer an outline thereof in the right place, in connection with kindred materia of mysticism; as also of another mediæval little book, likewise of no certain date, viz: *"The Letters of R. Aqiba,"* of an equally mystic tenor, as forerunners to the Qabbala, before we arrive at the luminous heights of Gebirol and the Vedanta philosophy.

Shiur Qoma, or the method of depicting the magnitude of the Creator and His creations, is exaggerated enough in the Qabbala, but it is not invented there.[1] We often meet with it in the Talmud and the Midrashim; we find it already systematized in the *Sepher Yezirah* sketched above. It is the same anthropomorphism with the intention of picturing God's infinitude by fabulous numbers and monstrous quantities; but that was then and even now taken literally by many, and the God of the Bible was described as the gods of India, Greece, Bactria and Persia. The middle ages produced most monstrous tracts of that description. Such is our treatise, *"Shiur Qoma,"* measurement of the height of God, a mystical booklet delineating the Deity as a monster-man with colossal magnitude and huge human passions. Maimonides, especially, combated it with might and main. While many Rabbis, contemporaneous with and after him, sided with the anthropomorphism of the booklet, claiming to find it in Bible and Talmud. The Zohar popularly utilized such anthropomorphisms of the grossest kind, though totally clashing with its sublimized metaphysics, without much caring for consistency and logic. It is by turns most rationalistic and metaphysical, calling God *Aïn and Ain-Soph,* the Nothing, the Unknowable, the Infinite, discarding even any and all attributes from His

---

1 Prof. Graetz opines, they are invented and not to be found in the Talmud.

being, as idolatrous and blasphemous; then again remembering the popular taste for the material and the monstrous, after having screened the idea of God against all anthropomorphism, it opened the door to the grossest kind of it, in depicting the Sephiroth and even the first Sephira, their sum total, the double and alter-ego of the Infinite, as a celestial man, with mythologic shape, color and limbs, representing him fully as the Hindoos do their monstrous idols. It did not intend to teach idolatry, but it actually created idols, with all the accompanying follies and superstitions on one hand, and all the jugglery and necromancy on the other hand; to such a degree that even today one may find in the Orient and in the Occident, too, persons otherwise shrewd and sensible, entangled in the meshes of the Zoharitic "Practical Qabbala," believing that the *Zaddick* or holy-man is capable of working wonders and incarnating the Deity in his own person. Further on we shall meet that book again.

LETTERS OF R. AKIBA.

Here is another specimen of naive allegory and monstrous anthropomorphism. It is a similar little mystical tract called: "Letters of R. Akiba," popularly attributed to that famous teacher of the II. cent. P. C. It narrates: [1] "The body of the *Shechinah* has an extension of 236 times 10,000 parasangs, viz: 118 times 10,000 from the loins and below, and as many times from the loins and above. It is an evident allusion to Ezekiel's Mirkaba (I. 27). But these parasangs do not resemble ours. Each divine parasang has 1,000 times 1,000 yards. Each divine yard has four *zareth* and a *palm;* each *zareth* contains the length comprised between the two extremities of the world." Now Talm, Babl, Hagigah 12a narrates that "*Adam, the first,* occupied the space between the earth and the firmament, and when he disgraced himself, God placed his hands upon him and made him small." The same treatise, 14a., claims that R. Akiba explained "the two thrones" of Daniel VII. to mean that one was prepared for God and one for David. The same R. Akiba vouched for the messianity of Bar-Kokhba, the leader of the

---

[1] אותיות ר"ר עקיבא. גופי של שכינה.—1579 Edition, p. 15, Letter h.

Jews against Rome (120 P. C.) That rebellion cost the Jews their last national existence and their best blood. Of course, he died a martyr, and if he was an enthusiast, he was no hypocrite. This goes to show that the anthropomorphism of Talmudic literature is a stern fact; thence it came into the Qabbala, and is not its invention.

Here is a further analysis with specimens from the "Letters of R. Akiba," containing chapters from different hands and diverse times and embodying different views, from naive allegory to monstrous anthropomorphism. (Ib. 2a.) R. Akiba said: "These are the twenty-two letters with which the *Thora* was delivered to the tribes of Israel. They are all engraven as bright gems with a flaming pen into the venerable crown of the Holy One, blessed be He. At the moment the Holy One was about to create the world, at once they stepped down and stood before Him, each claiming the honor of beginning (the first word in the narrative of) the creation. At first came forward the *Thau,* (the last letter of the Hebrew alphabet, numbering 400). The Thou began: "Master of the Universe! Mayst Thou be pleased to begin thy creation with me, for thy Thora begins with the Thou!" "No," replied the Holy One. "Why not?" "Because," God explained, "the Thou is the mark (*thou* means mark in Hebrew) of the wicked to be prepared for their destruction." . . . . So we learn when the Holy One ordained the destruction of Jerusalem, He bade the death angel: Go to Jerusalem and divide off the righteous from the wicked ones. The forehead of the righteous mark with the *Thou in ink,* the initial of תחיה, life. While the wicked ones mark with the *Thou in blood,* foreboding death, תמות. Thereupon Divine Justice pleaded: "Master of the Universe, let the righteous ones, too, be inscribed with the bloody Thou!" "Why so?" "Because they neglected their duty to preach and inculcate better conduct to the sinners." To which God said: "I knew

---

1 Puterkob Edition, 5644. A similar allegory is narrated in the Introduction to the Zohar, I. 2 b, but much more artificial and abstruse, hence, to all appearance, of later date. While the Midrashim have the simplest form of that legend.

perfectly well that had they done so, it would have been in vain; they would not have been listened to." But Justice replicated: "Nevertheless it was their duty to remonstrate and that duty they neglected!" The Holy One felt convinced and the righteous of that generation were treated alike with the wicked ones. (inscribed with the bloody Thou).

Each of the letters of the alphabet stepped forward, in its turn from the last to the forefirst, before His Divine Presence, each raised its ingenious claim, each backing it by an appropriate verse from Sacred Writ, and each was refuted and refused that honor by the Deity; the refutation too proven with a verse from the Bible. At last came the letter Betha, b, ב: "Lord of the Universe, mayest thou be pleased to begin thy creation with me *Betha,* the initial of: Blessed be God," *Baruch Ihvh.* And at once the Divine Presence assented, saying: blessed be Thou indeed. Hence do we read in Genesis I. i, בראשית ברא, the creation story begins actually with the letter B. The Aleph, now, the first of the alphabet, remained alone, mute, silent and humbled. Then the Supreme Lord called out: "Aleph! Aleph! Why sayest thou nothing?" "I am the weakest of all; I number but one; I have nothing to say." Almighty replied: "Fear not, thou art indeed the head of all. Thou art one and I am one; the Thora is one and Israel is one. . . . . The Ten Commandments will begin with thee, O Aleph!" (אנכי י״ה אלהיך)

The same ingenious allegory is remembered by nearly all the Midrashim, but much shortened and epitomized. To all appearance it subsisted in full, and they, relying upon that, abbreviated the naive story. One feature they mention which we do not find in this little work. It is quite a good point and bold enough. The Midrash has it this way: "The Holy One said to Aleph: Where the Thora begins *indeed* (the Ten Commandments), it will begin with the Aleph (אנכי)." This intimates that the Thora begins not with Genesis, nor with Exodus, but with the "ten words." A passage of the Talmud states that plainly, alluded to elsewhere.

As to the age of the composition of this little treatise, I would not say anything definite. It is written in a fair pure Hebrew, as in the Mishna. It has the least of actual mysticism and no attempt at philosophizing. It has only some traces of the earlier Mishnaic mystic allegory or parable. But we find here already *Metatron* with all that halo of pomp and circumstance, which among the later Christian sects, surrounded the Messianic Ideal, and while the Qabbalists built up with these materials, their great first Sephira, the Gnostics did their Demiurgos. Even the Crown, כתר, appears already here in its embryo; not yet personified, as later in the Zoharic literature, but simply as the crown on the head of the Supreme King of the world. These Crown gems are the twenty-two letters of the Thora; the Thora being the world's foundation and the Supreme Law, not only of Israel or mankind, but even of God Himself, so that even His dicta are ever proven and supported by a verse from the Thora. Our little book places and combines, interprets and comments upon the twenty-two letters of the Alphabet, in different ingenious manners. It reads them from the first to the last; then from the last to the first; then again first and last letter, second and forelast one, by pairs; then by pairs, the first and middle one, etc., as אל . בם or backwards, חשרק then it speculates upon their meaning as words: Aleph, a lord, Baith, a house, etc.; then their value as notaricon or initials of sentences; then their numerical value א—1, ב—2, ת—400, etc.; then their shape and form are ingeniously interpreted. Some letters have a double form, why so, is explained. Thus the same twenty-two letters are turned, combined and twisted in all possible shapes and ingeniously interpreted, all allegorically, not fully mystically. These allegories appear later to have acquired authority, naively taken as positive facts and truths, made to mean mystic philosophems and became gradually the Qabbala. From an innocent infantile tale, the book proceeded to be considered as religious legends and finished as mystic philosophy. Here are some more instances in corroboration of this view: (Ib. 10a.) "R. Akiba discusses the same twenty-two letters as notaricon. The letter Aleph אלף represents the initials of the Hebrew words אפתח לשון פה, I shall open the tongue in the mouth of men to chant my praises and crown me daily in all the corners of the world—for which I have created it. . . . Because of the 248 human limbs, the mouth alone is made to sing the praises of God. . . . . Even so the mouth and its tongue liken the sea and its waves. As the sea ever broadens and opens, even so the mouth. As the sea is full of pearls and gems, even so the mouth (with pearly teeth.) As the sea is an ever living well, so is the mouth. As the ocean waves press one upon another, even so the tongue (speech) in the mouth. As the sea swallows up the ship, even so the (evil) tongue in the mouth. As the sea roars and thunders, so does the (wicked) mouth. As the sea waves are aroused by the storm, even so the tongue by the passions. As the sea pours out its waves, even so the mouth (the thoughts). As the sea is encompassed by its shores, even so the mouth by the lips. As the sea contains great impurities, even so the mouth. As the sea waves are awe-inspiring, even so fearful is the (bad) tongue. As the sea casts up mire and dirt, even so does the mouth, its idle or slanderous words. As the waves are rising and falling, even so the tongue proud and fawning, etc."

(Ibid. 10b.) "If there were not the Thora, there would not be the world. If not the world, there were not the Thora. From Is. XXV. 1, אמונה, אומן, is argued that "God has given to Israel two faiths on Sinai, one for Israel and one for the Messiah." Christians and Mohammedans acted upon that. We have seen in our Messiah Ideal that Jewish teachers deny that view.

(Ibid. page 12b.) "The Holy One bears seventy distinct names בפירוש His veiled unexpressed names are innumerable. . . . . The distinct ones are not given, out of reverence. They are in the twenty-two letters of the alphabet, differently arranged from right to left, left to right, by pairs, several combinations and diverse places, אב, אלבם, אתבש, תשרק, These Divine names stand forth on many crowns of fire, of flame, lightning, *hashmal* and thunderbolt, all facing the Divine Throne. Surrounded by a thousand hosts of the Shekhina and myriads of heavenly armies, they are led on as the king, with trembling and shaking, with fear and terror, with beauty and splendor, glory and magnificence, with strength, wisdom and knowledge, with fire pillars, lofty columns of flames and awful thunderbolts. Their light is like lightning and the aspect of the *hashmal.* They are venerated and adored with hymns of holy! holy! holy! They are marching in grand procession, throughout all the heavenly spheres and at last are brought back in triumph to the Divine Throne when the *Hayoth* of the *Mirkaba* exclaim: "Blessed be the names of His Glory forever and aye!"

QABBALA AND METATRON.

Here I believe to find a forerunner of the Later Qabbalists. Of this gorgeous mystico-allegorical material they perfected their Sephiroth. The *Crown,* the Mirkaba, the Hayoth and the myriads of angels making up the heavenly court, later systematized by the mystic philosophers. So *Metatron* makes here his appearance, the later *Crown* or *Adam Qadmon,* the highest Sephira, also termed here the *Lord of the Presence,* Metatron "by the throne," the Mirkaba, viz: the man-figure on the throne, of Ezekiel's vision, Chapter I. 27. So we read: (Ibid. 13a.) God said: "Aleph is (the notaricon of) איברתיו, לקחתיו, בקדתיו. I have created, chosen and installed him as *Metatron,* my servant. . . . . Contemplating the degeneration of Adam's children, I removed my Shekhina to Heaven and translated Henoch, son Jered, to on high (Gen. vi. 22) to be my witness there with the four Hayoth of the Mirkaba. I have placed him over all my treasures and hidden things in the heavens, have turned over to him all the keys and made him lord above all the lords, to administer to my Throne of Glory and my palace divine . . . . to attend upon my mercy-seat . . . and be in the presence of my majesty in the heavens above, with all their higher and lower mysteries. I have exalted him (Metatron) to his high stature by 7,000 parasangs. I have adorned his throne with the splendors of my throne. His body I have made transparent and changed into flaming torches; have rendered his aspect as the thunderbolt, his face as the rays of the sun, his eyes as the lustre of my throne; his robes are adorned with grandeur and splendor and a beauteous crown of royalty sits on his brow. I imparted to him from my own majesty and the beauty of my Throne of Glory. I called him by my name *Idid,* the Lord of the Presence (Shekhina), Grand Master of all the mysteries. I have placed his chair close to the gates of my sanctuary, there to render justice and give judgment. All my court lords are bid to take orders from him. . . . He is to command in heaven on high and on earth below, to smite princes with the rod of his mouth, to install and to depose kings in their dominions . . . to reveal my mysteries and promulgate my behests."

(Ibid. 14a.) "Ninety-two names bears Metatron. . . . . They are all borrowed from the Supreme Divine Name, the שם המפורש, of the Mirkaba, engraven on the Divine Throne, for God took from his own name and placed them to that of Metatron. . . . The divine Seal-bearer, the prince of the Presence, of the Thora, of wisdom, of the Palace, of all nations' genii, the exalted angels in Heaven and on earth."—Here we have even more pronounced the full-fledged Logos of Philo and Neo-Platonists, the first Sephira, Crown or Adam Qadmon of the Qabbalists, the office and charge of the Christ, the Messianic Ideal of Christology. This treatise may be the connecting link between the sober prophetic mysticism of Isaiah, Ezekiel, Sachariah, Daniel, etc., and the later one of the Essenes, the Apostles, the Gnostics, the Alexandrine philosophers, the Mediæval Jewish mystics down to the Zoharitic system contemplated.

(Ibid 13b.) "Even more, daily is Metatron sitting in the high heavens, gathering around himself all the souls of still-born infants, or those of babes at the breast of their mothers, or children at school, dying in their prime. He brings them beneath the wings of the Divine Throne, places them according to their grades and classes and teaches them *Thora.*" This quaint poetry may be the source of the legend that Jesus of Nazareth was especially fond of children. A similar tale the Mohammedans tell of Mohammed, the Parsees of Zoroaster and other Orientals of their own ethical heroes. The twenty-two letters of the Alphabet are thus ingeniously interpreted and speculated upon, from the first to the last, then from the last to the first, backwards and forwards, and made the medium of ethical meditations. The letters are gems in the Divine Crown. Gradually the poetic mystic is emboldened: (Ibid 17a.) "All these letters are of fire, looking like lightning and rays of light, each measuring 21,000 myriads of parasangs, all fastened upon the crowns, resembling the luster of the thunderbolt. They are engraven by the finger of the Most Holy One." Here we have the name and the measurement of the famous booklet Shiur Qoma spoken of here, its name and its method, anthropomorphism. "The twenty-two letters are, again, (Ibid. 17a.) the seals of the Holy One, by which all the holy names[1] are sealed. . . Each name of the Mirkaba has a seal, while the Holy One is sitting upon a fiery throne, surrounded by fire columns. These divine names, שמות המפרשים, each in a light-halo, with hosts of fire-armies around. When man is bold enough to use those holy names, at once the world is in danger of collapsing in a universal conflagration. But soon it is found out that the earthly wings are connected with the heavenly wings and sealed with the seal of the Eternal. At once the heavenly hosts relax in their ire, and Divine Mercy מדת רחמים takes the place of Divine Justice." We believe this sketch enough to give the treatise its place, ethical, allegorical and semi-mystical, between Ezekiel and Daniel on one hand and the Rabbinical mysticism on the other.

ANTHROPOMORPHISM. GRAETZ.

Graetz says on this theme:[2] "As the orthodox Mohammedan religious teachers strenuously opposed the exaggerated rationalism of the *Mutazilites,* and fell into the opposite extreme representing the Deity in a bodily form, attributing to Him immense extensions and gigantic proportions, even so acted the Jewish partisans of the old doctrine who deemed the contemporaneous rationalistic innovations as an apostacy from Judaism, and conceived the silly notion of the corporeality of God. They, too, desired to take the biblical expressions: "the hand,"

---

1 The text reads כשמות, שמות is correct. 2 Geschichte d. Juden, V. 231.

"the foot," "sitting" and "walking" of God, etc., literally. The Aggadic interpretation of the Scriptures, oftentimes using sensual metaphors and sentences unintelligible to the masses, induced them to such a belief. That theory hatched out by an imbecile, and expressed in a mysterious way, found partisans. It gives a minute description of the divine Being, limb for limb, measuring His height from head to foot in Persian miles, "parasangs," [1] speaking in a heathen manner of God's "right eye and left eye," upper and under lip, of God's beard, etc., of things . . . . blasphemous even to mention. In order not to belittle the grandeur and sublimity of the Godhead, it extends to infinity His every limb and believes to have done enough in declaring, that the miles of the measurement of the divine limbs surpass the entire world. To such a grossly depicted and miledescribed God, the theory gives a special household in heaven, with seven palaces or halls. In the highest one God is sitting upon a sublime throne, whose extension is of fabulous dimensions. The throne prostrates himself thrice daily before God praying: "Deign to sit down upon me, for Thy burden is sweet to me." These *halls* are populated with myriads of angels, whose names are compounds of Hebrew and barbarian (no doubt Persian) sounds. The highest angel is *Metatron,* and of him is fabled, conforming to Christian and Mohammedan models, (Henoch book) that he is Henoch, originally a man, translated into heaven and changed to a flaming fire. He is placed at the side of God and is called the "little god." Such we find in Zohar Idra Zuta III.: The forehead, which is uncovered in the Most Holy Ancient One, is called Grace... For that supernal head concealed in the Unknown Infinite expandeth its emanation and this is comprehended in the forehead.—(VI.) The eyes of the head of the Most Holy Ancient One are two, really making one, that watch and sleep not. So in Ps. 121, 4: "The keeper of Israel slumbereth and sleepeth not." "And therefore are there no eyebrows nor eyelashes unto His eyes." In all the Oriental symbolisms was Divine Providence represented as a huge eye without eyelashes or brows, emblematic of

[1] The method no doubt hails from Parseeism.

its never ceasing vigilance. Greek mythology describes Argus, jealous Juno's servant, with a hundred eyes, but with eyelashes, foreshadowing his final sleep and death, at the hands of Mercurius. See Ovid's metamorphosis on that.

Idra Zuta V: From his nose, from the opening of his nostrils the spirit of life rusheth forth upon the "small visage" (the lower Sephiroth.) Ib. VI: From the beard of the Most Holy One emanates the influence and decoration of all (*i. e.* from divine strength emanates the harmony and fitness of all creation.) Ib. VIII. "When the Most Holy Ancient One, the most hidden one, desired to manifest himself, he conformed all things under the categories of male and female." . . . . This intends to express that the dualism of the sexes is inherent in the Infinite as it is in nature, as the leading principles, the two poles of being. Both the Idra Rabba and Idra Zuta are largely occupied with such speculations. They are often sublime, but as often they trespass the narrow space "from the sublime to the ridiculous," yea to the blasphemous. They do not mean at all to depict the deity as a bodily monster, but rather to discard all bodily representations, just by such extravagant magnitudes, baffling all our fancy. But there are silly persons who delight in the marvelous and to whom no stupidity is too foolish for belief. Such descriptions became therefore schools of the grossest superstition in the Occident and the Orient, to Jew, Christian and Moslem. These passages are sufficient samples of the least attractive chapters and verses of mysticism. They are legion; we quoted but a few here. Really they occupy the major portion of those treatises. They express mostly abstruse philosophems, in picturesque, metaphorical language, with copious poetical tropes, in a language, the ancient Chaldeo-Aramaic one, very imperfectly known, and selected expressly for the purpose to be obscure and to admit of any and every interpretation. The sound metaphysical minor parts of these mystic books are but for the few thinkers, for the select ones, intentionally veiled and expressed in riddles on account of their real boldness. The major portion of the treatises is but poetry, a flowery bower, an Arabian kiosk for the hidden metaphysics, a screen against the eye of the vulgar, sweet-meat and play for the naive ones and the marvel-hunters. As the Orient offers its paupers *hashish* and opium to beguile their tedious and wretched existence; as the Occident bids the same social strata, alcohol and cards; as the Roman classes offered their masses "bread and circus-plays" (panis et circences ludi), even so did former generations offer mysticism as a relief from the harsh actualities. The Zohar is of the latest date; but its wonder-lore has an ancient background. It hails from Hinduism, Parseeism, Esseneanism, the mysticism of Mishna, Talmud, Aggada, Yezirah, Letters of Aqiba, *Shiur Qoma,* etc. But side by side with such puerile and vanquished mythological views, they contain all speculations worthy of true philosophy and noble metaphysics. In one word, Mose de Leon simply compiled all that his time brought down from antiquity, the best and the worst, the grain and the husk. The reader must use his own judgment and separate the wheat from the chaff, remembering the well-known mediæval: "Credo quia absurdum est."

CHAPTER V.

GEBIROL'S PHILOSOPHY.

We have seen above that the Qabbala and the Zohar are metaphysically and rationally, as well as mystically and religiously, the heirs to and descendants of the doctrines of Vedanta, Philo, Neo-platonism, *Sepher-Yezirah,* etc. But there is, besides these, another link between these progenitors and their offspring. That link is Gebirol and his philosophy. We shall follow here the writings of that leading star on the horizon of Jewish-Arabian literature, in his "*Meqor Haim,*" or "*Fons Vitae,*" and his well-known poem, "*Kether Malkhuth.*" We shall utilize the lucid exposition of that system by Prof. Graetz. We leave to him all the responsibility of the exact rendition and follow him mostly on this subject. It is a most abstruse and complicated system, originally in Arabic; then translated and retranslated into Hebrew, Latin and modern tongues. Therefore we prefer to follow the master-historian Graetz on this theme, leaving to him all the honor with all the responsibility for the exactness of the rendition of the system. We shall only venture to intersperse occasionally our own remarks in explanation or as a free criticism of the theory, as passed through our prisma.

Salomon ben Jehuda Ibn-Gebirol,[1] of Cordova and Malaga, known as Avicebron or Abu Ayub Sulaiman Ybn Yachia, born in 1021, died in 1070, was philosopher and poet, thinker and singer, scientist and writer, "every inch in him was song and thought;")[2] every one of his features was great and surprising; he was cosmopolitan, scientific, national and patriotic. Gebirol was, after Philo, the Talmud, and the Sepher-Yezirah, the nearest blood-relation to Qabbala and Zohar in their best phases. He was their progenitor in the best, most logical and audaciously rationalistic elements these latter ones may contain. Everything that has come down from India, Chaldea and Persia,

---

[1] It is Prof. Munck who rendered that name to history in his Melanges de Philosophie. [2] Graetz Geschichte d. Juden, vi. 31.

from the last prophets and the Aggada, the Greek and the Alexandrines, from Philo, Neo-platonists, Apochryphæ, Talmud and Midrashim, from the Mohammedan and Spanish-Jewish thinkers, down to Saadia and to the very dawn of Maimonides—all that was sifted and filtered through the vast brain, the sound logic and the bright fancy of that great thinker and greater poet, the forerunner of Spinoza's Ethics, Ibn-Gebirol. Ibn-Gebirol's system gave the Qabbala its rationalistic theories; the mystical philosophems and the anthropomorphic vagaries it took from the just epitomized and discussed books: *"Sepher-Yezirah"* and *"Shiur Qoma,"* etc.

GEBIROL'S METAPHYSICS AND "SUBSTANCE."

God is essentially the Arch-Substance, one and unique; whose unity is integer and unbroken. It is not as the numerical unity, capable of increase and decrease, of division and alteration. In that unity is the difference between essence and form, substance and accident not thinkable and really does not exist there. This thesis as also the existence of God, Gebirol postulates as self-evident and not necessary to prove. For since the universe is, God must necessarily be, for all existence, spiritual and material is in God. "Thou, Oh God, art alone, thou art the only Being from whose light-rays all came forth and in whom we all live."[1] These ideas are apparently identical with those of Spinoza's *"Substance."* Yet they are, closely seen, a biblical heirloom, a rationalistic definition of *"Ihvh-One"* pushed to its philosophical and literal extreme.

"The unity of God is the only allowable divine attribute.[2] The Arch-Substance is therefore unknowable and inconceivable by man, since it is above all sublime and infinite. Man's intelligence can guess it only by virtue of his own spirituality, contemplating the universe."[3] Here we have the Qabbalistic Infinite, the Unknowable, the Ain-Soph, and even Adam Qadmon and the Sephiroth world. God by Himself is unknowable, only when manifested in creation, he is revealed to man in his

---

1 Often repeated in Meqor Haim and Kether Malkhuth.

2 Kether Malkh. begin. 3 Meqor Haim I, 5 and II, 5.

brain or reason by reflection. Here we find Qabbala, Spinoza and even Hegel.

Opposed to this divine Supreme Being, full of light, one and infinite, stands the finite world as a dark, chaotic, broken, inert mass. In what relation stand these earthly, divided, composite, poor beings to the absolute and supreme Substance? Have they been called into existence directly and immediately by that original Substance? Does the divine fullness pervade this wretched low world? In the reply to these questions lies the center of gravity of Gebirol's system. It cannot fraternize with the orthodox conception of a direct creation out of nothing; nor with that of Aristotle, the heathen hypothesis that side by side with the deity there was primordeally an original matter, the arch-material of the universe, which matter, the divine Mind has but shaped and moulded. Against the one his philosophic consciousness felt aroused; against the other his religious conscience revolted. The one seems to draw down the Infinite into the finite; the other leaves a deep gap between God and world. It does not allow any logical connection between them to bridge over the abyss; how could pure mind produce inert matter? The direct creation belittles the God idea, bringing it into unmitigated contact with this low, earthly realm. To accept that God did but give a form to the original matter, independently, previously and from all eternity existent, that would limit the divine omnipotence and dispirit the world, pre-supposing that God and the world are a heterogeneous duality.

The answer to these questions is peculiar to Gebirol's philosophy. It is as follows: "There is in the Arch-Substance a creative, spending, motive force which manifests itself as the Will or the Word of God. In this divine Will, which is of the identical nature as the divine Essence, there slumbers an infinitude of perfect beings. That Will resembles an endless light capable of permeating with its light an infinitude of worlds. From this Arch-light, the divine Will emanates, without mediation, motion or lapse of time, forces which are of the same nature as the Will Himself, simple, infinite, spiritual, creative powers which are capable of continuing further to operate and to influence. At first emanate from that Will two forces; the one is the capacity of producing and forming an infinitude of beings; the other of sustaining and giving them permanency, the chief condition of all being, the universal form and matter of existence, (forma universalis et materia universalis.) These forces are apparently two-fold and separate, yet they are identified. It is the divine Will which unites them so that the form is never without its matter and the matter never without its form. They are not absolutely identified; they are united by the intermediation of the divine Will; the divine Will is, so to say, the spiritual space holding them together. They are different from the Will though forming with that but one attribute of God; they stand to each other in the relation of writer, writing and writing material." This last sentence and the entire passage are weighty and important to the extreme. They open a new vista in the history of philosophy. They show Gebirol as a most influential link between Philo and Spinoza, between monotheism and pantheism, the Greek and the Mosaic mode of thought. Later on Malebranche, etc., took up this view. He elaborated it, but only Spinoza gave it its full import.

GEBIROL AND SPINOZA.

This passage comes very near to Spinoza's identification of thought and extension, of mind and matter, yet it is not so fully: "The form is never without its matter, and matter never without its form; they are not one, but made one by the divine Will." Gebirol pretty nearly arrived at Spinoza's bold guess, but missed it by a narrow door. He said: "Form and matter ever go together." Spinoza made further the one bold step: "Form and matter are one and the same thing, but appear as two to men, when looked upon from different standpoints." This is the great advance of Spinoza over Gebirol. Alike to this latter one is the French philosopher, Malebranche. Closer yet is Geulinx, who said: "Mind and matter are different things, but ever going together in parallels, as two independent clocks do, finely harmonized to do so by the cunning watchmaker." Behold, in what a dilemma Gebirol feels to be! Anxious to harmonize Plato and Moses, to uphold the biblical doctrine of God, creator of all, yet not identical with mind and matter; God Supreme Cause, yet not harboring in his being form and body, he says: "They are different from the Will (of God), yet forming with that Will but one attribute (of God). They, viz: God's Will, the forms and the bodies, stand to each other in the relation of writer, writing and writing material." They are three combined, but not identified; just as Geulinx's watchmaker with his two harmonized clocks, eternally going in parallel, yet differentiated.

THE DIVINE WILL—SPINOZA.

Let us return to Gebirol's theory. He says: "The form is never without its matter, and matter never without its form; they are held together by the divine Will, forming with him but one attribute of God. They are standing to each other in the relation of writer, writing and writing material; that means that matter and form, or body and soul, are in the Will and all three are in God. This bold doctrine is qualified and mitigated by the other utterance. God is the writer, writing His letters upon the writing material, viz. emanating beings, the world. God impresses the forms upon the universal matter. In such a manner Gebirol believes to smooth over the embarrassing alternative between "creation out of nothing"[1] and "eternal matter besides God," the great discrepancy between Genesis and Plato; he postulates that form and matter, both are issued from the one divine Substance and both held together by the Divine Will, as their spiritual space. But the difficulty remains. If they both emanate from the one divine Will without actually being there, then it is a creation from nothing, which he would not accept as logical, and if they are but two phases of the same thing, differently colored rays from the one original sun-light, simply two aspects of the divine Will—or without metaphor: if form and matter are but one thing appearing as two to the human eye, (something which he never said), then he accepted pantheism, then is the biblical standpoint sacrificed and Gebirol is the forerunner of Spinoza!—Whether he was known to him? That

1 Ex nihilo.

is hard to answer. Apparently he was not, for it is but Prof. Munck who, in 1857, exhumed the name and writings (in Hebrew and Latin translations) of Gebirol as identical with Avicebron and restored them to Hebrew history and philosophy. It is thus not probable that Spinoza knew his system directly; though it is not absolutely impossible. At any rate he knew his leading theories, indirectly, through the medium of Maimonides, Qabbala, etc.; no doubt veiled and distorted; leaving to his own genius room enough to sift, clear and perfect it in his own Ethics. It must be remembered also that Gebirol's "form and matter standing in their intimate relation to God as writer, writing and writing-material," closely seen, is identical in substance, though mitigated in expression and intentionally altered in wording, with the pantheistic formula often quoted in these pages from Aristotle, Philo, Maimonides' "Code and Guide," and lastly from Qabbala, viz: that "in God is thinker, thought and thought-of-object one and the same." It is evidently the same idea, but veiled and ambiguously expressed, with the intent not to break down the bridge behind, connecting with the biblical view.

GEBIROL'S UNIVERSE—CRITICISM.

"All substances flowing forth from the divine Will participate in this, their origin; they are connected with each other and so all with the Will, and consist likewise of a spiritual basis and a spiritual form. "Thou, O God, hast issued Thy Will from Thy essence, the artificer, to draw being from nothing, as rays flow from the source of light. He draws from the light-fountain without bucket, and effectuates all without means. . . The force reaches to the extreme margin of the lowest creature."[1] Here Gebirol emphatically accentuates the creation of matter from nothing; he sacrifices Plato to Moses; what for, then, begin with rationalism to close with naive belief? What for try to prove what can be accepted but as an article of faith? Here is in place the remark of *Rabed* to Maimonides: "What cannot be answered is best not to question."[2] That biblical belief is

1 Kether Malkhuth.

2 Yad Mada Repentance, V. 5. Abr. b. David's remark.

but poetically, not seriously, meant by Gebirol. God is identical with his Will. All substances flow from the Will and participate in this their origin, viz. are co-substantial with it; hence is God, His Will and all things co-substantial! Further: "The divine Will is an eternal, infinite attribute of God; that Will, thought or word of God is the divine creative power and co-eternal with God; hence has that will ever been creative, and ever manifested in creation; hence is the universe with mind and matter co-eternal with the Will and with God. The Divine Will being an eternal attribute, and its contents being the universe, follows then the logical conclusion that the universe is as eternal as that Will and as its source, the Deity himself. Further, it is a general assumption that the Bible teaches creation as a free and spontaneous act of the Deity. But this is incompatible with Gebirol's premises, according to which the "Original Substance and the divine Will must necessarily create and have been creating since all eternity; the fulness of Deity must needs come out; it is in the nature of the divine power to manifest itself in creative activity."[1] Thus we see that the ambiguity of Gebirol, while it deprives his system of the salient plainness and perspicuity of Spinoza's *Ethics,* nevertheless does not spare it all its drawbacks. The same difficulty is to be found in its moral as in the metaphysical doctrines. The biblical assumption is that the human soul is free to choose its course, and hence it is responsible for its actions. According to Gebirol, the human soul is an emanation of the deity, and must needs follow its higher instincts, hence can there be no question about free will, responsibility, etc.[2] The fact is, the logical consequence of Gebirol's philosophy is Spinoza's metaphysics and ethics. The same is the case with the Qabbala and the Zohar, as far as logically followed up. But Gebirol, Qabbala and Zohar did not go to the last extreme result of their own premises. They prized the biblical ethics higher than their own logic. Spinoza, not caring for consequences, followed up steel-cold, pitiless reason and logic, and the result was the *Ethics.*

---

[1] Fons Vitae, III. 15, V. 68, etc. [2] See Graetz, Geschichte d. Juden, VI. 48.

"In the meantime, the further the beings depart from their divine arch-source, the more they lose in the simplicity and strength, light and spirituality of their origin, and become more and more manifold, complex, divisible, weak, dark, condensed, *bodies,* and hence perceptible to the senses. The beings emanated from the divine Will form a descending scale of grades, of which the higher ones are more spiritual, noble and energetic than those standing beneath them. Entire existence is borne by the all-embracing origin of beings, the universal matter, they make up its component parts. The last degrees are the space and the world of bodies which have their forms in their quantity and proportion, in their shapes and colors. These lowest beings are on account of the distance from their Origin, the divine Will and the first emanations, dim, condensed, inert, hence lowered down to passiveness. The light streaming from above, they can but weakly receive; they can therefore emit but shadows in place of substantial formations."[1] All this is exactly and identically the theory of Qabbala and Zohar concerning matter, bodies and shells. "Between the Arch-Substance and the last condensed and embodied scale of beings, there must be intermediate degrees which stand in connection above with the divine Will, and below with the earthly world. Without such a connection, there would be not only a bottomless gap between the highest and the lowest, but the last one could not subsist a moment even without the beneficent influence from above."[2] There are three such intermediate grades—the universal reason, (intellectus universalis), "the highest, tenth *Sphere,* cast in the silver of truth and the gold of the spirit." Then the universal world-soul (anima universalis) and lastly the general nature. These are three descending degrees of the spiritual element of which each higher degree encompasses the lower one, encircles and permeates it. The world-spirit has been emanated by the two first forces from the divine Will, and nature is in connection with the world of bodies, spending to them life and movement. The middling

1 Fons Vitae, I. 3, II. 6, 10, III. 13, 32, etc. 2 Ib. III. 1-8, and Kether Malkhuth.

grade, the world-soul is the space of the armies of spirits and angels, and also the nine Spheres of the stars, spiritual and endowed with souls, participate in the world-soul.[1] In that manner the entire scale of beings is in continual connection with its links. The lower degrees receive from the higher ones, turn to them in love and longing and are held up and borne by the spiritual space, the Divine Will. The entire universe, spiritual and bodily, is filled with the Supreme Being by means of the Will, and not a single being is completely void of it. However different the spiritual is from the bodily, nevertheless that difference is not one in kind, but only in degree; a difference of more or less, of higher or lower. They are all related to and resemble each other; they rest also upon the two forces of universal matter and universal form. The bodily world too rests upon spiritual ground; it forms the reflex and mirror of the spiritual world, the lower world receives impressions and traces from the higher one.[2]

GEBIROL AND QABBALA.

Nearly all this we find again in Zohar and Qabbala, with only a change of name, garb and arrangement. The divine Will there, is the Adam Qadmon here. The other forces there, are the Sephiroth here, with a superior array of pomp and titles, triads, groups, combinations and proportions, connected above with the first Sephira and the Infinite, and below with the material world, which too is but a condensation, the farthest and last emanation from the higher, spiritual world. Even the word *Sphere* is to be found there. The Zohar and Qabbala made the last step; they boldly drew the last conclusion. Gebirol only ventured into the realm of the unknowable; he made a simple guess and built up his hypothesis. His successors, emboldened by his attempt, took that mystic hypothesis as a proven fact and built new, aerial castles upon it. This world being but a bodily condensation, a last hardened impression of the higher world, they audaciously, as the biblical Nephilim or giants, built new Babel towers to storm heaven; they claimed the ability to influ-

---

1 Fons Vitae, III. 24, IV. 19, etc. 2 Ib. II. 1–12, 23, 30; III. 1, 21, 27, 36, etc.

ence and to dictate to God and his hosts; that the *Zaddik*, the Qabbalist, is even superior to the angels. Such utterances by the scores we find in the *Laws of Manu;* that the Brahmanas, the Hindu priestly aristocracy, the highest caste, are superior to the gods and to nature; that they can supersede these and create other powers in their stead; that the world is made and subsists on their account, etc.[1] Something akin we find also in the rabbinical Aggada, that the "world subsists by the virtues of the righteous, the Zaddik."[2] And the same doctrine we find in the Qabbala in all its extravagance. Indeed, since the Sephiroth world, the higher realm is influencing the lower one, this lower one must be too capable of reciprocity and influencing in turn the spirit-world. The Qabbala is thus but an elaboration and expatiation of the systems of Gebirol, Philo, Neo-platonism and all its hoary predecessors in metaphysics and mysticism. There is no doubt that the Parsee Magians laid claim to the same pretensions and on the same authority as the Brahmans. "There is nothing new under the sun." Gebirol's bodily world, mirroring the spiritual one, is identical with the rabbinic and Qabbalistical "light-mirror"[3] repeatedly alluded-to in this treatise. This, too, corroborates the doctrine advocated in this and my former works, of the parallelism of philosophical views all over the world.

GEBIROL ON THE HUMAN SOUL.

"The soul originates in the world-spirit (intellectus universalis), participates in it, is of the same substance with that, simple, spiritual, infinite and eternal. It permeates all the beings, bears them in her own essence, in spiritual transfigura-

[1] Manu, Duties of a King, 313: "Let not the king provoke Brâhmanas to anger; for they could instantly destroy him and his army. . . By them was made fire to consume, the ocean undrinkable and the moon to wane and increase; they could create other worlds . . and deprive the gods of their station. . . Brâhmanas must be honored in every way, for in them is a very great deity (313-319) . ." Manu on castes, 3; "On account of his pre-eminence, his superiority of origin and his particular sanctification, the Brâhmana is the lord of all castes."

[2] צדיק יסוד עולם. [3] אספקלריא דנהור.

tion, and conceives them in the twinkling of an eye. From the fire of the soul, the body is created, and from nothing it sprang into existence. "The godhead dwells there in fire." Uniting with the body and becoming a person, the soul enters into intimate connection with the sensuous world; but just for that it becomes estranged from its higher origin. Its sublimer capacities and impressions from the spirit-world become paralyzed. The obscurity of materiality envelops it and dims its original lustre. It becomes condensed, so to say. It resembles then a clear mirror fixed to a thick, dim body. In order to be enabled to work up and raise itself again from darkness to light, the Creator conferred upon the soul in its bodily existence the capacity of sensual perception, that through the knowledge of the lower world-sphere it may rise to the realms of the higher world. If the soul turns to its origin, the world-spirit and hence to the Arch-Substance, it can soar up and vanquish the sensual, earthly narrowness. If it remains in this lower one, it loses its own higher being and the connection with the higher sphere."[1] That the soul is immortal is a matter of course according to this conception and needs not to be proven any further.

MAN A MIKROCOSM.

"Man forms in his composition of soul and body a world in miniature, mikrocosmos. He is in construction and arrangement a true image of the higher world. The essence of the world-mind, the *intellectus universalis,* the most sublime, holy and simple in the scale of substances, is unified in him by means of the soul and the breath of life. By the contemplation of himself, soul-endowed and of spiritual origin, man can understand the nature and the connection of the higher world. He can have even a dim conception of the deity.[2] The noblest part of man therefore is his capacity for knowledge, by which he encompasses and penetrates the universe. By that he can attain at eternal beatitude. For this felicity he is created; that is his highest good, his final object. The acts of man should corres-

[1] Ibid. I. 5; II. 5; III. 24, etc.; V. 65, and Kether Malkhuth.
[2] Ibid. III. 6, 44.

pond to his mental cognition, his practice to his theory. By means of correct cognitions and activity conforming to them, man is capable of freeing himself of the tightening bands of nature, of the dimness and darkness adhering to him as a bodily being, and enter into immediate relation with the higher world."[1] Gebirol followed Philo, Neo-platonsim and Saadia from rationalism to mysticism; he followed them also in their method often alluded-to of allegorizing Scripture. In that way he may have imagined that he stood yet upon biblical grounds. The Qabbala took from that philosophy all of its metaphysics and rationalism, and pushing these to their extreme, it landed on the shores of mysticism. So Gebirol's "Supreme Divine Will," etc., and "*Man, a true image of the higher world,*" developed into Adam Qadmon and the Sephiroth theory. Once there, the mystics embarked upon the boundless and bottomless ocean of obscure supernaturalism and miracles, known as the "*working Qabbala,*" finding all the materials in the "Book of Creation" and of "*Divine Height,*" discussed in these pages, which elements infinitely increased during the centuries of the crusaders with their religious wars and superstitious beliefs.

---

[1] Ibid. I. 1, etc.

CHAPTER VI.

HINDU PHILOSOPHY AND QABBALA. THE VEDAS.

Having attempted to trace back the origin of the Jewish philosophy or Qabbala and to show its development from preceding systems, we now arrive at the last link of the world-wide chain, and that appears to me to be the principal source of the Qabbalistic doctrines. My noble predecessors in that study, especially Adolph Franck, stopped at Parseeism. Since that time the Sanscrit science, the knowledge of the Vedas, Upanishads, Vedanta, etc., has appeared in the West and I have profited thereby. There can be no doubt entertained that Jewish philosophy has made its start from there, and these pages will make this evident. We have seen the Qabbala is derived from the mysticism of the Yezirah-book, from Gebirol, Aggada and Talmud, from Philo and Neo-Platonism, from Gnostics and Zoroasterism. But more than all that, it clearly shows to have been derived from the ancient Hindu mysticism, from the philosophy of the Vedanta, Upanishads and Vedas. Hence must we give here a careful survey of that hoary doctrine. We could not overlook that, since Hindu thought plays so great a part in universal and in Jewish philosophy.

So, naturally, we begin with the Vedas: The Vedas are the most ancient and most sacred part of the Holy Books of India. They are a vast collection of hymns addressed to its many gods, as taught by popular polytheistic Brahmanism, composed in prehistoric antiquity, during a long string of centuries by the *Rishis*,[1] the inspired poet-priests of India. They are accepted by the believing ones as most important revealed truths and of undisputed divine authority. Those sacred hymns are primarily composed for divine service and are considered by the Brahmans with the same respect as our own III. Book of Moses, Leviticus, the priestly and sacrificial part of the Pentateuch, combined with the books of Psalms, composed for the ancient Temple service in Jerusalem. We give here but a few select specimens

1 See Zend Avesta and East. Religions, p. 71, etc.

from the Vedas, so as to acquaint the reader with their character and tenor. But more so in order to find out the sparse chips and rare kernels of that philosophy, which passed from there into the Upanishads, a later collection of the Sacred Books of the East, and from these finally into the Vedanta philosophy. This is a system brought forward in our present study, as the principal source of the rational and of the mystic philosophy of the Qabbala and all its predecessors mentioned just above.

VEDIC HYMNS.

Part I., translated by F. Max Mueller, Oxford, 1891, (p. 1), Mandala X., hymn 121: *"To the Unknown God."* "In the beginning there arose the Golden Child. As soon as born, he alone was the lord of all that is. He established the earth and the heaven. . . . Who is the God to whom we shall offer sacrifice? He who gives breath, he who gives strength, whose commands the bright gods revere, whose shadow is immortality and death. . . . Who is the God to whom we shall offer sacrifice? He who through his might became the sole king of the breathing and twinkling world, who governs all this man and beast. . Who is the God to whom we shall offer sacrifice? He through whose might these snowy mountains are, sea and river . . . by whom heaven and earth were made fast; he by whom the ether and the firmament were established; he who measured the air in the sky... he by whom the rising sun shines... he to whom heaven and earth look up, trembling in their minds . . . by whose commands the waters went forth, holding the germ and generating light . . . he who alone is God above all gods . . . who begat earth and heaven . . . " This lofty hymn, which approaches so nearly the monotheistic God-idea, has been suspected, says F. Max Mueller, as younger than the Vedas generally are. But since its verses frequently occur in the Samhitas and the Brahmanas, it cannot be more modern than one thousand years B. C. *The Golden Child, Hiranyagarbha,* the golden embryo, the germ, may allude poetically to the sun-god, or to Pragâpati, the lord of Creation, or to Brahmân, long dormant in the creative world-egg, the mythological germ of heaven and earth. Hence the Golden Child Hiranya-garbha or Pragāpati are but other names for "The Brahmān" brooding in the creative egg, which he burst in two and made heaven and earth out of its two halves. This *"Golden Child,"* lord of creation, is probably the source of that ancient universal legend, symbolizing the growing sun, the day of the annual 25th of December. It is remembered in Syria as Apollo, in his crib, in a cave illumined with candles; in Christology, as the Messiah with the light, cave, crib and candles on Christmas night; in Judea, as the Maccabean celebration of lights, and in Eastern Asia, as the birth of Buddha with his crib, cave and candles. It is the same legend with different names and draperies. But this Veda verse is also the material of which is made up the Adam Qadmon, the Logos, Sophia, etc., of the Qabbala, Apochryphæ, Neo-Platonism, etc. Thus here in the very first verse, the opening of the Veda, we find the corner-stone of our Qabbala and most of the other mystic doctrines, and what we shall see later on will corroborate this surmise.

POLYTHEISM IN VEDAS.

Yet before proceeding, we must caution the reader not to assume that the hoary Vedas are all spiritual, monotheistic and rational, as is the first hymn quoted, which is comparatively modern. In their great totality, they are poetic, mystic, polytheistic, grossly idolatrous, in the first stage of nature worship. Here is a specimen, such they are in their grand totality.

(Ibid. p. 14.) Mandala I. 6. To Indra and the Maruts (the god of the bright day and the storm-gods): "Those who stand around him while he moves on, harness the bright red (steed), the lights in heaven shine forth. They harness to the chariot on each side, his two favorite bays, the brown and the bold, who can carry the hero. Thou who createst light where there was no light, and form where there was no form, hast been born again with the dawn. Thereupon they (the Maruts) assumed again the form of new-born babes, taking their sacred name... Thou, O Indra, with the swift Maruts who break even through the stronghold, hast found in their hiding-place the bright ones. -

The pious singers have shouted after the giver of wealth, the great, the glorious (Indra).... May the Maruts be seen coming with Indra, both happy-making. . . . We ask Indra for help!" . . . This seems to be a hymn to the god of the day and his atmospheric companions. The god is riding in the sun-chariot, accompanied by his satellites. Where we would speak of dawn and morning, the Vedic poet speaks of them as of living and intelligent beings, capable of understanding his prayers and powerful to reward his praises." (F. Max Mueller.) Numerous such hymns are addressed there to many of the Vedic gods, great and small, all representing the forces and the phenomena of nature; crude conceptions and rude forms, metaphors and hyperboles, witnessing to a primitive, uncultured society whose sages and priests have not yet passed the stage of imagination and poetry, vigorous and lofty, but mostly naive and childish. Yet they show the juvenile human heart as yearning for God and striving to overleap the boundary between the temporal and the eternal, and to connect itself with the overpowering universe and its mysterious Rule of Providence, who is ever manifesting itself and ever hiding in the impenetrable immensity of space and eternity. Further on, we shall come back to this part of the Vedic hymns and elicit the sparse seeds of rational ideas, later elaborated in the Upanishads, etc.

VEDIC HYMNS—II. PART.

Translated by Herman Oldenberg, Oxford, 1897.

A large number of hymns are addressed to Agni, the fire-god, a leading one in the Vedic mythology, as everywhere in the East and West. Agni, fire, was the noblest representative of man and his messenger to the Deity.

HYMNS TO AGNI.

Agni, the genius of fire, was considered as the messenger and mediator between man and the gods, as the flame rising to heaven from the altar, as the priest bringing to heaven man's offerings and prayers. Fire is the greatest benefactor of civilized man, his supreme treasure, preserved on the altar, as the communal palladium. The holidays and divine worship were inaugurated by kindling of fire among Hindus, Parsees, Druids, etc. Its distinct trace is preserved in all the cults even to this day. (See Zend-Avesta on that.) That great force hidden in every combustible object could but elicit awe and wonderment.

(P. 1.) Mandala I. 1: "I magnify Agni, the Purohita, the divine ministrant of the sacrifice, the Hotri-priest, the greatest bestower of treasures. Agni, worthy to be magnified by the ancient Rishis and by the present ones—may he conduct the gods hither. May one obtain through Agni wealth and welfare, glory and high bliss of valiant offspring." Children were thus still considered as good and desirable things. The later view in the Upanishads, Vedanta, Buddhism, as also in Hebraic *Ecclesiastes,* declared such too as "vanity of vanities." "Agni, whatever sacrifice and worship thou encompassest on every side, that goes to the gods. May Agni, the thoughtful Hotri, he the god, come with the gods." The gods were simply the personifications of nature's forces. *Elohim,* a pre-Mosaic term for the gods, meant originally the Forces, too. "Whatever good thou wilt do to thy worshiper is thine. Thee we approach day by day; thee who shinest in darkness, with our prayers and adoration. Thou who art the king of all worship, increasing in thy own house, (light and fire was the emblem of the Deity and its worship.) O Agni, be easy of access to us, as a father to his son. Stay with us for our happiness."

Mandala I. 12. "We choose Agni as our messenger, the all-possessor, the Hotri of this sacrifice, the all-wise. Agni they constantly invoked, with their invocations, the lord of clans, the bearer of oblations, the beloved one. Agni, when born (in the flame of the sacrificial wood) conduct the gods hither for him who has strewn the Barhis (sacrificial grass.) Thou art our Hotri.... Awaken them, the willing ones. Sit down with the gods on the Barhis. Burn against the mischievous, against the sorcerers, O Agni! By Agni, Agni is kindled (by fire, fire is kindled.) Praise Agni, the sage, who drives away sickness." Everywhere in folklore is light and fire the sovereign remedy against sickness, the devil, evil influences, etc.

The day is God's domain, night the devil's. "Be the protector, O Agni, of the offerer of sacrificial food who worships thee as his messenger. Be merciful, O purifier to man, who invites thee and all the gods to the feast. Conduct them hither. Praised by us, bring us wealth, good children and food. Mayest Thou be pleased with our praises."

Mandala I. 13, is an Apri Hymn. Oldenberg says: (p. 9.) "This hymn belongs to the class of Apri hymns, which were placed among the Agni hymns, destined for specified offerings and addressed to Agni and other deities." The reader will remember that we have, elsewhere, spoken (Zend Avesta p. 216) of the genius of rain and clouds called Ap-bri, the cloud-gatherer, the Latin "nubes cogens" and the Homeric "Nephel-Egereta." A similar genius we find in Talmud Tanith 2 and Sanhedrin 113. That may be identified with Apri, fire, Agni, viz: the lightning and the thunderbolt elicited from the shock and born in the dense clouds, a personified force found everywhere. Thus the Apri-genius of the Vedas may be identical with the Ap-bri of the Midrash Tilim 78, and the Ap-bri of the Hebraic Holiday poetan. That Apri-hymn chants: "Being well lighted, O Agni! bring us hither the gods and perform the sacrifice. Make it rich in honey and convey it to the gods," etc. We submit the hint to scholars without insisting upon it; it is a mere conjecture. The Qabbalistic poetan of the Hebraic ritual, finding the genius Apri invoked in eastern myticism, naturalized it as Ap-bri, אף-ברי. Similarly a poetic Qabbalist has heathen genii issue forth from the sound of the new year's cornet שופר.—Mandala, v. 25. "Address thy song to the god Agni . . . for his help. He is our Vasu. May he help us against our enemies. Shine wealth on us, excellent Agni, for our beautiful praises. Agni reigns among gods . . . and among mortals. . . . Serve ye Agni with prayers... He gives the worshiper a strong son, of mighty spells, excellent, unconquered, who brings renown to his parents . . . Agni gives a steed swiftly running and victorious. Sing mightily to Agni!" Thus, in exchange for song and sacrifices, the worshiper expects of him wealth, strength, brave children, spells, a swift steed, and above all, victory in battle. Even so is Mandala, v. 28: "Agni, kindled, has sent a light to the sky (the flame burning upwards); kindled, thou reignest over immortality. Thou attendest for welfare the man who prepares the sacrificial food. . . . Let him acquire all wealth. . . . Make our householdership easy to conduct. . . . Sacrifice unto Agni! . . . Exalt him!"

MANU AND QABBALA.

The Vedas have a limited number of semi-supreme gods, or powers, and an infinite number of subordinate genii. Each god is leading and represents a full side and visage of the Deity, and together they represent all the aspects and phases of that same, Supreme Godhead standing behind and upholding them all, veiled in unbroken, unrevealed majesty, as the clouded sun disc sending forth his infinite irradiations. Mandala I, xlv. 1 (p. 42), reads: "Sacrifice here, thou, O Agni, to the Vasus, the Rudras and the Adityas, to the (divine) host that receives good sacrifices, the Ghrita-sprinkling, offspring of Manu." Here is the view expressed in the Vedas, that "Manu procreated the divine hosts, the gods." Compare there X. 53, 6, also Bergaigne Rel. Vedique, 1, 69. Exactly the same is the theory of the Qabala: The Unknowable One emanated Adam Qadmon, the Hebraic Manu, and he emanated the Ten Sephiroth and the host of subordinate spirits, the prototypes of the bodily creation. Christology with the angelic hosts is another such parallel view.

In proof of this, viz., that each Vedic god represents but a trait of the one and the same Supreme Being, that each is considered as the Deity's representative and symbol from that special standpoint, that the many Hindu gods are thus but the many phases of the Only One Deity, the rays from the effulgent majesty of the Supreme Unknowable, we quote the following: (p. 49) Mandala I. 59, 1-2: The other Agnis (fires) are verily thy branches, O Agni. In thee all the immortals enjoy (the sacrifices). . . . Thou art the center of human settlements; like a supporting column thou holdest men. The head of heaven, the navel of the earth, is Agni; he has become the steward of both the worlds. Thee, a god, the gods have engendered, to be a light to the Aryā. .

(P. 371) Mandala, v. 3: "Thou, Agni, art Varuna (sky) when born. Thou becomest Mitra (sun) when kindled. In thee, O sun of strength, the Visvedevas (all the gods) dwell. Thou art Indra (atmosphere, heaven) for the mortal worshiper... Without metaphor that means, fire is a heavenly aerial force, when born. It becomes light when enkindled; all the divine forces center in it. Thou art the universal space and air for mortal man. All the gods have their forces in Agni, while all of them, inclusive of Agni, are but phases or attributes of the one Supreme Deity." Finally we quote Mandala, 1. 11, 6 (p. 391): "Thee, O Agni, who wert hidden, dwelling here and there in every (log of) wood, the Angiras (a priestly tribe) have discovered. Thus thou art born, produced by attrition, a mighty force. Thee they call the son of strength."... Thus the Vedic gods are but personifications of the great forces and bodies of nature. Varuna, Mitra, Rudra, Indra, Agni, Dyaus, etc., are heaven, sun, storms, sky, space, fire, light, day, etc., while Brahma, Vishnu and Siva symbolize the forces of creation, preservation and destruction ever going on as the ebb and flood in the ocean. The substance thereof is one and single, undivided, spiritual, eternal and infinite. It pervades the universe and all its individual beings, bodies or minds. That unique substance illumines and pervades, vivifies and energizes the world, as the air penetrates the bodies or as light is translucent in the ether. That unique essence is the substance of the universe and its infinite multiplicity of bodies and minds; that is termed, in the Vedas, in the Indian theology and philosophy, *Brăhman*. Brăhman is the only One, the Supreme God. He is also termed Atman, Source, Essence, Self, One. He unites all nature's forces as their only reality. He is also termed Existence, *That-Which-Is*, the Impersonal, That, Sat and Highest Atman. That, Sat, Atman, Brahman, One, Absolute, differentiated and became many, emanating the creatures, pervading and sustaining them. He is the Atman, the spiritual essence of all nature. *Brahman* is also the essence of man, in whom he is conscious. The best of mankind recognize him in their own Self. He is identical with the human Self, but obstructed by the fettering body. Hence, when the body is dead the Self is unfettered, and again resumes its original condition. That is *Nirvana.* But as long as men have desires and do not realize their identity with the Divine Essence, they are born again and again, assume new bodies, transmigrate and are subject to all tribulations, until they are purified from all desire, when they are reabsorbed in Brahman: Nirvana. This string of ideas goes through Vedas, Upanishads and Vedanta philosophy. It was entailed in part upon Plato, Neo-Platonism, Philo and the Alexandrian dreamers. It had its adepts in Talmud, Gnostics, Aggada, among Arabs and Jews, to Gebirol and Maimonides. And all this is Qabbala and Zohar, as we shall see in the second volume of this work.

UPANISHADS AND QABBALA.

Having attempted to show succinctly the matter and the spirit of the Vedas, we now pass to the Upanishads. These connect with and follow the Vedas, Brahmanas and Samhitas in time and in authority. They, too, are considered as inspired and authoritative, but only next to the Vedas. We mentioned that the Vedas have primarily a practical purpose, as hymns and prayers at the sacrifices and divine worship. Theoretically, they enliven and deify all nature, and represent the cosmic bodies and forces as living deities, for the worship and veneration of man. This idealization and personification are to be found yet throughout the Middle Ages. Even Maimonides, in his rabbinical and philosophical works, as seen in this volume, ascribes to the heavenly bodies a special governing conscious mind or angel, just as the soul rules man. Another scope have the Upanishads. They are a kind of philosophical and spiritualizing commentary upon the Vedas. The Upanishads are accepted as inspired and orthodox; nevertheless, they address, it appears, only the chosen spirits, the educated and thinking portion of the Hindu people. Though claiming to be in full harmony with and dependent upon the Vedas, they nevertheless produce new aspects, startling thoughts, and are at times, when looking between the lines and behind the metaphors, exceedingly rationalistic, yea, iconoclastic, a method followed by the Qabbala, too. The Upanishads stand to the Vedas in about the same relation as the Talmud and the Qabbala to the Pentateuch.

THE UPANISHADS AND SCHOPENHAUER.

It was in the sixteenth century P. C., during the reign of the Persian King Akbar, that Hindu literature began to be known in western Asia. But it was only in 1775 that western Europe took any notice of it. In that year Anquetil Duperron, the traveler, discoverer, and first translator of the Zend Avesta, obtained a manuscript of the Persian translation of the Upanishads. This he retranslated into French and into Latin, and in 1801 and 1802, etc., the Latin version was actually published under the title of "*Oupnek'hat*, i. e., Secretum tegendum"—Deep Mystery. This Latin translation being in an unintelligible style, and its author having been much decried since his Zend-Avesta translation, was not much considered by the learned and entirely neglected by the world at large. Until the great pessimistic philosopher, Schopenhauer, devoted his assiduous attention to that newly discovered branch of literature, and had the intellectual and moral courage to speak out that "the ancient Hindus may have had perhaps more to say about philosophy and fundamental truths than many of our modern writers of the West, and that such truths, or rather guesses of truths, may be buried in the poetic jargon and tasteless poetry of the Upanishads."

In his "Welt als Wille and Vorstellung" (1818, in the preface to first edition, p. 13) he says: "If the reader has received the benefit of the Vedas by means of the Upanishads, the discovery of which is, in my eyes, the greatest privilege of this century, and if he has received this initiation with an open heart, he will be well prepared to hear that every one of the statements of the Upanishads may be considered as a necessary result from their fundamental thoughts. . . . Indeed, how wonderfully does that *Oupnek'hat* breathe throughout the holy spirit of the Vedas! How is every reader of that incomparable book stirred by that spirit to the very depths of his soul! How does every line display its firm, definite and harmonious teachings! From every sentence, deep, original and sublime thoughts arise, and the whole is pervaded by a high, holy and earnest spirit.... Indian air surrounds us, and original thoughts of kindred spirits. . . . And oh, how thoroughly is there the mind washed clean of all early engrafted Jewish superstitions, and of all philosophy that cringes before those superstitions. In the whole world there is no study, except that of its originals, so beneficial and so elevating as that of the *Oupnek'hat*. It has been the solace of my life; it will be the solace of my death... In[1] most of the pagan philosophical writers of the first Christian centuries, we see the Jewish theism—which, as Christianity, was soon to become the faith of the people—shining through; much, as at present, we perceive everywhere pervading, in the writings of the learned, the native pantheism of India, which is destined, sooner or later, to become the faith of the people. "Ex Oriente lux."—This is the drastic opinion of Schopenhauer on the Upanishad philosophy which in its essence and kernel, no doubt, is important. Yet, by the way, we must demur to, we must raise a protest against his heated exaggeration. At the side of the Bible, the Vedas pale and fade in thought and in ethics, and cannot hold out any comparison. However interesting it may be for the truth-seeker to examine those ancient naive philosophems, still, great truths, real, new light, they will not yield to the unbiased reasoner. The pessimism of Schopenhauer is much more striking and salient in this, his view, than is the excellence of the Hindu writings. His peevish pessimism was so thoroughly dissatisfied with the serene optimism of "Jewish theism" that he preferred even the crudities, the juvenile extravangances of the Vedas and the vague, dreamy doctrines of the Upanishads to the substantial, realistic and virile teachings of the Pentateuch, to the noble stirring strains of the Psalms, to the lofty, invigorating Prophets, yea, to his own Mount Sermon. Schopenhauer, enraptured at the "holy spirit" of the Vedas and railing at the "Jewish and Christian superstitions," was greatly blindfolded by his pessimism. He forgot that the main object of all "holy writings" is that "the people live by them," be patient, hopeful, optimistic, striving and never despairing of the final success of goodness, of

[1]Loc. cit. I, p. 59.

effort, of reason. Read the prophetic harangues of the Deuteronomist, repeating again and again as a protest against Baal and Indra, against Babylonian and Hindu pessimism, his manly and consoling teachings: "Listen, Israel, to the laws and statutes, God teaches and bids you to realize, in order that you *should live ... possess your lands ... live long and happily ... live and not die,*"[1] pointedly say the Rabbis. This is the scope of healthy legislation. Finally we find this most witty coincidence: This Indian pantheism, so much extolled by Schopenhauer and triumphantly opposed to "Jewish" theism, is the very doctrine taught in the Jewish Qabbala! Again, this very philosophy of the Vedas and the Upanishads, opposed by Schopenhauer to Christianity, underlies its very Christology. Our dissatisfied philosopher upbraids the Jewish and the Christian doctrines and extols the Vedic pantheism, while really he was too hasty; he has overlooked the fact that that Vedic pantheism is the very backbone in the mysticism of both, the Judaic philosophy and the Christian theology, apparently both hailing from their Hindu neighbors.

Brâhman unknowable and incomprehensible is but another name for the Christologic "God the Father" and the Qabbalistic "*Ain Soph* or *Aïn.*" While the personal Brahmān, the Creator, the Golden Child, etc., is the Indian name for the Messiah, Son of God, the Savior, etc., on one hand, and on the other for the Qabbalistic *Adam Qadmon,* Lord of Creation and the Sephiroth. . . . Thus it comes to pass that that very doctrine, assumed and extolled by Schopenhauer as a great and a new discovery, as the savior of the world from the old "Jewish and Christian superstitions," that Indian scripture, "alone beatifying and holy," with that saving dogma, was well known to Jewish mysticism and is the very substance of Christian mysticism! Nearly a century has passed since Schopenhauer penned over-hastily this bitter Christo-Judean criticism and his Hindu panegyric. The vapors and roseate clouds over the newly discovered Upanishads have been since clarified and scattered. One sees now more clearly. A new salvation doctrine they do not contain. They were known

1 וחי בהם, ולא שימות בהם.

and utilized by both Jewish and Christian thinkers. Nor are they to be considered as flagrantly opposing all theism; a conciliation is possible. So especially has that Hindu doctrine been reconciled with theism, in both the Jewish and the Christian camps. That doctrine has a twofold pole. Looked at practically from the standpoint of "*practical reason,*" as Kant says, theism is right. The world is a tangible reality, governed by a wise Providence, consciously shaping means to ends. To all human purposes our senses and our reason are reliable, and so is the sensual world. But reasoned from an abstract standpoint, that transcends our senses and our reason, we can say neither yes nor no. From the point of view *of theoretical reason* the other view tallies: The universe is but a fleeting panorama, a manifestation of the only reality, the Deity. And such pantheism is not a denial of God, but rather a doubt whether the world is. Thus the entire hot controversy between theism and pantheism is, theologically and ethically, without importance. There is no atheism involved. It is a scare-crow for the ignorant, in the hands of the cunning. So were the Jews reproached by the pagans with atheism because they would not believe in idols.—Schopenhauer, further on, designated the Upanishads (Loc. cit. II. p. 428) as "products of the highest wisdom; he placed the pantheism taught there high above the pantheism of Bruno, Malebranche, Spinoza, Scotus Erigena, etc." Here, too, I cannot coincide. The Hindu pantheism is verging towards theism, and is nearly identical with that of Bruno, Spinoza, etc. Theism pushed to the extreme becomes pantheism. The open-eyed sage holds to the golden mean, theism. Schopenhauer closes: "In India the primitive religion of the human race will never be pushed aside by the events of Galilee. Indian wisdom will flow back upon Europe." . . . To this I say, with all due deference for so great a man and thinker, that a century has passed since that prediction, and we find that not theoretical pantheism, but practical theism, is more and more dominant in both, in India and in Europe. So Rammohun, Roy, the great Hindu reformer, discarding the authority of Vedas, Puranas and Laws of Manu, pointed to the Upanishads and the Vedanta philosophy as offering sound doctrines of theology and ethics. And while he discarded the mysticism of Upanishads, Christology and Qabbala, he found in their purified monotheism the anchor of salvation for India. He stated that, "The adoration of the invisible Supreme Being is exclusively prescribed by the Upanishads and the Vedanta." (Rammohun Roy, Kena Upanishad, Calcutta,p.6.) Thus Rammohun found and advocated in the Hindu scriptures identically the same, what now thinking men find in our Bible (see my Zend Avesta, p. 87): A positive world, ethics and God, a scheme "for men to live by."

SCHELLING AND F. MAX MUELLER ON IT.

F. Max Mueller says (Upanishad, part 1, 65): "It was in 1844, when attending Schelling's lectures at Berlin, that my attention was drawn toward these ancient theosophic treatises (the Upanishads).. It is true they are later than the Samhitas and Brahmanas, but the first germs of their doctrines go back to more than 800 B. C. Even the younger Upanishads are anterior to Buddhism. Some mention Alaha, and are of the Mohammedan period. Schelling and his school used rapturous language about them. At all events, they, like the Aranyakas (hermit discussions), belong to what Hindu theologians call *Sruti,* or revealed literature, in opposition to *Smriti,* or traditional literature. . . . The earliest of these Upanishads will always maintain a place in the philosophical literature of the world among the most astounding productions of the human mind."

Thus, though not going to the full extent of the eulogy of the great but biased Schopenhauer, not finding there the philosopher's stone, nor the theologian's salvation doctrine, one will nevertheless fully coincide that the study of the Upanishads and of the subsequent Vedanta is highly interesting and profitable. It reveals to us the pure old sources from which Christian, Jewish and Mohammedan thinkers have, in part, drawn their experiences, mystic or rational. That study, furthermore, shows us the continuity of human thought since Brahma and Manu to Spinoza, Hegel and Schleiermacher, the identity of the human mind and the unity of the human race.

The Upanishads,[1] Hindu mysticism, unmistakably drift towards a modified, mild pantheism. The one unknowable, undifferentiated substance permeates all. God is the essence and spirit. The world is but the garment, or yea, perhaps only the shadow of the Deity. God, Brāhman, is both immanent in and transcending the universe. *"That"* is the essence, the life, the thought, the energy, the seed of all the creatures. He is the soul of man. He alone is real. The world is but phenomenal, fleeting, changing, as the waves, the bubbles on the ocean. But Brāhman is also transcending the universe. He is the ocean; the universe is an isle, drifting on the bosom of the divine abyss. The Lord, Creator, is not Brāhman, the impersonal, undifferentiated, divine substance and essence of all existence. No! the immediate creator of the visible world is Brahmān, the personified God, he is the Demiurgos, the architect of creation. The relation between them, between Brāhman, the unknowable, impersonal, incomprehensible, *divina essentia*, and the Brāhman, the personal king, immediate Creator, Lord, Isvara, preserver and destroyer of the created world, is the same as between *Ain-Soph* and Adam Qadmon of the Zohar. The popular gods are but nature's great bodies, or its forces and agents or man's phantoms! The Hindu philosophers of the Vedanta ignore them entirely. They offer no sacrifices, nor care they for the popular notions. Divine service is insituted to appease the cravings of the human mind, that yearns for God, desiring to come in touch with the universal Mind. Divine service administers to God within man. It lifts him up from this mud and mire to higher planes, until the purified soul is reinstated to the bosom of God, Brāhman. He needs neither our praises nor our sacrifices. Man and the entire universe entune spontaneously their hymns at His glorious manifestations. So is the mother happy at the child's smiles and grateful utterances. Even so, perhaps, is God at our prayers. Hence, at any rate, prayer does good to man. God, Brāhman, is above it. He is all in all, and all is in Brāhman. He is the being, the existence, the essence, above

[1] Following very often F. Max Mueller, Oxford, 1879.

time, space and shape. This is the Theos of Greece, the Being of Parmenides and the Infinite of the Qabbala.

We have considered the sires and sister systems of the Qabbala, their strong affinity and family features with Jewish mysticism and rationalism. But it appears to us that its fountain-head, the great source from which it began to run its course, is to be looked for farther back in antiquity. The great philosophic reservoir of all such systems, the hidden Albert and Victoria Nianza Lake of Qabbala and its above sketched predecessors, is Hindu philosophy, the Vedas, Upanishads, Brahmanas and Sankara's Vedanta philosophy especially. The Vedas are the Hindu Bible and the Upanishads are the mystic books, the eastern *Qabbala.* They are a collection of books, commenting on the Vedas, the liturgy, the sacrifices, the laws and the doctrines of Brahmanism, just as the Jewish Qabbala, with the Zohar, comment on Thora, Talmud, ritual, Aggada, etc. As Jewish mysticism, so they contain often some exquisite gems of true philosophy, even of bold, unflinching rationalism, combined with a deal of superstitious beliefs, vanquished notions, allegoric and mythic tales, ceremonies and observances, mental and moral rubbish of by-gone times; empty, sonorous words, with much pretence and priestcraft. Such, at least, they appear to the alien reader, the uninitated, who may, to all appearance, misunderstand the text with its eastern quaint expressions, figures and hyperboles, with the infinite ceremonies and rites, all having a symbolic import, entirely hidden to the foreign reader. But the most curious is that they often teach nearly identical views of Jewish Qabbala and Greek philosophy, amalgamated with the mythology of both. This goes to show the identity of the human mind, aspirations and thoughts, propagated from the East to the West. "There is nothing new under the sun."

We shall give a sketch of that most interesting *Upanishad* philosophy, as unveiled in the *Vedanta* and expounded by Sankara. But first we offer some literal extracts from those Upanishads (meaning philosophic sessions or lectures), following the translation of our revered just departed friend, the great philologist and Sanscrit scholar, Prof. Frederick Max Mueller, of Oxford University, England, in his Upanishads I. 54, Oxford. He kindly expressed to me his interest in this labor (see introduction to this volume), and this chapter is reverently dedicated to his glorious memory, he having now assumed the state of Nirvana.

UPANISHADS ON CREATION.

[1]"Aditya, the Sun, is Brahman . . (All is Brahman. All is derived from him and returns to him) . . In the beginning this was non-existent (viz., being without shape, color, etc., hence not reached by our reason nor our senses; it was non-existent—for man, as Ain-Soph is termed אין in Qabbala.—It became existent; it grew. It turned into an egg." (See Manu's Laws, B. I.12, etc.; see Kellgrou, Mythus, De ovo mundana, Helsingfors, 1849.) "The egg broke open. The two halves were, one of silver, the other of gold. The silver one became this earth, the golden one the sky; the thick membrane, the mountains; the thin membrane, the mist with the clouds; the small veins, the rivers; the fluid, the sea. . . Born from that was the sun, Aditya. Shouts of hurrah arose . . . and all beings arose" (viz., Brâhman, the divina substantia, the shapeless seed of all existence, assumed a shape, created forms. He was the root, the nucleus out of which the universe developed. He thus manifested himself by creation). (Upanishad I. p. 54, by F. M. M.) (Ibid., 93) "In the beginning there was that only which is (Το ὀν), One, Only, without a second (the Eleatic God, One) (ἔν και παν), one and all, and that One is the only true existence. Others say, in the beginning there was that only which is not (Το μη ὀν); One only, without a second, and from that which is not, that which is, was born (i. e., Brahman, the immaterial being or essence, unreached by our senses, and hence, for us, non-existent, became materialized by creating the universe, or nature. Thus the original non-existence developed into (sensual) existence. The abstract *Sein* came into concrete *Dasein* . . . . viz: "The One only, without a second (the unknowable Brahman) thought, may I be many, may I grow forth? So I sent forth fire, water, earth.

[1]Upanishads, by F. Max Mueller, Oxford, 1879, p. 54.

. . . Water and rain produce food" . . . which produced or developed the animal kingdom. Thus the pure, undifferentiated Being, Brāhman by his simple thinking, or by his will (see above Gebirol's philosophy), developed the elements, earth, sky, man, etc. Even so the Eleatic philosophers, Xenophanes (fifth century B. C.) and his successor, Parmenides, attributed thought to the One Only Being, or God. They taught that the Deity created the universe by thinking, that divine thought is creation. We saw in this volume that this remained the leading doctrine from Aristotle to Maimonides, the Qabbala and Spinoza. This is the meaning of their well-known proposition that: "In God is thought, thinking and thought-of object, one and the same." The latter, as the Eleatic Zeno, returned to absolute monism, declaring the sensual world as mere appearance and illusion, a bubble in the sea. Such, too, is the view of Vedanta, the world is but phenomenal. (Ibid., 94.) "Of all living things there are, indeed, three origins only, that from an egg, from a living being and from a germ. The Being (Brāhman) thought, let me now unite those three products of mine (fire, water, earth) with the *Living Self,* the Atma (the breath רוח), and let me then reveal (develop beings) names and forms." Viz., Brahman developed the elements of the material universe and allied himself to them, viz., permeated them with his own self; his own unknowable essence is their only substance; he is ever immanent in them. Here is an attempt to show how the immutable, unknowable, transcendental, pure, ever one and undivisible Self-Existent, brought about this universe material, various and perishable. The preceding and the following remarks are the would-be reply to that question. Of course, it is unsatisfactory, for the entire theme, as Kant has honestly ackowledged, transcends our senses and our reason. Exactly the same difficulty we meet in the Eleatic system, in Xenophanes, Parmenides, and even more so, in Zeno, just as in the Qabbala and in Spinoza's pantheism. "We see the creatures entering into the lion's cave; we see none coming out." Everywhere, in the Hindu Upanishads and Vedanta, in the Greek Eleatism, in Qabbalism and in Spinozism, we find a simple monism expanding into a huge complicated pantheism, a unity developing into a multiplicity, an immutable being—

Sein—becoming a changeable, perishable creation, *Dasein*. How does that take place? None of those systems makes it plain. All they say, Upanishads or Qabbala, is but allegory, poetry, names, words—yea, priestcraft. The transcendental remains out of human reach. Here one remembers the pointed remark (mentioned above) of *Rabed* to Maimonides, on a similar occasion: "What one can not satisfactorily answer, is best to let alone and never raise a question."

(Ibid 96.) "The earth (food), when eaten, becomes (in part) fæces, flesh and mind. So is water threefold; it becomes liquid, blood and breath. And so is fire (in oil or butter); when eaten, it becomes bone, marrow and speech (thought). . . . That which is the subtile portion of curds when churned, rises upwards and becomes butter. In the same manner, the subtile portion of earth (food), when eaten, rises upwards and becomes mind, etc."

In some sense, the Hindu philosopher is more consequential and fearless than the Greek, the Qabbalist, or even Spinoza. He has his abstruse Brăhman develop into fire, water and earth, and he now continues, with fearless logic, to show that earth, fire and water again elicit and unfold mind, breath and speech, that means spirit, thus boldly showing the primordial identity of all, mind and matter, Brahman and universe, thought and extension. That is a most uncompromising monism; one element pervades all, and all diversity is but appearance, illusion. At any rate, we see here the parallel lines running identically in the Hindu Upanishads, the Eleatic philosophy and the Hebraic, eastern and western Qabbala, up to and inclusive of the rationalistic Spinoza.

UPANISHADS. PART II.

Translated by F. Max Mueller, Oxford, 1884. P. 10.

Katha Upanishad II. 12: "The wise who by means of meditation on his Self (man's spiritual essence) recognizes the *Ancient* (Godhead, the Supreme Cause), who is difficult to be seen, who has entered into the dark (So I. Kings viii. 13: God said to rest in the clouds), who is hidden in the cave, who dwells in the abyss, as God, he, indeed, leaves joy and sorrow behind." That means, he who has recognized his own essence, or Self, as really identical with the Highest Self, or Brahman, he is above all worldly joy and sorrow. By the very fact of his recognizing this identity, he is reunited to him, though yet in the body. That is especially interesting, as also that God is designated as *"The Ancient."* Just so He is in the Qabbala and Zohar. The impersonal, Unknowable God is termed *"the Ancient of Ancients,"* while Adam Qadmon is the Ancient of Days. Even so in Daniel, vii. 13.[1]

(P. 11.) "The knowing (Self, the conscious essence in nature) is not born, it dies not; it sprang from nothing, nothing sprang from it (it is immaterial); the *Ancient* is unborn, eternal, everlasting. . . . The Self, smaller than small, greater than great, is hidden in the heart. A man who is free from desire and grief sees the majesty of the Self by the grace of the Creator. The wise who knows the Self as bodiless within the bodies, as unchanging within changing things, as great and omnipresent, does never grieve. That Self cannot be gained by the Veda, nor by much learning. He whom the Self chooses, by him the Self can be gained. But he who has not first turned away from wickedness, who is not tranquil and subdued, he can never obtain the Self by mere knowledge." The last lines strongly remind one of Paul's doctrine of grace, not work, nor knowledge, etc. While the entire verse means: Man's spiritual essence is identical with the divine Essence, as soon as everything human, bodily, impure is eliminated from consciousness. One is divine when one feels to be divine. That is Self-apotheosis by *ascetism.* That is the Qabbalistic view. It is at the base of all Christology.

(P. 18.) Ibid., v. 5. No mortal lives by the breath that goes up and by the breath that goes down. We live by another in whom these two repose. . . . This reminds one of V. M., viii. 3: For man lives not upon bread alone, but upon all that issues from the mouth of God. (Ibid., 8): "He, the highest Person, who is awake in us while we are asleep . . . that is Brahman, the Immortal." (Ibid., 9): "As the one fire after it has entered the world, though one, looks different, according to whatever it burns (consumes by its flame), even so the One Self within all

---

[1] In Zohar: עתיק יומיא—עתיסא דעתיקין.

things, becomes different according to whatever it enters, and exists also without." That means the One Divine Substance changes its appearance, according to the body it temporarily assumes, wherein it is immanent and is yet extra mundane.—(11): "As the sun, the eye of the world, is not contaminated by the external impurities seen, even so the One Self within all things is never contaminated by the misery of the world, being himself without (the world)." (12) "There is one ruler, the Self within all things, who makes the one form manifold"—viz., the same one Divine Substance assumes all visible forms. (15): "The sun does not shine there, nor the moon and the stars, nor these lightnings and much less this fire. When he shines, everything shines after him; by his light all this is lighted"—viz., all energy, all force, all activity is derived from God. Nature is dead, inert; all life centers in the Deity. The Deity is the undifferentiated, only one Substance. That is the truth and reality underlying all fleeting appearances. Just all the sensual, visible objects are unreal. All reality resides in the non-sensual incomprehensible, Highest Self, Supreme Essence, Brahman. (P. 21) vi. 1: "There is that ancient tree whose roots grow upwards and whose branches grow downwards. It is the fig tree whose branches grow downwards, strike roots and form new stems, one tree growing into a complete forest.—That is Brahman. All the worlds are contained in it, nothing is beyond that. (4): If a man could not understand this before his body decayed, then he has to take up a body again"—i. e., must be born again; he cannot attain at Nirvana, and is not ripe for being absorbed into the Deity, the goal of all nobler human aspirations. (5): "As in a mirror, so (Brahman may be seen clearly) in the body, as in a dream, as in the water. . . . (6): Having understood that the senses are distinct (different from the Atman), and that their rising and sitting (waking and sleeping) belong to them in their distinct (separate) existence, a wise man grieves no more"—viz., his essence being the Atman, or Brahman, not the ephemeral senses nor the body, so he cares not for them; they being strangers to the real spiritual man, pleasure and pain become indifferent to him. (7): Beyond the senses, is the mind; beyond the mind is the highest (created) being (the intellect); higher than that is the Great Self; higher than the Great, the highest Undeveloped (Brahman, Atman). . . . (9): His form is not to be seen; no one beholds him with the eye. He is imagined by the heart, wisdom, mind.—This is identical with the view of the Pentateuch and Prophets. (10): When the five instruments of knowledge—the five senses—stand still together with the mind, and the intellect does not move, that is called the highest state (ecstasy). (11): This firm holding back of the senses is called *Yoga*. . . . (12): He, the Self, cannot be reached by speech, by mind or by the eye. How can it be apprehended, except by saying "He is"? (14): When all desires cease in the heart . . . when all the ties on earth are severed, then the mortal becomes immortal—here ends the teaching." This seems to have been the ideal of Schopenhauer, and that is Buddha's pessimism and Nirvana. In Vedanta, Nirvana means yet existence continued in Brahma. Buddhism finds all existence a misfortune, hence Nirvana means total extinction, blowing out the light, no longer to be. Schopenhauer seems to border on that.

MUNDAKA UPANISHAD. CREATION A SPIDER'S WEB.

(P. 27) I. i: Brahman was the first of the Devas (gods), the maker and preserver of the world. He told the knowledge of Brahman to his eldest son Atharvan. (2): Whatever Brahman told to Atharvan, Atharvan told to Angir, he to Satyavaha, and he to Angiras.—Here is the claim to revelation and then to tradition. (4): "Angiras told to Saunaka: There is a higher and a lower knowledge. The lower one is: The Rig-Veda with the other Vedas, the ceremonial, grammar, meter, astronomy, etc. The higher knowledge is that apprehending the eternal. (6): That which cannot be seen nor seized, having no family and no caste; no eyes, ears, hands nor feet, the eternal, omnipresent, infinitesimal, imperishable—that the wise regard as the source of all beings. . . . (7): As the spider sends forth and draws in its thread, as plants grow on earth . . even so does everything arise from the Indestructible. . . . (8): The Brahman swells (develops) by means of brooding (by warmth and thought).

Thence are gradually evolved matter (food), breath, mind, the worlds (elements), the immortal . . . (P. 95) II. Adhyaha I. Brahmana, verse 20, reads: As the spider comes out with its thread, or as small sparks come forth from fire, even so do all senses, all worlds, all Devas, all beings come forth from that Self . . . the True of the True.

WORK OR NIRVANA?

(Ib. 30): It begins with a pompous description of the sacrifices, the priests, the ceremonies, and their import, but concludes with a philosophic sneer and half-veiled radicalism whispered into the ears of the initiated. (II.1.): "Practice the sacrifices, etc., diligently. This is the path that leads to good works. . . Oblations lead to the place where the Devas dwell." . . . (6): "Come hither, the brilliant oblations say, and carry the sacrifices on the rays of the sun. . . ." (7): But frail, in truth, are those boats, the sacrifices, the eighteen . . . in which this lower ceremonial has been told. Fools who praise this as the highest good are subject again and again to old age and death (must be reborn and learn better). They have not reached the goal of wisdom. . . . (8) Fools dwelling in darkness, wise in their own conceit, puffed up with vain knowledge, go around and around staggering, like blind men led by the blind. . . . (9) Children living in ignorance consider themselves happy. . . . (10) Considering sacrifices and good works as the best, these fools know no higher good. . . . They enter again this world, or even a lower one"—viz: they must continue their migrations until they become wiser. Here is a most astonishing piece of radicalism: Ceremonies and good works, both are of little avail. They bring reward, but not the highest reward. They are not essential; they are but formal! . . . Some such ideas seem to be implied even by certain Hebraic philosophers, especially in Maimonides' *Guide,* and also elsewhere. They looked from the highest standpoint, the absolute one. All other considerations were minor, and as yet clinging to earthly objects, hence unworthy of the sage. That is bold reasoning: "Fools dwelling in darkness . . . wise in their own conceit . . . puffed up with knowledge . . . staggering . . . like blind men led by the blind . . . etc., etc."

That reminds one of the sarcasm and the deep insight of the reformer of Nazareth. Mark, the ideas are only hinted at, as if intentionally obscure. The pithy sentences are broken off, unfinished, as if to veil the sense and make it unintelligible to the ignorant and avoid the wrath of the priests. What, then, is really important? He answers: (11) "But those who practice penance and faith in the forest, tranquil, wise, living on alms, depart, free from any wish, to where dwells the immortal and imperishable." . . . Only wisdom and ascetism are important, elucidating: (12) "Let a Brahman after he has examined all . . . which is gained by works, acquire freedom from all desires. Nothing that is eternal can be gained by what is not eternal. . . . (13) To the pupil who is no longer troubled by any desires, and enjoys of perfect peace—to him the wise teacher truly told the knowledge of Brahman, the eternal and the true." . . . Closely looked at, that is Buddhism disguised. Neither Vedas, sacrifices nor good works are of much avail; all that is perishable. Only Nirvana, the identification with Brahman, is desirable, and Brahman himself is the All-Substance, the undifferentiated Existence. That is what Schopenhauer termed the "Solace of my life and of my death." That is fatalism, pessimism. And that is also the last thought of Spinoza: "The universe is a fleeting panorama. God alone is its reality. All is necessity, the cast-iron logical results of pitiless circumstances, and human effort can change nothing." Well, that may be so in the universe, but would the human world thrive with such fatalism and pessimism? Human society without endeavor, effort, work, based on hope and perseverance, such a society could not succeed. Hence come the theism and the legislation of the Bible—utilitarian!

BRAHMAN OMNIPRESENT.

(P. 34) II. i. 1: This is the truth. As from a blazing fire sparks, being like unto fire, fly forth a thousandfold, so are the various beings brought forth from the Imperishable and return thither also... (2) He is both without and within (the world), without breath or mind, higher than is the Imperishable . . . (as

Ain-Soph is higher than Adam Qadmon or God the Father above the Son). . . . (3) From him is born breath, mind, sense, ether, air, light, water, earth, the support of all. . . . (4) Fire (sky) is his head, his eyes the sun and moon, the quarters his ears, his speech the Vedas disclosed (well interpreted), the wind is his breath, his heart the universe, from his feet came the earth; he is indeed the inner Self (essence) of all things. . . . (II. 2, 11): "Brahman is before and behind, right and left, below and above; Brahman alone is all this, is the best. (III. 1, 5): By truthfulness, penance, right knowledge and abstinence must that Self be gained." Similar views are entertained by western mystics of all other denominations. The monastic orders apparently repose upon such assumptions, a development from Indian ascetism· (III. 2, 3): "The Self cannot be gained by the Veda, by understanding or by learning. The Self chooses his own" . . . viz., by divine grace, Paul's doctrine cited above: Not work and law, but grace brings salvation. Mosaism bids law and works. (4) Nor is Self to be gained by one who is destitute of strength, without earnestness or meditation." . . Some such thoughts we read of the Rabbis and Maimonides: "The Shekhina does not rest upon laziness nor discouragement, nor weakness, but upon the wise and strong."[1] (8-9) As the flowing rivers disappear in the sea, losing their name and their form, thus a wise man, freed from name and form, goes to Brahman and becomes Brahman." This is the pure Hindu *Nirvana*. To lose one's identity, be detached from all the ties of the world, be reabsorbed in God and make one with Him.

TAITTIRIYAKA UPANISHAD.

(P. 54) II. 1, etc.: "From the Self sprang ether; from ether, air; from air, fire; from fire, water; from water, earth; from earth, herbs, food, seed; from seed, man. Man thus consists of the essence of food. . . . From food are produced all creatures on earth. They live by, grow on, and return to food. . . . Different from this is the inner Self—it is breath. . . . Breath is the life of beings. . . . Higher than this is mind—higher yet is

[1] אין השכינה שורה לא מתוך עצלות, עצבית

understanding—still higher is bliss. . . . He who knows Brahman as non-existing, becomes himself non-existing. . . He wished: May I be many, may I grow forth! He brooded . . . and sent forth all that is. . . . Then he entered into it, became *Sat* and *Tyat,* defined or undefined, real and unreal. The Sattya (true) became all this: therefore the wise call it Sattya (the True)." All this is an attempt to show how the undifferentiated one Substance, incomprehensible and invisible, produced the infinity of sensuous beings of the universe.

BRIHADĀRANYAKA UPANISHAD.

(P. 85) IV. 1, etc.: In the beginning, there was Self alone. He looked around and saw nothing but his Self. . . . He feared. . . . Anyone who is lonely fears. . . . He thought there is nothing but myself, why should I fear? His fear passed away. But he felt no delight. Therefore a man who is lonely feels no delight. He wished for a second. He was so large as man and wife together. He then made this his Self to split in two, and thence arose husband and wife (pati-patni). Therefore Yagnavalkya said: "We two are thus (each of us) like half a shell." (Roer translates: "Therefore was this only one half of himself, as a split pea is of a whole.") Therefore the void which was is filled by the wife." Now compare with Genesis ii. 18-24: Ihvh Elohim said, it is not good that Adam shall be alone. I shall make him a help-mate at his side. And Ihvh formed all the beasts and the fowl and brought them unto Adam. Adam gave them each a name . . . but he found no help-meet at his side. Then Ihvh made Adam fall deeply asleep, when he took one of Adam's ribs and built it into a woman and brought her to Adam. Then Adam said: "This time, indeed, she is bone of my bone and flesh of my flesh. She shall be called woman, for she is taken from man. Therefore will man leave father and mother and cling to his wife, and they will form one person." This entire tradition and the part of Adam and Eve seem to be a higher and more refined concept of the Hindu Yagnavalkya-pair. But the Talmud and Aggadas, on this, seem to be nearer the Indian tale. We have quoted this in these pages. According to that Rabbinic legend, Adam was first made Androgynous, a man-woman, and then separated into two bodies, just as in the Upanishad. Generally the Pentateuch remembers the pre-Mosaic legends, but purified and refined, and with a higher moral on the top; while the Talmud brings it closer to the original, popular version. This, I hope largely to verify in our later studies on the traditions of the Pentateuch and the Babylonians. (P. 292.) Strikingly we read in the Maitrayana Brahmana Upanishad II. 6: "In the beginning Pragâpati (Creator) stood alone. He had no happiness when alone. Meditating on himself, he created many creatures. He looked on them and saw they were like a stone, without understanding, and standing like a lifeless post. He had no happiness. He thought, I shall enter within, that they may awaken . . . and He entered within them." . . We may here, further, remember that the Divine Agent in this Indian tale is the Self, the Creator, the second Brahmân, the Emanation of the supreme, unknowable and impersonal Brâhman. And this is the identical part of *Adam Qadmon* in the Àramaic Qabbala, and of the *Adam Harishon* of the Talmud and Aggadas. Again: The Genesis tradition just quoted implies the matrimonial connection of Adam and Eve and their parenthood of the human race. The Hindu legend continues so explicitly: (Ibid. 3) "He embraced her and man was born. He and she were successively metamorphosed into bull and cow, stallion and mare, he-goat and she-goat, etc., down to the ants, and brought forth all those species." While the Hebrew version is infinitely more rational and euphemistical: "Ihvh brought to Adam all the beasts, etc., and as he named each, so is its name" (Genesis ii, 19). So in the Hindu myth. The Self, thinking the *"nama-rupa,"* names and forms of all beings, brought about their creation. (P. 86, Ibid. 4-6): "Thus he created everything that exists in pairs. . . . Hence he became the creation. . . . Each god is but his manifestation, for he is all the gods." This is the exact meaning of the frequent expression in Genesis: "Ihvh-Elohim."—(7): "At present all this is developed by name and form, so that one can say, He called so and so, is such a one." This corresponds to Gen. ii, 19: As Adam named each animated being, such is its name.—Apparently the tradition of our Gen. ii. has at its back the similar legend of the Upanishad. But there it is purified and rationalized. With the Hindu is all pantheism: Brāhman the Impersonal develops Brahmān the personal Creator, who develops man, who develops woman, and both develop the human race. They metamorphose and produce the living species. So all creations are but developments of the Brahman, the Emanation of the Supreme Brāhman, the Highest Atman. So (Ibid., 17) it reads: "In the beginning Self was alone. He desired, Let there be a wife for me, that I may have offspring." . . . Is this more intelligible to man's limited understanding? Hardly! The Genesis is more simple, popular, and rational withal. Ihvh-Elohim, the Being, containing all the powers and capacities, created heaven and earth, sun, moon and stars, man and woman and all other beings. How and why? Genesis does not claim to answer. That is above human comprehension. The Hindu tries to solve it, but his philosophems contain little true philosophy. It reminds of Goethe's "Where ideas fail, words cunningly supplement them!" The Upanishad closes. (7) He, Brahman, entered creation. He cannot be seen; breathing, he is called breath; speaking, he is speech; seeing, he is eye; thinking, he is mind. All these are but names of his acts. He is unknown, without predicates or attributes. Let men worship him as the Self, Existence, Essence containing all." That is Spinoza's view. That is pantheism. That was "the solace of life and death" of Schopenhauer. That is Qabbala. But it is far less intelligible than theism, while it is more dreary and cheerless. Reader, think and choose!

BRIHADĀRANYAKA UPANISHAD IV. 1.

THE SELF ALONE IMPORTANT.

The same idea of pantheism, that everything, from the highest to the lowest, is but one unique substance, Brahman, is again repeated here, ingeniously and tenderly (iv. 1), as follows: (P. 108): "When Yagnavalkya was going to leave his house and enter upon his hermit life, his wife Maitreyi inquired of him: My Lord, if this whole earth full of wealth belonged to me, should I be immortal by it? No, he replied; there is no hope of immortality by wealth. (So said Nazareth: Rather will a camel pass through a needle's eye than a rich man go to paradise.) She inquired: What, then, shall I do with that by which I do not become immortal? And he answered: Come, sit down, and I will explain it to thee: Verily a husband is not dear that you may love the husband (for his own sake), but that you may love the Self in the husband, therefore, a husband is dear. Verily, a wife is not dear that one may love the wife, but that one may love the Self (within her), therefore a wife is dear. Verily sons are not dear that you may love the sons, but that you may love the Self in them; therefore sons are dear. Verily wealth, cattle, are not dear for themselves, but for the Self within them, they are dear. Verily the Brahman class, Kshatra class, the worlds, the Devas, everything is not dear for its own sake, but for the sake of the same Self in them it is dear. . . . Whosoever looks for anything elsewhere than in the Self, is disappointed. . . . All is that Self. . . . As the sound of the drum, the conch-shell, the lute, cannot be seized (with the hands) but with the ear, even so the Great Being. From Him all was breathed forth. As a lump of salt, thrown into water, dissolves there and cannot be taken out again, but wherever we taste, it is salt, thus verily, O Maitreyi, does this great Being, endless, consisting but of knowledge, rise from these elements and vanish again in them."

It is such vast, world-wide, hazy conceptions that charmed a Spinoza, Schopenhauer, etc. Disappointed with the visible human world, they stretched forth their Briareus arms after the mighty All. Did that satisfy them? I fear, not!

(P. 132-139) Ibid. III. 7-8: "Gautama asks Yagnavalkya: What is the string holding the worlds and the creatures together, and who is their Ruler? Answer: Vaya (air) is the thread and Brahman is the Ruler! He who dwells in the earth, in the water, in fire, in the sky, air, heaven, sun, space, stars, ether, darkness and light; he whom they do not know and whose body they all are, Brahman, is the Ruler within, and he is thyself. He who dwells in all beings, even in mind, knowledge and seed—all are but his body; he is the Ruler and he is thyself. *Akshara,* the imperishable, is neither coarse nor fine, short nor long, fire nor water; it is without shadow, air, ether, taste or smell; without eyes, ears, speech, breath, light or mind; having no within nor without. By the command of that Imperishable, all exists, moves, acts. . . . That Brahman is unseen, but seeing; unheard, but hearing; unperceived, but perceiving; unknown, but knowing. There is nothing that sees, hears, perceives, knows but it (the impersonal, undifferentiated, all-containing Substance, Supreme Self, Brâhman). (P. 139) Ibid., iii. 9: "How many gods are there and what are they? Answer: There are as many gods as there are powers and capacities in nature and its creatures. They are graded in power, but infinite in numbers. The one Supreme God is Brâhman, *That,* the principle of every Self. (P. 149) That Self (Atman) is to be described by No! No! He is (without attributes) incomprehensible and imperishable, is not attached and not fettered, does not suffer nor fail." (This is the Qabbalistic אין, the Non-Existent, one of the designations of the *Ain-Soph.*) The same is repeated (p. 160) in Brihadaranyaka, iv. 2. 4—(p. 180) Ibid. iv. 4. 22—(p. 185) iv. 6. 15—in exactly the same wording. Man is like a tree; his hairs are the leaves, his skin the bark, his blood the sap, his lumps of flesh are the layers of wood, etc. Now, when the tree is felled it grows again from the root. From what root does man grow after death? From Brahman! the principle of all, the root of new life," (p. 151).

Ibid. iv. 1. 1 (p. 152): Ganaka sitting to give audience, Yagnavalkya approached him, and the king asked: For what object did you come—for cattle (as a price) or for subtle questions? "For both, your Majesty!" he replied. The sage did not lose the sense for a good joke. Ib. iv. 4.22 (p. 179): "The great unborn Self who consists of knowledge does not become greater by good works, nor smaller by evil works. . . . Knowing this, the people of old did not wish for offspring. What for offspring, they said, for us who have the Self? Having risen above the desire of sons, wealth, they wander about as mendicants. . . . The Self is to be described by No! No!" (23) This eternal greatness of the Brahmana does not grow larger nor smaller by work. . . . Quiet, subdued, satisfied, patient, he sees Self in Self, sees all as Self."

We have above repeatedly called attention to Paul's favorite doctrine, that not virtuous deeds, nor religious ceremonies and sacrifices, nor fulfilling of the law are the sure road to salvation, but solely faith and divine grace. By this doctrine, he was at last emboldened to supersede the Mosaic Code, and inaugurate what he termed the New Dispensation of Grace and Faith, and that idea revolutionized the world. The Gentile, Roman world hastened to accept it and range itself under that philosophy and that flag. Now that view, we see, is taught and insisted upon in the Upanishads. These tenets were thus well known in Eastern Asia. Paul could not have imbibed them in Judæa, nor in Athens, nor in Alexandria. They were not taught there. They hailed from India.

Ibid. iv. 5 (p. 181). Here we find again the narrative of Yagnavalkya instructing his wife concerning immortality. We have seen that above, in almost the same terms, only verse 13 here reads otherwise: "As a mass of salt is altogether a mass of taste, thus indeed is the Self altogether a mass of knowledge." That God is pure knowledge, we find also among Jewish philosophers. There are many aspects to such an idea.

Ibid. v. 2. 1 (p. 189): "The threefold descendants of Pragapati, gods, men and Asuras or spirits, dwelt as students with their sire. The gods asked: Tell us something! He told them, Da! The men asked, tell us something. He answered, Da! The spirits asked, tell us something. He answered, Da! Did you understand? They answered: We did understand. You told us Damyata, be subdued; Datta, give; Dayadham, be merciful. The divine voice of thunder repeats the same Da! Da! Da! That is: Be subdued, give, be merciful! Let that triad be taught—Subduing, Giving, Mercy." That no doubt is sublime. It is taught by Rishis, Buddha, Nazareth and Mohammed, just as well as by Moses, Rabbis and the Prophets. Pragapati means father of creatures, the Adam Qadmon of Qabbala. V. iv. 1 (p. 190), mentions and repeats Brahman as the great, glorious first-born (for the Supreme Self, the Highest Atman is nameless). V. v. 1: "In the beginning this (world) was water. Water produced the true, Brahman; Brahman produced Pragapati,

Pragapati, the Devas (gods)." Highly interesting is this, especially. Nearly all the philosophers, from Plato to Spinoza, could not get over the abyss of matter and mind—how to reconcile them and reduce them to one principle. They nearly exhausted their ingenuity upon that most difficult problem of philosophy, and really they hardly succeeded more than smoothing it over with words. The Upanishads alone most naively say: "In the beginning this universe was water; water produced Brahman, Brahman produced Pragapati, the creator of Devas, man, bodies and spirits." This seems to be an assumption that water or matter was the origin of all. So taught the Ionian philosophers. But we must not forget that, according to the Upanishads, there was something, and ever was, before creation, something impersonal, undifferentiated, unknowable, more refined and subtle than even mind, Devas; something mysterious and really nameless, which they style Atman, Highest Atman, *That* or *That-Which-Is,* and usually, Brāhman, as neuter, the Incomprehensible. He is the Essence of Existence, the Self of all the Selfs. He is the unique and only Substance of the universe and he bore the second Brahmān the personal one, the Pragapati or Creator. Thus the Upanishads believe to have bridged over the gap between matter and mind by assuming one supreme Substance, differentiating itself into mind and matter. The difficulty is not overcome, but it is interesting to see the Hindus grappling with that problem long before the West.

VI. iv. 1, etc. (p. 219), prescribes for sexual relations, which are not translatable. Such we find also in Qabbala, Zohar and in Cordex *Ioreh Deah.* Here is some of the Hindu version: (13) "When the monthly illness arrives, a woman should for three days not drink from a metal vessel, nor wear a fresh dres, nor be touched by a Soudra (slave). At the end of three days she shall bathe and the husband make her pound rice (for the sacrificial ceremony). (15) If a man wishes a white son with knowledge of one Veda and long life, he and his wife should eat of boiled rice with milk and butter. If he wishes a reddish son, with two Vedas, etc., he and his wife should eat of boiled rice with coagulated milk and butter. If he desires a dark son, with three

Vedas, etc., they should eat rice with water and butter. And if he craves for a learned daughter, etc., then they should eat rice with sesamum and butter. And if he wishes a learned son, a famous one, a public man, a popular speaker, then they should eat rice with beef and butter. Towards morning he offers a sacrifice, with a prayer to Agni . . . washes his hands, sprinkles her with water and pronounces a benediction." The Zohar contains much more of such untranslatable rites and formulæ. Everywhere mystics presupposed in both, nature and Deity, a male and a female principle. The *Sephiroth* were divided into male and female forces, and by the union of both all development and creation proceeded. This was symbolized in matrimony. The Christological Trinity originally comprehended male, female and offspring.[1] Such speculations we find everywhere. What means that? Philosophers, Hindu, Alexandrian or Qabbalistic, saw everywhere such two principles in the universe, male and female sexes, positive and negative electricity, two poles of the magnet, the cloud, the lightning, etc. Hence they searched for its cause—in the Divine Essence.

SVETÂSVATARA UPANISHAD. YOGA. SPINOZA'S EPITAPH.

That treats of the highest themes of philosophy. (I. i. p. 231): "The Brahman students asked: Is Brahman the cause? Whence are we born? Whereby do we live and whither do we go? At whose command do we abide, whether in pain or pleasure? Should time or nature or necessity, or chance or the elements be the cause, or he who is called the person (Purusha, the personal Brahman)?" The question is very bold and frank. Let us see the answer: "The sages, devoted to meditation and concentration, have seen the power belonging to God himself, hidden in its own qualities. He, being one, superintends all those causes, time, Self, and the rest. We meditate on him who (like a wheel) has one felly with three tires, sixteen ends, fifty spokes, twenty counter-spokes and six sets of eight; whose one rope is manifold, who proceeds on three different roads and whose illusion arises from two causes." This answer is neither plain nor frank. It

1 See Mosheim on trinity at the Council of Nicaea. 325, P. C.

is timid, ambiguous, intricate and puzzling. Sankara (800 P. C.), the best commentator, tries to solve the riddle as meaning: "The *Isvara* or Creator is represented as a wheel with one felly, viz., the phenomenal world; the felly having three tires or hoops to bind it, viz., the three qualities of nature." . . . . Another explanation is: "The one felly may mean the chaos and its two products in a general form and its individual products." The other numbers are explained, too, in some way, but not satisfactorily. The query is not answered, the answer not understood, and if understood would not be satisfactory, simply because the question transcends the human level, and as usual we are paid off with words.

The *Yoga,* viz., ecstasy and concentration of our thoughts upon things divine, eliminating all earthly concerns, plays a great part with the Hindu hermit philosopher. "When the Yoga takes place, then there is no longer illness, old age or pain" (P. 242, ii. 12). Yoga is thus described: "Fixing the thought on the tip of the nose, . . . on the tip of the tongue, on the point of the palate, on the middle of the tongue, on the roof of the tongue, . . . different heavenly sensations and ecstatic states are produced, . . . by means of which perceptions the mind is supposed to be steadied, because it is no longer attracted by outward objects." (See Yoga, Sutras, i. 35.) (14) "As a metal disc (mirror) tarnished by dust shines bright again after it has been cleaned, so is the one incarnate human person satisfied and free from grief after he has seen the real nature of the Self (divine)." In Talmud, Aggadas and Qabbala we meet frequently with the expressions of "mirrors illumined and not illumined, wherein the Deity is visible to the diverse seers."[1] The Upanishad just quoted seems to allude to such a mirror of the Rishi. The same does the following verse (P. 243, ii. 15): "When, by means of the real nature of his Self, man sees as by a lamp, the real nature of Brahman, then having known the unborn, eternal God who is beyond all nature, he is freed from all fetters. . . . (17) "The god who is in the fire and in the water, who has entered into the whole world, who is in the plants and trees, adoration be to that

[1] אספקלריא המאירה....שלא מאירה....
This suggests that the prophet sees the Deity, as reflected in his own mind, more or less clearly, not as *per se.* Here Talmud, Upanishad, Mystics and Spinoza are at one.

god, adoration!" There is no doubt that the Hindu hermit philosophers distinctly surmised the One God of the universe behind their popular mythologic gods, the forces of nature. Hence their great attraction for Jewish and Christian monotheistic thinkers in Gnosticism and in Qabbala. P. 248, iii, 3, 20 and 21: "The Self smaller than small, greater than great, is hidden in the heart. A man who has left all grief behind sees the Lord, the passionless by divine grace. . . . I know this undecaying *Ancient* one, the Self of all things, who is infinite, omnipresent . . . and eternal." The Upanishads insist upon the identity of the Divine Essence with the human essence. Mosaism teaches the soul as created, yet a divine breath, while the Qabbala essentially entertains the Hindu view: the soul originating in God and returning to him. If Schopenhauer accepted this view in earnest, it was truly "the solace of his death," as he said. As to Spinoza, the force of his logic could but accept it in full earnest: Everything rooted in God, and hence man's essence, too—and so he lived and died serene and hopeful, without desire, regret or fear, in communion with his Divine Father, as becoming a Jewish sage or a Hindu Rishi. His earthly life was not a happy one, but seeing God in his heart, he did not grieve long, shrugging his shoulders at his pigmy enemies, he lived and died as a sage. Spinoza set to the following picture of the Hindu poet in Maitr. Bra. Upanishad, vi. 30: "Having settled down in a pure place, let him study, speak and think the truth. Henceforth, he becomes another man; his fetters are cut asunder. He knows no hope, no fear, no desire. He is blessed in the true God." Upon his tombstone might be engraved: He lived, he thought, he spoke, he wrote the truth. He knew no fear, no desire, no disappointing hope. He is blessed in God.

P. 249, IV, iv. 2-4: "That Self indeed is Agni, Aditya, Vayu, Kandramas (fire, sun, wind and moon). It is water, the starry firmament, Brahman and Pragapati. Thou art man, woman, youth, old man; the bee, the parrot, the thundercloud and the seas. Thou art infinite and parent of all the worlds. . . . (13) He who is the sovereign of all the gods, in whom all the worlds rest, who rules over all, to that god let us sacrifice an oblation.

. . . (14) He who knows him in the midst of chaos, creating all things, enveloping every thing, passes into peace forever." P. 257, v. ii. and 12: "By means of thoughts, touching, seeing and sympathizing the incarnate Self (Brahman pervading the bodies) successively assumes in various places, various forms . . . choosing many shapes and uniting himself with them, he is seen as one and another, through the qualities of his acts and of his (temporarily assumed) body."

P. 260, vi. 1: "Some men, deluded, speak of nature and of time (as the causes of things). But it is the greatness of God by which this Brahma-wheel is made to turn. . . . By his command, by him the knower, the time of time, this work (of creation), earth, water, fire, air, ether, unfolds itself . . . he being in truth different (from them and all his productions). . . . He is their beginning and primary cause. He is above all forms and all time . . . the support of all . . . the Deity of Deities, the Lord of the Universe . . . His power is revealed as manifold, inherent, acting as force and knowledge. . . . That only God who spontaneously covered himself (with the world) like a spider with threads drawn from (himself), the first cause. . . He is the one God, hidden in all beings, all-pervading, free from qualities (undifferentiated). . . . The sun does not shine, nor the moon, the stars, the lightning, much less the fire. By his light, all this is lightened. . . . He makes all, he knows all, he is self-caused, the time of time. He creates, sustains and dissolves the world's existences. He first created Brahmān and delivered the Vedas. . . . Through the grace of God has the wise Svetasvatara truly proclaimed Brahman to the best of Ascetics, as approved by the Rishis. . . . This highest mystery of the Vedanta should not be given away to one whose passions have not been subdued, who is not a hermit, a mendicant, devoted to contemplation, who is devoted to God and to the Guru (teacher) as to God." The last sentence we find literally in Treatise Abboth: "Let the fear of thy teacher be to thee as the fear of God." But even the admonition to be careful with delivering the lessons to none but the worthy is also often to be found in the Talmud, moralists, Aggadists and Codices.

MAITRĀYANA BRAHMANA UPANISHAD.

P. 303, v. 5, 1: "Thou art Brahma, thou art Vishnu, thou art Rudra Pragapati, Agni, Varuna, Vayu, Indra and the Moon. Thou art Anna, Yama, the Earth and all. In thee all things exist! Lord of the Universe, glory to thee! Thou art the Self (Essence) of all, the maker of all. Thou art all life and joy. Glory to thee, the tranquil, the hidden, the incomprehensible, without beginning and without end!" VI, 17: "In the begin Brāhman was all this. He was one and infinite; infinite in the East, West, South and North, above and below. The Highest Self (Existence) is not to be fixed, is unlimited, unborn, not to be conceived. He is like the ether (everywhere), and at the destruction of the universe, he alone is awake. . . . He awakens all this world by his thought only; by him it is meditated and dissolved. He is the light shining in the sun, he is every (kindled) fire, he is in the heat digesting the food in the stomach. Thus he who is in the fire, in the heart and in the sun, they are one and the same."—There is no denial of the grandeur and beauty of some of the hymns and meditations of the Upanishads. Often they remind of the Psalms, as also of the hymns of the Hebraic Common Prayer Book. Compare such with those beginning: "O, Master of the universe," or Great is the living God.[1] Some verses there are almost identical: So the Hebrew: "And when all is to be destroyed, He alone will rule in awe"—and the Hindu: "At the destruction of the universe, He alone remains wakeful."—Such parallels we could quote very frequently. Ibn Gebirol in both his philosophy and his poetry came nearer yet to the Indian poet-priests, verging upon their pantheistic modes of view. While the Hebraic hymn-writers kept strictly within the Mosaic theism, dominated by the personal Godhead.

ECSTASY. BEATITUDE. SUBLIME MORALS.

(P. 318) VI. 18: "This is the rule for achieving that. Restraint of the breath and the senses, meditation and fixed attention, investigation, absorbtion, this is the sixfold Yoga.

---

[1] יגדל אלהים חי. ארון עולם.

(Meditation and Ecstasy.)—When beholding by this Yoga, he (the sage) beholds the bright maker, Brahman, the Cause. Then the sage, leaving behind good and evil, makes everything to be one in the Highest Indestructible . . . and no sin approaches him. There is the superior fixed attention: If one presses the tip of the tongue down the palate and restrains voice, mind and breath, he sees Brahman by discrimination. . . And when after the cessation of mind he sees his own Self as the Highest Self, he becomes selfless, absorbed in thought. This is the highest mystery, viz: final liberation. His Self, serene, abiding in the (divine) Self, obtains imperishable bliss."—(P. 326) VI. 29: "Through the practice of Yoga, a man obtains contentment, power to endure good and evil, and tranquility. . . This secret should not be revealed but to the initiated."—VI. 30: "Having settled down in a pure place, let him study, speak and think the truth. Henceforth he becomes another man. His fetters are cut asunder; he knows no hope, no fear, no desire. He is blessed in the true Brahman. Freedom from desire is the highest prize. He, possessed of desire, will and imagination is a slave: The opposite is free."—(P. 332) VI. 34: "As a fire without fuel becomes quiet in its place, so do the thoughts, when all activity ceases, become quiet in their place . . . for thoughts alone cause the round of births; let a man strive to purify his thoughts. What a man thinks, that he is; this is the old secret." Moleshott, the known physiologist, said: "What a man eats, that he is." That is materialism; the former axiom is spiritualism. "By the serenity of his thoughts a man blots out all actions, whether good or bad, and obtains imperishable happiness. . . The mind is pure when free from lust. It is impure when in contact with lust. . . When a man, having freed his mind from sloth, distraction and vacillation, becomes as it were, delivered from his mind, that is the highest condition." Akin to that is: "The Deity never rests upon one in laziness, discouragement or poverty," a known saying of the Rabbinical Moralists.—"The mind, i. e., passions, must be restrained in the heart till it comes to an end—that is knowledge, that is liberty; all the rest are extensions to the ties which bind us to this life. That happiness which belongs to a mind which, by deep meditation, has been washed clean from all impurity and has entered within the Self (reduced itself to its true spiritual essence) cannot be described here by words; it can be felt by the inward power only. Water is water, fire is fire, ether is ether; no one can distinguish them. Likewise a man whose mind has identified itself with the Divine Self, attains at liberty... Mind alone is the cause of bondage and of liberty for men. Attached to the world, it becomes bound; free from the world that is liberty."—So Buddha also and all ascetic moralists.—(P. 338) VII. 1-8, enumerates the many Hindu gods, great and small as but the forces, activities and bodies of nature, representing as many traits and phases in the Deity. Agni, Indra, the Maruts, the Visve-Devas, Mitra-Varuna, Sani, Rahu, Ketu, etc., they enter again into him, they look out from him; he who is wise, the center of all, the imperishable, the pure, the bright, the tranquil—he is, indeed, the Self, within the heart, endowed with all forms.... within him all creatures are woven ... He is the highest Lord, the master and guardian of all beings, holding all in their places. In him all the gods are resumed. He abides in the fire, he is in the heart and he is in the sun; all being one and the same... To thee who art this, clothed in all forms and settled in the ether, be adoration!"

No doubt this is pantheism and not theism. But it is the noblest mode of pantheism. It is the very opposite of atheism. It rather denies the world and identifies all with God. It teaches that God is the sole energy, the only real Substance, the Providence of the universe, and the essence or Self of man. At the same time it does not deny the world as others do. It represents it as the garb, the temple, the visible manifestation of the Deity. At any rate, it is strongly verging towards theism, and by no means its irreconcilable foe, as generally assumed by the ignorant. Therefore must its study interest us greatly. But it is more. It is the oldest system of philosophy and visibly of immense influence. From it is derived and modified that of Zoroasterism, viz: Ormazd and Ahriman, the two Parsee Supreme Principles, as evolved from the mysterious Zrvana Akarana. They are originally Indian conceptions. Closer even has

Buddha followed the philosophy of Kapila and the Upanishads. Nay, Buddism is nothing else but a practical application of the Upanishads, taught to the people at large. While the Rishis kept it a secret from the masses. Greek mythology, polytheism and blind supreme fate are but another modification of that Hindu polytheism; the Greek and the Indian gods are, alike, but phases of Brahman. But even Greek rational philosophy has Hinduism as its necessary antecedent. Plato, assuming matter and mind as co-eval and primordeal, vaguely postulates for both a common origin, which darkly refers them back to the undifferentiated prime Substance, as does the Vedanta. Nearer still is Neo-Platonism, another modification of the Vedanta by Greek masters. Are the Unknowable and the Logos anything else but the two Brahmans, Father and Son? Such, too, is Philo, etc., and their Alexandrian Logos doctrine. Further unfoldings thereof are the Jewish philosophers, Maimonides, Yezirah, Gebirol and the Qabbala, etc., of course, with strong Jewish modifications. Many elements thereof penetrated earlier into Jewish Aggadas and the Talmud, as shown above and in the second part of this treatise. The Qabbala and the Zohar are wholly and thoroughly a derivation from Vedanta and Upanishad philosophy. Finally Böhm, Spinoza, Schelling, Hegel have drawn therefrom, directly and indirectly. Finding thus that Hindu Brahmanic philosophy is the very first source of rational and mystic speculations, influencing us to this day, hence is that of the greatest importance for the study of philosophy, and of Qabbala in special, as above acknowledged by F. Max Mueller.

OBSCURITIES IN SACRED BOOKS.

The leading views of the Qabbala are, no doubt, elaborated from the system of the Upanishads and the Vedanta. Not only are these leading ideas essentially identical, but even the form, veiled and obscure, the metaphors, the rhetoric, the symbolism, the hyperboles, are patterned from the Hindu originals. These Upanishads are a commentary of the Vedas and other Brahmanic Scriptures. The Zohar is such on the mosaic Bible. The first are the product of many Hindu Rishis or Saints. The latter claims to be by R. Simon ben Jochai, and other rabbinic worthies and teachers, yea perhaps by higher authorities and divine inspirations. In both, we find grand and imposing, ratinal and bold thoughts of strikingly identical tenor. In both are whole chapters of obscure, unintelligible, puerile, superstitious, exploded notions, vanquished samples of priestcraft and children's goblins, *"Koehler Glauben,"* in form and tenor unworthy of their better parts. Why are the Unpanishads often so varied, obscure and enigmatical? That is easily answered: They treat often of questions transcending human ken, themes intrinsically very obscure, which often the Rishis did not know and that they would not acknowledge, but paid off with words. . . . And what they did know and could answer they would not, since it was not prudent, they did not dare speak plainly, but used artifice. Brahmanism, Vedas, cult, sacrifices, rites, etc., were grossly idolatrous, polytheistic and full of priestcraft. Could they openly say so? Could they declare all that to be of no avail and superstitious? They dared not! Hence they had to use poetry, hyperboles, metaphors and riddles. They did not express, but imply and hide and veil their teachings meant to be intelligible only to the initiated. Frequently such passages become intelligible only on the score that they were veiled or falsified from the very start, or later intentionally garbled and changed. The bold idea was mutilated and the verse filled up with a piece of superstition, or commonplace, to suit better the vulgar and the tradition, better in harmony with masses and priests. Often I scan a verse or even a chapter, which at first has poor sense, or none. But when I leave out part of it, apparently used as a dilution, or as a screen, or as a later interpolation, I find there excellent sense, even in flagrant opposition to the public teachings of the hierarchy; hence mutilated, changed or obscured. And let us not shout: "Priestcraft!" Let us be thankful that there were in all times and countries some good honest men who dared hint at the truth (and let us guess it even veiled) at the risk of starvation and the fagot. For the greatest benefactors of mankind are often to be found among those neglected in a garret. Often again the Hindu texts are unintelligible from sheer ignorant, stupid corruptions and negligent copying of originals, or from meddling additions and insertions by ignorant scribes and commentators. Often again, the verse is mistranslated and misunderstood by the European translator, or even by the Hindu one, who has forgotten the original meaning of the technical words, or of the rites and allusions after a lapse of thousands of years. When the Sanscrit science will be more advanced, scholars will apply more freedom in their interpretation and rendition of the texts, and these will become more intelligible and more useful. Hence the obscurity, the maze, the misunderstandings and monstrosities in the sacred books.

Withal, the leading Hindu ideas are luminous, intelligible; often imposing, grand, worthy of our attention. On the whole, the system is well digested and often well and finely expressed. Especially, it is so in the Vedanta philosophy, which we shall now discuss. Thus we close the chapter with the fine Hymn of the (P. 303): Maitr. Brahmana Upanishad V. 5, 1: "Lord of the universe, glory to thee. Thou art the Self-conscious Essence of all. Thou art the Maker and the life, the Lord of joy, glory to thee, the deeply hidden, the incomprehensible, the immeasurable, without begin and without end!"

CHAPTER VII.

VEDANTA PHILOSOPHY[1] AND QABBALA.

The late erudite, Professor F. Max Mueller, a literary and scientific representative of the 19th century, recently demised after a glorious career of great activity, various achievements and epoch making initiative in philology, philosophy and religion—has prepared himself by half a century's training to be enabled to give us an insight into the Hindu Vedanta Philosophy. During this last half-century, he carefully studied both, Arian and Semitic languages, and thus acquired a thorough knowledge of Sanskrit religion, philosophy and literature indispensably necessary for his task to issue a reliable publication and, in part, a translation of the Rig-Veda, the bible of the hoary religion of the Hindus. He then published his translation of the *Upanishads,* treatises which expound the Vedas. Finally following the commentaries of Sankara, he gave his "Lectures on the Vedanta Philosophy." We shall offer here extracts from Vedas, Upanishads, Vedanta, Sankara, following mostly F. Max Mueller. Then, by a careful perusal of their contents, I believe the reader will find our convictions confirmed that, the leading philosophical features and doctrines of the Hindu sages are strongly reflected and reproduced in our Qabbala and Zohar, just as we have surmised in the preceding pages in quoting extracts from the Hindu history and Sacred Books.

Extracts from "Vedanta Philosophy" by F. Max Mueller.

(P. 7-8): "I wish to claim your sympathy for the profoundest thoughts of Indian thinkers, about the soul. . . Schopenhauer, certainly not a man given to exaggeration, thus delivered his opinion: "In the whole world, there is no study so beneficial and so elavating as that of the Upanishads. It has

[1] In this chapter, I follow sometimes Thibaut, Deussen, Colebrook, etc., but mostly F. Max Mueller's "Lectures on Ved. Philosophy," verbatim or in extract, accompanied by our own comments and arguments.

been the solace of my life, it will be the solace of my death."—F. Max Mueller adds thereto: "If these words need an endorsement, I should willingly give it, as the result of my own experience during a life devoted to the study of many philosophies and many religions."

W. JONES, COUSIN, SCHLEGEL.

(P. 9) Sir William Jones remarks that: "It is impossible to read the Vedanta or the many fine compositions in illustration of it, without believing that Pythagoras and Plato derived their sublime theories from the same fountain with the sages of India." (Works Calcutta ed. I., pp. 20, 125 and 127.) This is just what I thought, concerning the leading Vedanta traits. They are strikingly similar to, if not identical with the Qabbala. F. Max Mueller demurs to Sir W. Jones' saying: "If that means that those Greek philosophers borrowed from India, few would adhere to it. For what was possible (to think out) in one country, was possible in another also... Nevertheless, the similarities between these streams of thought in India and in Greece are very startling, nay sometimes most perplexing."—Hence the best explanation is, that they were derived from the same source. The same thought-wave traveled from East to West. The priority and first impulse belongs to India. We shall find our great F. M. Mueller sometimes afraid of his own initiative and far-reaching guesses. He had to count wih the powers that be. After mature reflection, I venture to say that great philosophical ideas are rather likely to travel from country to country, from sage to sage, and propagate their impulse than otherwise. So with the Greeks and so with the Qabbalists; they too received that impulse from the East. All great thoughts are slow developments from preceding germs deposited and matured during æons of growth in congenial soil. Only in poetry, sprang Minerva full-armed from the head of Jupiter. Hence must propagation best account for their simultaneous appearance in different countries. Victor Cousin (Vol. I. 32, Histoire de Philosophie), says: "When we read the poetical and the philosophical monuments of the East, especially of India, we discover there many a truth, and truths so profound, contrasting so favorably with the results of the European genius, that we are constrained to bend the knee before the philosophy of the East and to see there the native land of the highest philosophy." Frederick Schlegel (Language and Philosophy, p. 471), says: "The Indians possessed a knowledge of the true God, conceived and expressed in noble, clear and grand language . . . Even the loftiest philosophy of the Europeans, the idealism of reason, as set forth by the Greeks, appears in comparison with the abundant light and vigor of oriental idealism, like a feeble spark in the full flood of the noonday sun, ever ready to be extinguished." —This testimony he bears, especially concerning the Vedanta philosophy.

VEDANTA. TOLERATION.

(P. 11) "What distinguishes the Vedanta Philosophy from all other philosophies is that it is at the same time a religion and a philosophy."—It corresponds to our treatises on religious philosophy, taking the Bible, etc., as their text and point of departure. Just such a treatise is the Zohar, and such is the commentary of Sankara, the 19th century emancipated both.

(P. 15) "Vendata is derived from Veda, the Hindu bible and means: The end of Veda, its conclusion and object. It recognizes its dependence on the Veda and insists upon the harmony between religion and philosophy. The Veda is thus acknowledged as the highest authority on all religious questions. Veda originally means *knowledge* and corresponds to the Greco-modern word Bible (and the Hebraic Thora, meaning doctrine teaching). The Veda consists of three portions, the *Samhitas,* metrical prayers and hymns; the *Brahmanas,* treatises on worship; and the *Aranyakas,* meditations of the forest-dwellers or hermit-sages, the most important parts of which form the *Upanishads.* These last ones are philosophical treatises and their fundamental principle might seem with us subversive of all religion. . . . The whole ritual and the sacrificial system of the Vedas is ignored or rejected, even the Vedic gods are no longer recognized. And yet these Upanishads are looked upon as perfectly orthodox, nay, as the highest consummation of the Brahmanic religion." . . .

RELIGIOUS HYPOCRISY AND SINCERITY.

Let us remark the following analogy: The same freedom is maintained in Hebrew literature. The thinkers, as long as thinking and not acting, had full liberty of thought. They could even utter it if veiled in cautious language, so as not to offend the ignorant or give a handle to the malevolent and the hypocrites. We find in Talmud, Aggada, Midrashim, Apochryphæ, moralists and philosophers the greatest freedom of thought and speech, coupled with the severest morality and modesty. So Maimonides was an Aristotelian thinker, an exact writer and the Chief-Rabbi of the Egyptian Congregations. These ever revered and clung to him. It was the invidious hypocrites who threw stones at the dead lion's grave. Gebirol and Spinoza would ever have remained inside the synagogue, if meanness had not borrowed the guise of orthodoxy to ostracise them. The great rule in Judaism was that thinking is free and the highest mode of divine worship,—just as with the Rishis and sages of the Veda and Vedanta philosophy. But it was not carried to such a pitch as claimed by F. Max Mueller. The God and the doctrines of the Bible had nothing to fear from criticism. The Vedic myths had, and there is the difference.—"This freedom of thought was brought about by the recognition of a very simple fact, which nearly all other religions seem to have ignored. It was recognized in India from very early times that the religion of a man cannot be and ought not to be the same as that of a child, and that with the growth of the mind, the religious ideas of an old man must differ from those of an active man of the world. It is useless to attempt to deny such facts. The faith of the child is one. . . . Others are the convictions of manhood. . . But when the evening of life draws near, when to agree with the spirit within is dearer to man than to agree with the majority of the world without, he musters again his beliefs, and parting with non-essentials, he clings all the more firmly to the few strong and solid planks left to carry him to the harbor, no longer distant from his sight. . . . It is hardly credible how completely all other religions have overlooked these simple facts, how they have tried to force on the old and wise, the food that was meant for the babies, and how they have thereby alienated and lost their best and strongest friends. It is, therefore, a lesson all the more worth learning from history that one religion at least, and one of the most ancient, most powerful and most widely spread religions, has recognized this fact, without the slightest hesitation."—This is telling. F. Max Mueller, no doubt, had experienced the sting of intolerance. Who has not? Yet we must not forget that Greece too allowed her philosophers freedom of thinking—as long as they did not claim freedom of acting, contrary to the public polity or religion. Alcibiades and his friends, and especially Socrates, were cruelly persecuted for blasphemy only after the statutes of the house-gods had been broken down in Athens during one night. So Rome too was fairly tolerant, as long as the iconoclasts did not endanger the state polity and religion. Nevertheless, F. Max Mueller is right in seriously reflecting upon modern malevolence and hypochrisy donning the cloak of piety.

THE HERMIT SAGES.

(P. 18) "After childhood, boyhood and manhood, when a man's hair turns white and he has seen his children's children, he retires into the forest for meditation on the great problems of life and death."—Some such ideal seems Psalm 125. to have in view: Behold the blessed God-fearing man; thy wife, a rich vine, thy children as olive branches around thy table. Thou hast seen children, and children's children—peace in Israel—"At that zenith of life, the Hindu retreats and devotes to the study of the Upanishads. There are all the sacrifices and worship, the prayers and the gods of the Veda put aside to make room for the One Supreme Being, called Brahman impersonal Being, corresponding to the Hebraic Ihvh.

BRAHMAN, ATMAN, SELF, DEVAS.

(P. 20) "Brāhman is the Supreme Being. The soul of man is called Atman, Self (Athem, breath, נפש, נשמה, רוח. anima, ψυχη, πνευμα. Atman is the very soul, the essence of man It is used, in the highest degree, also of God, it is a mere pronoun, *ipse,* Self. Atman or Givatman is the living human Self; Brahman and Soul are identical, substantially the same. Brahman is the Highest Self, also termed Parama-Atman. Atman means merely Self, existence. Brãhman is Self-existence, Supreme essence. The Brahmãn is the personified God, the Creator, God manifested. All these terms are very ancient, found in Veda and Upanishads . . . and belong to a prehistoric layer of Sanskrit."—In some sense they correspond to the Hebraic abstract, יהוה, Being and the concrete אלהים, Divine Powers.—While the polytheistic gods of the Veda are the angels, the divine messengers and agents of Scriptures.

(P. 25) "More ancient than the Upanishads is the Veda. In the Vedic hymns, we see the first revelation of Deity . . . that behind this visible and perishable world there must be something invisible, imperishable, eternal and divine. . . . The leading deities of the Veda bear the unmistakable traces of their physical character . . . names of the great phenomena of nature, fire, water, rain, storm, later becoming mythic gods and heroes. . . . This sheds its light into the dark corners of history even beyond the Hindu and Aryan nations. . . . These gods, Devas, the bright powers of nature, gradually cease to satisfy the worshiper, who begins to postulate *One God* behind nature's pantheon . . (27) In these ancient Vedic hymns already, say 1500 B. C., we see incipient traces of the yearning after One God. . . . Many gods are invoked, each representing a phase of the one, same and only Deity. . . . So is Indra (air) called the Maker of all things; the Sun, Savitar or Pragãpati, the Lord Creator is the Lord of all living beings, the *One* is the great Divinity of all the gods (R. V. III. 55. 1). (28): From these invocations of the unknown, natural agents, the Veda proceeds to the discovery of the one unknown, unseen God, the maker of heaven and earth, the Lord and Father, the Divine Essence Brãhman; he of many manifestations, persona, masks, faces, *pratika,* but one in substance, ignorantly worshiped as many by the Vedic poets."—So is the Supreme made to say in the Bhagavadgita: "Even those who worship idols, worship me," (the One true God).

VEDIC DISCREPANCIES.

(29): "The Vedanta philosophy is to be found unsystematically and in wild growth, in the Upanishads, then carefully elaborated in the *Vedânta-Sûtras*, of uncertain date, containing but its quintessence and presupposing accompanying, oral teachings. The collection of these was best effected by Sankara, who reproduced in his commentary the full Vedanta Philosophy. His is an independent system; nevertheless it asserts its derivation from the revealed doctrines of the Upanishads and Veda . . when properly interpreted... for even the boldest Indian philosophers had to reconcile their teachings with those of the said "inspired" books, a task performed with great ingenuity and perseverance. Sankara acknowledges and professes that *"The Veda is eternal and the source of knowledge."*

In reading Sankara's bold hypothesis, cunningly claimed to be orthodox and in harmony with the Veda and Upanishads, one is frequently reminded of certain fathers of the church and synagogue. These were as independent as he was, and yet they asserted conformity with Scriptures. So, for instance, says Maimonides,[1] that if reason would require him to accept the Platonic doctrine of the eternity of matter, the Sacred Writ would not be in the way, and could be easily reconciled to and harmonized with such a view. So he enumerates Ten Categories of divine beings, emanations of the Supreme Unkowable and Ineffable God—identical with the Ten Sephiroth and the Ain-Soph of the Qabbala.—What is even more wonderful, he counts *Elohim* among these ten Emanations (Yad, Mada II., 7). On such an assumption he believes to reconcile the philosophical difficulties in the Bible and Aristotle. As the Jews, so the Indians did not acknowledge any contradiction in the Sacred

[1] The book and page of any quotations, other than the Hindu ones, we shall omit in this chapter, such being mentioned often enough here in their proper places.

Books. If they happened to meet there any such discrepancy it was declared to be the result of our ignorance, *avidya*, *nescience,* called by Sankara, and extensively used to reconcile his philosophy with the Veda. (32-35) "To us, Non-Hindus, Vedas and Upanishads offer the opportunity to watch the historical growth of philosophico-religious thought, and we are not offended at their variety of opinions, which is decidedly expected of individual teachers. So we find there: "In the beginning there was Brāhman.—In the beginning there was Self.—In the beginning there was water.—In the beginning there was nothing.—In the beginning there was something."—These last two sentences may be rendered by: In the beginning there was μὴ ὄν, and, In the beginning there was, τὸ ὄν.[1] We meet even in the Upanishads with contradictions, discussions about them and reconciliations of them. So Khand. Up. vi. 27: "But how could that which is, be born of that which is not? No, my son, that only which is, was in the beginning, one only without a second."[2] Thus the Upanishads try to conciliate the Vedic contradictory statements, which the Vedanta-Sutras and especially Sankara's Commentary, elaborated into a system of philosophy, perfectly coherent, clear and distinct, on almost every point of doctrine. This is more than can be said of the systems of philosophy since Plato to Kant."

THE TRUE BRAHMAṆA.

(36): "The study of philosophy in India was a religious duty, and was based on a moral foundation. The candidate must be properly initiated, introduced by a qualified teacher, after having first fulfilled the usual, civil, religious and household duties. He must have completely subdued his passions by penances and ascetism and gained six things: tranquility, restraint, self-

[1] This is rendered in the Qabbala by: God-Aïn and God-Ain-Soph. Mark also their parallelism in Gen. I, 1-4.

[2] See Thaitt Upanishad, II. 7. Sacred Books of the East, XV. p. 58. The same question about יש מאין is raised in Midrashim and in Qabbala, which Corduero settled best by declaring that "*Aïn*" is simply the Unknowable, Infinite, emanating the visible universe.

denial, long-suffering, collectedness and faith." . . We shall remember that the Hindu hermit philosopher aimed at sanctity too, just as much as at speculation. The modern thinker ever requires and postulates rather doubt. So, according to Descartes and Bacon, philosophy begins with: de omnibus dubitare.—The Hindu sage must surrender all desire for rewards here or hereafter,[1] for wealth or gaining a name in history. (36.) "In ancient India such claims of self-abnegation were real; there was no posing and no shams... The ancient Brahmans hardly had a public to pose to... in the forest, before a few ascetic students, living on herbs!... Many of the temptations to which our modern philosophers succumb did not exist in those days... of the Upanishads. Nor did they pose to foreigners and other countries... who were barbarians to them. Nor did the foreign press report on them... Thanks to these advantages, their works, two to three thousand years after them, still rivet our attention. While with us, in spite of reviews and advertisements, the book of the season is often the book of one season... They never cared for the public, the critic, the publisher, and made their work as perfect as possible. Hence it lasted for thousands of years.—The Upanishads hold up to their sage, the philosophical student, the following ideal (Brih. Up. IV. 4.23): "He who knows the Self, after having become quiet, subdued, satisfied, patient and collected, sees self in Self, sees all as Self (man and all in God). He overcomes evil. Free from evil, from spots, from doubt, he becomes a true Brāhmana."—There are many Aggadas strikingly parallel to that.

(41.) "To be able to mistrust the evidence of the senses, was to the Brahmans the very first step in philosophy... There are minds perfectly satisfied with the things as they appear... and not able to believe that what is invisible is alone real and eternal... while the visible is unreal, changeable, perishable, phenomenal."—Here is a fine instance of rationalism combined with mysticism: Mistrust your senses and rely only upon

---

1 So Antigones of Socho:
אל תהי כעבדים המשמשים את הרב על מנת לקבל פרס....אלא המשמשים על מנת שלא לקבל פרס.

your reason! So Bacon, Descartes and Kant renovated philosophy and science by beginning to doubt everything, asking for proof first. The Vedanta sages anticipated those European thinkers. Paul (2 Cor. IV., 18) appears to have taken the same view, but rather as a mystic than a rationalist. He says "We look not at the things visible, but at the things invisible, for the first are but temporal; the last are eternal."—We saw above that the Vedanta philosophers postulated also faith "*strddha.*" But F. Max Mueller explains that faith to be identical with Kant's plea for the data of "practical reason," without theoretical reasons, things which should be believed, without proof. But it is highly interesting to find that in gray antiquity, Indian Rishis declared to mistrust the senses, and to ask reason for proofs; that just what is accessible to the senses is doubtful, and that reason alone is a safe criterion! Would not our present materialists pause and reflect? . . . Indeed, the most interesting feature of the Vedanta philosophy is that it is the most ideal and the most rationalistic one—rationalistic just because it is ideal and non-sensual.

THE SAGE IN TALMUD AND MAIMONIDES.

The *true Rabbanite* is described in Treatise *Abboth* VI., thus: "Whosoever is busy with the Study of the Thora for its own sake, and disinterestedly, is greatly meritorious; he merits well, even of the entire world. He may be called a friend of God and of man; he is robed in humility and fear of God. He is on the road to become righteous, pious and fair, initiated in the mysteries of the Law, endowed with counsel, wisdom and strength... Indeed, this is the method of the Thora: Eat bread with salt, drink water moderately, sleep on the ground, lead a close life and study hard. Then is happiness thine here and hereafter. .-. Seek no other greatness and no other honors outside of thy knowledge. Desire not the table nor the crown of kings, for thy table and thy crown are nobler than theirs. Greater is the Thora than priesthood or royalty. By twenty-four degrees one acquires the priesthood, and royalty by thirty, but the *Thora* is acquired with forty-eight degrees or qualifications, viz: arduous study, close attention, careful speech, intelligence, fear of God, humility, serenity, purity, attendance on the sages, proper comrades, diligent discussion, deliberation, little business (and worldly cares), little dissipation and pleasure, much forbearance, goodness and patience, trust in the sages, patient suffering, modest behavior, contentment, no vainglory, worshiping God, loving mankind, righteousness and open to remonstrance; no scholar's pride, patient to the neighbor, inclining to and seeking for truth and peace, learning in order to teach and to practice... Great is the Thora, offering life here and hereafter..."

Here is another delineation of the true sage and scholar, following the Rabbis, after Maimonides in his great work, Yad Mada, Talmud Thora, I. 2: "We owe instruction and education to our children, children's children, and all free males. Education must precede work, for only that shows how to work, not vice-versa. We must first be educated, then learn a profession, next build a house, at last marry. Education begins at six years old. Every Israelite is obliged to learn, rich or poor, young or old, well or sickly, etc. The great sages in Israel were, some huers of wood, water-carriers, some even blind, but all were occupying with study to the end of their days—with Bible, Talmud, Qabbala or *Pardes,* viz: philosophy of nature and metaphysics.—(III.) Israel knows of three crowns—the crown of priesthood, of royalty and of Thora (knowledge). The first belongs exclusively to the sons of Aaron; the second to the descendants of David; the third is ready for every Israelite. The crown of knowledge is the greatest of the three. So hold our Sages: "A learned bastard is superior to an ignorant high-priest."—Learning outweighs all the other commandments, for wisdom induces good works; not vice versa. Let every one study whatever be his motive, for at last he will study for knowledge's sake. Whosoever aspires to that crown must leave off all other considerations, wealth or honors, for they do not well go together. This is the student's method: Eat bread with salt, drink water moderately, sleep on the bare ground, live closely, study laboriously, the result is proportionate to thy painstaking. If anyone says: I shall first acquire wealth then acquire knowledge—he will never gain that crown! Learning is not with the proud ones, the dissipated ones, the worldly, and business loving ones. It is with the humble, the lowly, the abstemious, the frugal ones, who work with their hands, for a small livelihood and devote most of their time, day and night, to study, desiring the company of the wise and renouncing all sensuous pleasures and idle pastimes, leisure and frivolousness. With all that, the scholar must work and earn a frugal subsistence by his handiwork. To appeal to the charity-box is a desecration of and a shame for the scholar and the Thora. Hence the rule: Love thy handicraft and hate assumed greatness! Let knowledge ever go together with some practical craft. It is a great merit for the sage to live by his handiwork. That was the habit of the *old Hassidai,* and by that he earns all the true honors of this life and of hereafter."—This is the ideal of the Saint and the Sage of Talmudic ethical teachers, the "pious," the *old Hassid*: high intellectuality united to true piety and self-abnegation. And that is identical with the ideal Hindu Sage, the Rishi, the retired hermit-Brahmana. I believe F. Max Mueller may be exaggerating by his claim that the Hindu sage discarded as a myth Veda, gods and worship. The Vedanta philosophy does not bear it out. It simply reconstructs Veda, gods and sacrifices, divested of mythology.—And even so acted the rabbinical sage. He, too, reconstructed Thora, heaven, law, cult. Even that reconstruction, the Talmud and Maimonides call *"Pards,"* Qabbala, the Vedanta of Judaism.

PHENOMENAL WORLD.

(42.) "The phenomenal world was to them like the mirage of the desert—visible but unreal... If asked why the Infinite should be perceived by us as qualified, the answer was: Look at the air of the sky; it is not blue, yet we see it, blue. Even so the One Infinite Being appears as many... just as the sun is reflected, manifold, in every wave of the sea. Of course, this is a mere illustration and *"omne simile claudicat."* The sun is a real body, with a form reflected on the wave. The *Highest*

Self has no form, is not reflected but abides in all... Brahman is really uniform and unchanging, but as far as he is permeating the bodies and reflected by them, he participates, as it were, in their states and conditions... he being the material and the efficient cause of the world.... The world is made not only by God, but also of God.... as the spider draws the threads of its wonderful web out of its own body.".. Now the reader will find this to be the view of the Qabbala also, as it is of Spinoza, too, though the Zohar does not express it so boldly and neatly: There Ain-Soph, and next Adam Qadmon, is the essence and sole substance of all existence; matter and mind are but two attributes out of an infinity of attributes inherent in the Deity. Hence is "the universe not only made by him, but also of him." He is the great reservoir whence all flows out and whither all returns; this is Qabbalistic doctrine, though not so plainly stated as in the Vedanta philosophy.

IMMORTALITY. NIRVANA. MERIT. GRACE.

(48): "A distinguished Brahman appears before Yama, the genius of death, and inquires what is death, immortality, the hereafter of man in relation to God? After long delay and efforts to evade the question, at last Yama, finding the inquirer fully worthy of and prepared to hear the truth, replies: Brăhman is the eternal reality of the world, and the human soul is one with Brahman. This is true immortality... The Self smaller than small, greater than great, is hidden in the heart of the creature."—Viz: God incorporeal, transcending and immanent in the universe, permeates and abides in man.—"A man who is free from desires and from grief, sees the majesty of the Self."—So say the Talmudists: "The Righteous sit in heaven, crown on head and enjoy of the majesty of Shekhina, נהינין מזיו השכינה "—This rabbinical view of hereafter and immortality is repeated again and again in Talmud and Aggadas, and is accepted by Hebraic philosophers down to Maimonides and Qabbala. "What Paradise is, no eye has ever seen, nor prophet predicted, but the righteous sit crowned, and enjoyof the splendor of the Shekhina, viz: grasp the truth in its fullest sense."—This seems to me to be but a Judaic version of the said Vedanta reasoning.—"That Self cannot be gained by the Veda, nor by understanding, nor by learning. He whom the Self chooses, by him the Self can be understood. The Self chooses his own."—Mark well: that seems to be the "*Sekhuth*" of the Rabbis and the "*Grace* of the New Testament. The New Testament Grace, is similar, unmerited and unacquired. It is conceived as a free gift from on high. The rabbinical view makes man dependent alone upon his doings. But it allows him some over-merit to be entailed upon his children and neighbors. Such modified "*grace*" or "Sekhuth," over-merit, seems to be the kindred idea of the Hindu one.

(51): "No mortal lives by the breath that goes up and down, called breath of life. We live by another in whom these two repose."—"Man lives not upon bread alone, but by all that the mouth of God brings forth" (V. M. 8. 3) may too refer to the life of both, body and soul. As to the Hindu here, he clearly distinguished between the organic life of the body, and the human Self or soul.—"He the highest Person who is awake in man while he is asleep, is Brâhman. . . Even so Ps. 121.4: Behold he sleeps not, the Guardian of Israel.—"As the one fire that enters the world is like unto any other fire it enkindles, even so is the One Self within all things it permeates, different in form, one in substance, existing within and also without."—God is immanent in and he is also transcending the world.—"As the sun is not contaminated by the external impurities it shines upon, even so the one Self within all things is never contaminated by the misery of the world, being himself without."—God is immanent in all things, but transcends them.—"There is one Ruler, one Self within all things who makes the one form manifold. The wise ones who perceive him within their soul, to them belongs true happiness, not to others."—"His form is not to be seen; no one can behold him with the eye. (Similar II. M. 33. 22. No man can see me and live). He is mirrored in and reflected by the heart, by wisdom, by mind. Those who know this are immortal."—Mark, here we see a radical difference between the Indian and the rabbinical sages. The former appear to rely for salvation upon intuition and divine choice. So do the Christian mystics, Paul, Calvin, etc. The Rabbis hope to acquire that degree by their own deeds and learning; so Maimonides, following them. Again mark, the immortality of the soul is postulated as an innate feeling, an instinct, no arguments are adduced to prove it; it is so with Indians, Greeks, Christians, Mohammedans, Rabbis and Qabbalists. The manner of the life hereafter is differently depicted by each, but all assume the immortality of the soul.—Like other sacred writings, the Upanishads indulge in the most fanciful descriptions of the hereafter, yet they emphasize a higher immortality: the only true one for those who had gained a true knowledge of the eternal Brâhman and their own identity with the Supreme. Man is immortal as soon as he knows the eternal Self within him."—Mark, that too appears to be the view of the Qabbala; and of Maimonides in a limited sense, viz: With the Rabbis and Maimonides, the aim of man here and hereafter is mental and moral development, knowledge. As with Socrates, so is virtue, with them, but a science, "The ignorant cannot be pious!" But during this life, our knowledge is obstructed by the body. After death, these fetters are burst and our knowledge is widened even to that of God—to know God is the highest aim—pretty much akin to the Indian doctrine. Of course, the Hindu crowns man with *Nirvana,* unison with the Supreme. The Rabbis, as monotheists, stop short of that. Yet closely seen, it comes pretty near; while the Qabbalists accept the full Nirvana view. F. Max Mueller opines: (55) "The Vedanta philosophy was the common property of ancient Indian thinkers, naturally withheld from children and the uneducated. It was entrusted to those qualified as the most precious thing to give,"—the patrimony of the elect, not of the commoner. That was the rule everywhere. Even at Sinai, we read: "Go and warn the people 'not to intrude.'" ... (II. M. 19. 21-25), not only in India. We find the same in Greek and Egyptian mysteries. The same is in Talmud, Aggada and Qabbala when there is the question of metaphysics: Maase Bereshilth and Mirkaba; all discretion was used, the commoner was hushed away from its precincts.

EVERYONE'S SECRET. BUDDHA.

(56) The *Maitrayana* Upanishad narrates: "A king surrendered his crown and, on his knees, besought a wise hermit: 'Thou knowest the Self, teach it to me. What is the use of the enjoyment of pleasures in this offensive, unsubstantial body—a mere mass of bones, skin, sinews, marrow, seed, phlegm, bile, etc.... a body assailed by lust, hatred, greed, delusion, fear, jealousy, hunger, thirst, old age, illness, grief, decay and death, all fades and perishes... heroes, kings, mountains, stars... what is the use of enjoyment, O Saint, tell me!'" No doubt there were some such thoughts that moved Buddha, induced him to reject the whole of Brahmanism, and to declare that religion is solely to diminish and alleviate human misery. Buddha was simply a Brahmanic Sage, no more and no less. "Nothing new under the sun." What then was his import? Why did he become an historic era? He told the people unreservedly what was kept as a secret and what the sages in the forest thought. "He gave out the secret of everybody"—as once said a witty French lady on a similar occasion—and boldly drew the conclusion.

UR, SINAI, KAPILA, NAZARETH, BUDDHA, MEDINA.

This is his import, hence is he an era, and became the Reformator of the East. Such may have been the case with Abraham. He told the people that the gods, the Chaldean books, ceremonious cult, human sacrifices, etc., do nothing for human salvation, that there is but one God in spirit, justice and reason, and that the practice of goodness is religion and saves.—May be that the actual import of Jesus of Nazareth and his era was that, and that alone: That he spoke out the secret of everyone; that he divulged the esoteric philosophy of his time, which the prophets, Aggadists and moralists had taught: That the priestly hierarchy, the sacrifices and the pompous ritual, were of small avail; that the heathen gods with the Roman cult, the Cæsarian polity, the legions, conquests and universal dominion, the abject superstitions, sublimized priestcraft and patrician astuteness—all that is of no use, and that human salvation is solely wrought out by "Thou shalt love the Eternal, thy God, with all thy heart," and "Thou shalt love thy neighbor as thy self." So Mohammed, too, simply cleared away the ruins of the long-before discredited Arabian idol worship. He hardly taught anything new. He cleared out the Augean Stables of the vulgar, and adapted the materials from the neighboring religions into his own. That Luther did nothing else but divulge "the secret of everybody," about the high usurpations of his time—every student of history knows. Closely looking, that may have been the case with his reforming predecessors, those of Balkh, Nazareth, Kapilavastu, Sinai and Ur of Chaldea. These men did what they could. But priestcraft and credulity soon twisted new bonds out of the very sinews of those great liberators. They elaborated new superstitious structures upon the very foundations and out of the material of these friends of mankind. Even so opines, in corroboration of this view, our immortalized friend and guide in this chapter, F. Max Mueller, (113): "We know by this time that most of Buddha's doctrines were really those of the Upanishads. He would retain the gold of Indian literature, but would not accept the rubbish... In the *Kalma Sutta,* he says: "Do not believe in (Hindu) traditions on account of their antiquity, or in anything because repeated by many, or because written down by some old sage. Do not believe as truth because attached to it by habit; do not believe on the authority of teachers, or elders, or conjectures.—After observation and analysis, when it agrees with reason and is conducive to the good and benefit of one and all, then accept it and live up to it." (Anguttara Nikaya, quoted in Transact. of the Parl. of Rel., vol. ii., p. 869).

Let us resume the narrative of Maitrayana Upanishad, VI. 1.34, Maitri delivers his teachings as a holy revelation: (59) "Slowly and cautiously the saint answers to the questions of the King: "Who made this body and who rules it? He on High, who is passionless, endless, imperishable, independent, Brăhman!—What for did he? Because he was alone, without happiness, so meditating, he created beings. These were lifeless like stones, without intelligence. He entered into them, awoke them, and became their subjective principle, though he himself remained unmoved. He who is in the fire, he in the human heart and he in the heavenly sun, are all one and the same; and he wo knows this, becomes one with the Only *One*. (VI. 17) .. "Let a man purify his thoughts; for what he thinks, that he is... (VI. 34). (61) A man who is free from sloth, distraction and unrest has attained at the highest point... is free, and his mind enters Brāhman—as water in water, fire in fire, ether in ether.... he obtains libertyand unison with Brāhman." That the human soul is a spark from the Deity, eternal, and reabsorbed therein (after its transmigrations) is no doubt the leading view of the Qabbalist, as of the Vedantist. It is also that of many Jewish philosophers. Orthodox dogmatists assume the soul to be created, divine and immortal. Maimonides seems to allow a soul only to the elect, to the thinkers—a most unorthodox and aristocratic opinion. Similarly, we find the rabbis answering to the question: What for did God create the universe? for His glory! and what for did he create man? To praise and glorify Him! Much nearer still comes the version of the Qabbalists, amounting to the bold assertion that without man, God was *Aīn*, Non-existent, and the universe could not be created before man had made his appearance. All this is duly enlarged upon in these pages, above and below.

TWO BRAHMANS, NESCIENCE, MAYA.

(71) "The ancient inheritance of the Vedanta philosophy from the Vedic hymns and Brāhmanas was Brāhman, from which the origin, subsistence and dissolution of this world proceed. (Vedanta Sutras I. 2). His only attributes are: That he is, knows and is perfect." (Just such is God defined by the Hebraic philosophers.) "Being so sublime, how is he the creator and ruler of the world? As creator, he is termed Brahmān!—Are there then two Brahmans; is not the supreme tenet that Brahman had no second one! Here the Vedanta philosophers emphasized that the exoteric, popular Brahmān is substantially the same as the esoteric, philosophical Brāhman, that there is but one Brahman, and as to the popular concept of

Brahmān as the Creator, that was due to ignorance, Nescience, "*Avidya.*" (Man knows not what God is, nor what is the world; hence it is foolish to speculate how God made the world.—The world is to man but phenomenal, and so is Brahmān phenomenal, but both these phenomena have their reality in Brāhman, the only One.—That is a bold and frank answer: Nescience!) "The created world is not nothing; it is phenomenal. There is something which we do not know. The world is neither naught, a zero, nor an illusion, *maya,* a fata morgana, as assumed by some Buddhists. (83.) The world and its bodies are something which we do not know, and such is Brāhman, its real Maker..." The Vedantists allow a qualified, personal Brahmān for practical purposes, particularly for worship, because for such, man requires a qualified God, a father, creator, etc., a *persona,* a *pratika,* a face or phase of the divine Substance, which is infinite in such faces or attributes. ThusBrahmān may be worshiped as a person and creator, yet is he identical with Brāhman, the Substance, high above all conditions and limits inherent in personality. So the Veda describes Brahmān as a being whose head is the heaven, his eyes the sun, his breath the wind, his footstool the earth, etc. Yet philosophically, man can predicate nothing worthy of Him... One can only say of Him: No! No! viz: one cannot comprehend and predicate of God what he is; one can only say what he is not." (84.)

Here Sankara reasons alike to Yezirah, Gebirol, Maimonides, Qabbala and Spinoza. So, too, the Qabbala teaches the Unknowable, Infinite Ain-Soph or Aïn; and next the emanated first Sephira, Adam Qadmon, who is the Creator and Ruler, ever personal and later claimed, by some even, to be incarnated. So also the Psalms and Gebirol: Silence is Thy praise. So Augustin: With regard to God, silence is better than a fight of words.[1] Sankara quotes (III. 2.27) the following dialogue: "Sir, tell me Brahman!"—The master remained silent. The pupil repeats

---

1 Quae pugna verborum silentio cavenda magis quam voce pecanda est. (De Doctr. Chr. 1. 6—Ps. 65. 2., לך דמיה תהלה.—Same, Gebirol, Kether Malkhuth.

the question again and again. The master at last: "We are telling it; the Self is quite still."

(85.) "Now what applies to Brāhman, the Great Cause, applies also to the universe, the Great Effect. It is real, it rests in Brāhman, but what we perceive and conceive is but phenomenal, the result of ignorance; our world, as we see it, is a dream; it is our subjective vision, our version of the things out of ourselves, our personal experience."

MĀYĀ.

Later on this view was pushed to its extreme. Not only the world is not what it seems to us, nay, it is nothing at all, a mere shadow, a fantasy, an illusion, the effect of ignorance, deception, *Maya,* inherent in nature, as a cosmic force. The Vedantists did not go quite so far: "The world is something which we do not know. It is real, though unknown to us, as Brāhman is. There can be no substantial difference between the cause and its effect. The world is ultimately Brāhman itself." (87.) Bishop Berkeley says: "The physical universe, as I see it and infer, is my dream and nothing else. Your and my dreams sometimes agree and sometimes do not."

THE SOUL-BRĀHMAN,

(88.) "The great promise is: There is and there can be but one Brāhman, cause of everything, matter and mind, body and soul. Nothing subsists outside of the Supreme Being, unlimited and without a second. Now *what is the human soul,* viz: our true Self, the Atman of Sanskrit? Not the animal soul, (Θρεπτικη), not the perceptive soul, (Αισθητικη), nor the thinking soul, (νοητικη), these are perishable, according to the Vedanta, but the Atman or Giva-Atman, the essence and real Self, the cause of our personality, as Brahman is the cause of the universe, the Highest Self? The human self is not our sensations, our thoughts, our mind, our knowledge, etc.—All these are perishable. The individual Self is identical with the Highest Self, Brāhman. It is not a part, a ray, a spark, a modification of that, but the whole of Brāhman, which is abiding in the universe, and in each individual being. The Soul is God; that is the view of Sankara (92.) But the Supreme Divine Self is eternal, omnipotent and omnipresent, while the human Self we clearly see is not? The answer is: Because the Supreme Divine Self in the human body is conditioned, fettered, obstructed. The *Upādhis,* obstructions are the very body with its organs and all its belongings" . . . Jewish and non-Jewish moralists have pretty nearly advanced this: The body is the prison of the soul. Jewish and non-Jewish philosophers have taught that the soul is a ray from the Divine Sun. They but repeated Hindu views, with their own respective modifications. But more: This entire, novel, bold and most important theory of Sankara, over two thousand years old, lies at the bottom of the Zohar system, or rather of the Qabbala. The idea travelled from the East to the West, and was adopted there unconsciously and with a Judaic coloring, but it exists there, though greatly shrunk. In the Vedanta, Brahman is the world-soul, permeating and vivifying all creatures; and wherever not obstructed, translucing them as their common soul. Instead of this bold tenet, the Qabbala assumes the soul to be a spark from the divine forge, a sun-ray, an atom from the universal spirit-ocean. The vast Vedantic view is thus shrunk in the Qabbala; but essentially it is there, only timidly expressed. It came from India with its concomitant theory, the transmigration of the soul, to us moderns a startling doctrine, yet adopted by nearly all the ancient thinkers and much emphasized in the Qabbala, in its literal popular sense; while with Sankara it is perfectly sensible, all-embracing, yea, sublime, viz: Brāhman being the essence and only One great Soul of the universe, all the new births are energized and enlivened by him alone, the one and same Divine Principle, the All in All. In this sense, this Brāhman-Soul conception would fit well into the system of Spinoza, too. According to that, there is but one Supreme Essence, source of all, matter and mind. The universe is to us but phenomenal, its reality is that divine Essence, which is the kernel and reality of all individual phenomena.

The fact is the philosophers of the Vedanta, the Qabbala and Spinoza bear a strong family likeness and affinity which points to their common derivation, and to which fact we wish to call the attention of thinkers. It is one of the leading objects of this volume, and this chapter in special, to which F. Max Mueller alluded, (as seen in the Introduction), when I called his attention to it.

SANKARA ON NESCIENCE AND SOUL

(97.) "The human Self is hard to define, just as is the Supreme Self, which it is in miniature. Both can be described by what they are not, and not by what they are. The Supreme Self is, knows, is perfect and blissful. The human Self is and knows, but on account of its bodily fetters it is not perfect nor happy. Only when it rids itself of that shell and contact, it rejoins its original and becomes again Brāhman. The body, senses, mind, thoughts, etc., are but fetters, clouds intervening between it and the Highest Self, obstructions deriving from our ignorance, nescience, *Avidyā*. And this ignorance is not individual and human; no, it is universal; it clings to and affects entire nature; nay, it overshadows for a time even the Supreme Brāhman. It corresponds to the *blind fate* of the Orientals. Nature is tainted by that. We cannot explain, why? We can only say: It is so; we must acknowledge the limits of our understanding and our knowledge, and say: our reason goes till hither and no farther"... "Hence comes our ignorance of our true nature and our belief in the objective world as it appears. To explain and analyze Avidya is as foolish as to see darkness by torchlight. It is our own inherent vice and impotence."... (100.) "But while temporarily we are enslaved by nescience, in the end we can conquer it by true science, the Vedanta philosophy. True, we cannot shake off our fetters; but by knowing them to be but fetters, they do lose most of their burdensomeness and irksome load. We cannot rid ourselves of our bodies, our senses, passions, illusions and temptations, of this phenomenal world, but we can soar above them and deprive them of their sting. We can thus conquer our freedom even before our death—even in our bodily fetters, even in this life."...

(103.) Sankara further discusses his great theory that the temporal (human) Self is the same as the Self of the Lord, quoting texts: "The Highest Lord is to be understood as the Self (in us), for in treating of the Highest Lord, the *Gâbâlâs* take him as the Self (in us), saying: "Indeed, I am thou, O holy Deity, and thou art I, O Deity."—This is thy *Self*, which is within all." "He is thy *Self*, the inward ruler." "That is the True, the *Self* and thou art it." "I (within) am Brahman."—"Brahman is mind."—Sankara adds: "We do not understand, that the Lord is the temporal (human) self, but that the human self, divested of its temporal character, is the Self of the Lord."

This passage refers to a hymn of the Gâbâlâs and their authoritative texts. Now it is very interesting to remember that the Jewish mediaeval, esoteric philosophy also is termed "*Qabbala!*" "*Qabbala*" means tradition in Mishnaic Hebrew, and mysticism, or secret doctrine in Aramaic. But *Qabbala* may at the same time allude to the Hindu Rishis, the poets of the Vedic hymns, the Gâbâlâs. As the Qabbalistic speculations are generally and greatly a parallel of, if not identical with, the doctrines of the Upanishads and the Vedanta, it was natural enough to tacitly acknowledge it by denominating them as Qabbala, viz: the secret teachings of the Gâbâlâs. Among the many Upanishads one is denominated Gâbâlâ Upanishad. If that came first to western Asia, all those doctrines may have been remembered there as Gâbâlâs, viz: the philosophy of the *Gâbâlâs*, the Rishis, the poets who composed the Vedic hymns and Upanishad speculations, and this may be implied, too, in Qabbala. Even so America is denominated, not after Columbus, but after Amerigo, who first published a treatise on that discovery, taking all the credit to himself. Again, those verses account for the salient doctrine of the authors of Qabbala, that God is not the Creator, but Adam Qadmon is, that the human figure was all-important for creation, etc., an oriental apotheosis of man. This may also allude to the Indian view that Brahman is identical with and incarnated in the human Self, and that all we know of the phenomenal world is not what that world really is, but what it appears to our mind, through the unsafe medium of our senses, percepts, concepts, thoughts, etc. It may mean finally, divested of its metaphor, that God Infinite is as incomprehensible to us as is the world, that we know neither what mind is, nor what matter is; that all our knowledge is simply imagination. Sankara closes (107): "The final result is that we should think of the Self within us as the Lord."—All this appears to underlie the Qabbalistic conception of Adam Qadmon, the Alter-Ego of the Infinite. F. Max Mueller opines (107): "This is not the Greek apotheosis of man, but an *Anatheosis,* a return of man into the divine nature. The German mystics call the former: *Vergoetterung,* the latter *Vergottung*. The former is blasphemous, the latter is but another expression for divine sonship, the highest object of the religion of Christ."—Even so the very same may be the meaning of the Qabbalistic Adam Qadmon, the *human face.* Even so is the man-figure in the Mirkaba of Ezekiel I. 26: "Above the firmament over their heads, was the likeness of a throne of Sapphire, and the likeness of a man hovered upon it."—Similarly it is alluded to in Is. VI. 1: "I saw the Lord high and sublime."...

BRAHMAN AND SPINOZA'S SUBSTANTIA.

(123): "The Brâhman of the Upanishads, defined by Sankara, is the same as Spinoza's *Substantia.*" Spinoza defines it as: "That which is in itself and is conceived by itself" (in se est et per se concipitur). It is infinite, indivisible, one, free and eternal.—Just as Sankara's Brâhman is called in the Upanishads: "unborn, undecaying, undying, without parts, without action, tranquil, without fault or taint."—He is the omniscient and omnipotent cause of the origin, the permanence and the disappearance of the world."—This is to Sankara, the real Brâhman, God of the real world. But the real God and the real world, we know not. We know but a phenomenal world and a phenomenal God, and this is a Brahmân and its popular representatives, the mythological gods, the forces of nature, Indra, Agni, etc. There is a higher and a lower Brahman. Even the lower one is adorned with the highest predicates man can bestow, while the higher, real Brāhman is above all praise and all predicates. This is intelligible in Sankara. His philosophy is a religious philosophy. He interprets the popular public cult. He makes plain that the many mythological gods are the manifestations of the One Deity as apparent to our senses, and that behind the appearance there is an unknown reality, a real world and its real Cause. That real Cause is Brāhman, while the phenomenal one, he terms the Brahmān, the personal Father and Creator of the sensual universe. Now this is exactly the view of the Qabbala: The Supreme Cause of all existence is unknowable, inconceivable, ineffable, above all attributes, praises, predicates, etc., just as Spinoza defines Substantia, and as the Upanishads and Sankara define the Higher Brāhman. This Absolute and Unknowable One, the Qabbala designates as *Ain-Soph,* Infinite (in time and space), nay, even *Aīn*, the non-existing, viz, non-phenomenal, not perceived by our senses. The phenomenal God, the Maker of the sensual world, is his first born, symbolized by the human face, the higher celestial Adam, Adam Qadmon. He emanated the Ten Sephiroth, viz: the ideal world, the prototypes of the universe, taking the place of the mythological forces and gods, who again emanated the sensual universe. Thus *Ain-Soph* and *Adam Qadmon* are in Jewish philosophy of the Qabbala, exactly the same as in the Upanishads and Vedanta philosophy, the higher Brāhman and the lower Brahmān with the popular gods. As Sankara tolerated for practical purposes, for popular worship and public cult, the mythological gods, but emphatically declared to the people that under these fictions, they worship but the real, unknown God, even so did Qabbala and Zohar introduce, under the lead of Adam Qadmon, the Ten Sephiroth with a host of angels for the wants of weak-kneed people, who need a God much nearer to them than the "Ancient of Ancients," the abstruse and hidden Ain-Soph. Nay, I venture to say that ideas similar to those of the Vedanta philosophy were well known and utilized by other Jewish philosophers than those of the Qabbala. So the Logos of Philo and the Divine *Will* of Ibn Gebirol are other versions of the Brahmān, the

Creator. Even Maimonides knows the distinction of: God, the Ineffable, nameless, above all praises, predicates and attributes, the hidden Supreme Cause of all existence, the Only One perfect Being—and his Ten Emanations, the ideal types of the created or emanated world, among which Ten Sephiroth he counts *Elohim and Ihvh.* So Sankara 800 P. C., Maimonides 1200, and Zohar 1300, were all not purely philosophers, but religious philosophers. The first commented on the Hindu Scriptures; the latter two expounded the Heb. S. Writings. In order to do justice to religion and to philosophy, they distinguished between God real and God apparent. Spinoza, who had retired from the popular world and taken refuge in the bosom of abstract philosophy, taught pure *Substantia* as the highest and as the Great Reality behind the world's phenomena. This One, the only Reality and Cause of all existence, no doubt, is the Supreme Deity which he defined: "Per Deum intelligo ens absolute infinitum, hoc est, substantiam constantem infinitis attributis, quorum unumquodque aeternam essentiam exprimit." (124.) Spinoza can be declared an atheist as little as Sankara, Maimonides or the Qabbalists. Only they were ostensibly representatives of their respective churches, and took care of their cult and theology, so as to bring them in harmony with their own philosophy. Spinoza was a private man and an independent thinker, who took notice of philosophy pure and simple. But in all, in Sankara, Maimonides, Qabbalists and Spinoza, the truly religious kernel of all theology and of all worship was deeply imbedded at the bottom of their soul.—(125.) "For all practical purposes of religion and of morality, that phenomenal Deity is all that can be required" with cult, sacrifices, hymns and symbols, while for the Vedantist, the sage, the knowledge and contemplation of the Grand Divine Reality, united to goodness and purity, is the only true worship.

(133-135.) "Sankara devotes much care and attention to distinguish in the Upanishads between the higher and the lower Brahman. So (IV. 3-14) he says: Are there two Brahmans? Indeed, there are two. When Brahman is described by negative words only, excluding all differences of name and form, due to Nescience—that is the Higher. But when he is described by such terms as (Khand, III. 14.2.), "the Intelligent, whose body consists of Spirit ... of light, ... distinguished by a special name and form for the sake of worship, that is the lower Brahmān ... while in reality the two Brahmans are one and the same Brahman, the one phenomenal and conceivable (by human senses), the other inconceivable, but absolutely real."—That is clear. Upanishad Prasna (V. 2) states that the syllable *Om* is the higher and the lower Brahman. The etymology of *Om* is difficult. It is a hoary symbol of deity, and means true! The devotee eliminates every thought and sensation, and concentrates his mind upon Brahman, exclaiming Om! Om! corresponding to our *Amen!*—With the poets of the Upanishads, however, the line of the higher and lower Brahman is not always so sharply drawn.

The same indistinction prevails in Qabbala and Zohar. The inconceivable God Supreme is termed Ain-Soph, the first Emanation is Adam Qadmon. But sometimes Ain-Soph is also applied to the latter. The one is designated as "Atiqa d'Atiqin," the Ancient of Ancients, the other as "Atiq Yomin," the Ancient of Days. But, sometimes even this distinction is omitted, and both are denominated by either name. I believe that the epithet *Aïn*, Non-Existent is never applied to Adam Qadmon. *Aïn* corresponds to the *Vedantic Non or Self-Existent*. This coincidence in Upanishads and Qabbala is very significant. The fact is that, in either system both the names are really identical, designating rather different standpoints and phases, than substances, hence the indiscriminate application of the names to either.

GOD, CONSCIOUS LIGHT.

(135.) "Paradise is acquired by virtue; knowledge alone makes one with Brahman."—The same high view of knowledge as the highest is entertained by Maimonides and Rabbis. He, Maimonides, does not identify the soul with God, but makes it, as the Talmud, abide in the Divine Presence and enjoy of His Aspect, coming near enough to the Hindu ideal of *Nirvana*.—

(136-137) Khand. I. 6. 6., describes Brahmān as seen within the sun, with golden beard, golden hair, etc., as an idol of the Hindu pantheon. While the real Brāhman is depicted entirely incorporeal and unqualified, only by negations, the impersonal germ of the world ... the light ... *conscious light* ... knowledge." The Everlasting has neither body nor color; no shadow, darkness or light; no air, nor ether; no eyes, ears, speech, breath nor mouth; no without nor within."—(Deussen System 146, Sutras I. 1. 5).—So *Mundaka Upanishad,* V. 2: "This is the light of lights ... by his light, all the world is lighted."—So Thomas Aquinas (I. 2 qu. 109, Art. 1 and 2) calls God the Intelligent Sun (Sol intelligibilis). The Qabbalist and Zohar, too, predicate Adam Qadmon as Light. But *Ain-Soph* is the very source emanating the light; light is only His habiliment, and He himself is inconceivable, light is His shadow. Qabbala and Zohar again describe the manifested Deity with the grossest colors and embodiments, with far less taste and poetry than Brahmān is by Hindu poets. They measure his face, forehead, nose, chin, locks, beard, cranium, arms, legs, toes, etc., etc., with all the minutia, ad nauseam, by Persian parasangs, fabulous myriads of dimensions and huge enormities, revelling in such pictures of monstrous volumes and sizes. All that is applying to Adam Qadmon and the other divine phases, trying thus to reach the spiritual Divine Infinitude by numerical monstrosities and bodily extravagances. Specimens thereof are given in Part II. of this work. No doubt all such eccentricities were imitations from Hindu pictures of the phenomenal Brahmān.

CREATIVE THOUGHTS. VERB. WORD.

(140.) "The eternal, divine thoughts, the Vedantist says, were names and forms (nama-rupa) identical with the (ειδη) *ideas* of Plato and the species of the Stoics. These names and forms became sensuous manifestations in the world. The creative thoughts of the Suprēme Being became the sensual bodies, these thoughts being the reality behind our phenomenal world. The Alexandrian philosophers called them *logoi,* and at last conceived them as one, the Logos of God. Metaphorically, Philo called the same Logos (Theosophy, p. 412): "The only begotten son of God (υιοσ μονογενησ) viz: the first ideal creation or manifestation of the Godhead."—These divine thoughts, or this first creation, this ideal prototype of the world in the thought of the Supreme, the Qabbala calls: the Ten Sephiroth, all contained in the first Sephira, Adam Qadmon. The Ten and their subordinates are the *logoi,* and Adam Qadmon is the Logos, the *"vios monageneys."* All the Ten are also called the Mirkaba, the Divine chariot, and they represent the world's original types, the ideal universe intermediate between the Supreme Infinite and the finite sensual bodies. The Nicean Council of the Church did nothing else but personify and localize that Logos as the first Verb or Word of God.

F. Max Mueller opines: "We feel quite ecrtain that the Greeks could not have borrowed that from India."—I must express my dissent in this instance. I believe that all these concepts, the Platonic *ideas,* the Stoic species, the Alexandrian *logos,* the Qabbalistic *Adam Qadmon,* and the Unigenitus of Trinitarianism, all originated in Hindu models and types, and thence were propagated to and condensed in Persia, Assyria, Greece, Egypt, Judæa and Rome. They were first meant as mere metaphors and gradually were rendered concrete and personified. All originally illustrated the philosophical idea that the Supreme, Unknowable Infinite did think the universe, which thought, Sophia, Logos, or Word condensed into and became creation, our sensual world.—(144.) Already in the Rig-Veda is word, speech (Vak) to be found in a hymn as a Power above the gods, a Logos or Wisdom: "I move along with . . . the god of storm and thunder, with the Devas. . . I support Mitra and Varuna, Indra and Agni (sun and heaven, air and fire). I am the queen, the gatherer of treasures, of wisdom, the first who deserves sacrifices."—(Just so is *Wisdom* frequently personified in the Old Testament, New Testament, Apochryphæ, Ben Sirach, Salomon's Wisdom, etc.). Thus speech or Word is shown as a creative power, in the distant past of India. Such passages, too, are found in the Brahmanas. (146.) So is found Sophia in Proverbs VIII. 22: "Wisdom calls aloud from high summits. On you, men, I call... Understand my cunning, O ye simple ones... Listen, for I utter mighty things... My tongue speaks truth and my lips abhor wickedness... Take my admonitions and not silver, for knowledge is superior to gold... Mine is counsel and advice, stratagem and strength... kings reign by me, princes and judges all."... Wisdom of Salomon (VIII. 1-4): "Wisdom reaches with her power from one world's end to the other, ordaining all to the best purpose... Her noble origin glorifies her community with God, and the Master of all, delights in her. She is initiated in the divine knowledge, and participates in the choice of his works.... (Ibid. IX. 2.) God, Thou hast formed man by Thy wisdom."—Even so Ben Sirach (I. 1): "All wisdom comes from the Lord, and she is with Him from eternity. Who can scan the height of heaven, the dimensions of the earth, the days of eternity, who can search out Wisdom? Before everything, Sophia was created. He Himself has created her."—Wisdom was as yet but a divine attribute; soon the attribute became personified in Judaea and Alexandria, hailing from India.

Similarly we find in *Pānkavimsa* Brāhmana (XX. 14.2): "Pragāpati, the Creator... had speech, Vak, as a second. He thought: Let me send forth Speech; she shall pervade all, and so she did."—In other passages, "Vak" is personified as his daughter or his wife. (So in the Old Testament and Apochryphæ wisdom is *"God's delight."*) "Vak" is the principal agent in creation. So in John: "All things were made by the *Word."*—In the *Sathapatha Brāhmana* (VI. 1. 1. 9) we read "Pragāpati, the Creator, first created Brahmān, whereupon *Vak,* Speech, produced all."

The first creation was thus Speech, the *Word.* Hence means Brahman, as also Veda, originally: *Word.* F. Max Mueller shows that Brihaspati is also called *Vakas-pati,* Lord of Speech, and *brih* is the root in Brahman, meaning an utterance, a creation"... a growth. F. Max Mueller, most learnedly and ingeniously, shows that *brih, vrih, vridh,* meaning: to burst forth, grow, the root in brahman takes in Latin the form of *verbum,* and in English *word,* hence brahman, verbum and word would proceed from the root brih, vrih, vridh, to burst forth. I add in corroboration of this that in Hebrew and cognate Semitic languages bara, ברא means undoubtedly to create, bring forth, pointing to a distant past, when Arian and Semitic were yet one. Hence Brahman means simply Creator. Remembering yet that in many passages quoted, Pragāpati is mentioned as preceding Brahman, that the Veda ever speaks of two Brahmans, that the world's creator is the second, the personal Brahmān, not the unknowable, impersonal Brāhman. These are solid arguments for the assumption that "brahman" was first conceived as the creative Word and Logos; then he became Brāhman and Brahmān. F. Max Mueller hesitates (150) as yet, saying: "That would be too good to be true." But the many hints from Hindu, Greek and Hebraic sources, accumulated, manifold, and the Professor's guess, appears to me fully verified. I therefore will not hesitate in assuming that the terms Brahman, Word, Verbum, Logos, Sophia, Will, Only Son and Adam Qadmon are synonyms and designations of the deity as revealed and manifested by the creation of the sensual world.

HINDU, CHRISTIAN AND QABBALISTIC VIEWS.

(151.) "Professor Deussen in *Sathapatha Brāhmana* (XI. 2. 3.) translates: "Brahman was all in the beginning. It sent forth the gods and established them over the worlds. This is one visible world, and above there is a higher world, with higher deities." . . viz: Brāhman had been raised to so transcendant a height that he could not communicate with the world, but by the Word or Logos, names and forms, the types of the world. He was so sublime above the worlds, that creation could be effected only by intermediary powers. The rupa-nama in India . . . the Logoi in Alexandria, Messiah or Adam Qadmon and Sephiroth in Qabbala, etc., are these intervening powers between God unknowable and the sensual creation. (153.) So we read in Maitrayana Upanishad (VI. 22): "Two Brahmans have to be meditated on, the Word and the Non-Word. By the Word alone, is the Non-Word revealed."—That means the Ineffable is manifested by the Logos, or the inconceivable Father by the Son, or the Ain-Soph by Adam Qadmon. This idea was first worked out in India. F. Max Mueller finally concludes (154): "When the Vedantists allude to the gods of other religions, they identify them with their own personal Brahmān, or with the several personæ, the personified phases of their impersonal, neuter Brāhman, the unchangeable Divine Essence, while the Brahmān is the active force of nature, endowed, too, with all the divine qualities. Thus *Ihvh* of the Old Testament, the *"Father"* of the New Testament, *Allah* of the Koran would be identified by them with the personal Brahmān, nature's active force."—I have remarked above that Maimonides, as other Jewish philosophers, gives no name nor attribute to the Supreme Infinite, and places Ihvh and Elohim among the Ten divine categories. Just so designates the Qabbala the Supreme by Ain-Soph; while Ihvh is common to the Supreme and the first Emanation, Adam Qadmon. Even some of the modern, petty pseudo-messiahs, as Sabbatai Zebi, dared sign themselves: "I am your *Elohim-Ihvh.*"—So are the Christian *Lord* and the Hindu *Isvara,* but the second Powers, the personæ or phases of the unknown God, intended for human understanding and worship. While the Great Reality behind was the unknown "Divina Essentia, substantia or natura divina." That was the common conviction of Vedantists, Christian and Jewish philosophers, and Qabbalists.

CREATIVE PERIODS, EVOLUTION AND KANT.

(158). "The Nama-rupa, logoi or types of the things sensual of the entire phenomenal world, were not denied by the Vedantist. He only claimed that he does not know their real nature; that they were the creation of Brahmān himself, the phenomenal God, *Isvara* or *Lord*... Kant also taught that the world and its sensual things are and can be only phenomenal; that the *Ding an sich* lies beyond our knowledge. The creation of the bodily world was no past, consummate, historical fact to the Vedantist. He speaks of repeated manifestations of Brahmān, and these repeated creations have no beginning and will have no end. At the conclusion of great periods (kalpas), the universe is taken back into, and sent forth again from, the bosom of Brahmān. And this alternation has no beginning and no end. This looks almost like our Darwinian theory of Evolution, eternity of the world, with continued change and improvement. That apparent change in the world is ascribed to modifications and forces in the Deity itself; but it conflicts with the idea of divine perfection and blissful contentment. So Sankara does not accept such a view. This apparent change, too, he ascribes to Avidyâ or Nescience, the real Brāhman being perfect and blissful, and the change in the world is caused by an original perversion; by ignorance and obstructions (Upadhis), just as the shortcomings and illusions of the soul are. For all practical purposes, the Vedantist would hold that the phenomenal world is real. It is not deception, *Maya,* illusion, nor total emptiness, as some Buddhists maintain. Hence man shall render himself here practically useful, perform his duties and abide by the laws. It leaves him a Deity, omnipotent and majestic, as any other religion. It respects and tolerates other religions. Kant, too, though declaring God transcending our reason, established his practical and moral philosophy for this phenomenal world. But the Vedantist again remembers here his double character, as religionist and as philosopher. As a religious philosopher he bases his moral law on the Veda, teaching it as revealed truth.—(163): "Before a man is admitted to the study of the Vedanta, a very strict moral discipline is imposed upon him, even by penance and fasting. He must learn to subdue his passions and ambitions, and quietly submit to mental and physical sufferings."

WRONG IN THE WORLD. UNIVERSAL SOLIDARITY.

What is the cause of wrong in the world? Whence comes pain, decrepitude, death, vice, sin? undeserved misfortune and the escape of the wicked? Brāhman, and even the Brahmān being wise, just, all-powerful, whence come tears, evil and wrong into the world? Western moralists and religionists rather evade that problem than answer it. They believe to settle it by establishing the great doctrine of the hereafter.

They prolong human existence beyond the bodily life, and so find space for just retribution and reward as a stimulant for virtue and a warning to vice. Beyond the grave, the reckoning will be made even. There the wicked will suffer and the righteous have his reward. The hereafter is the necessary complement of the doctrine of divine, just and wise government of the world. It is the other end of the arch in the rainbow of religion. The hereafter completes the God-belief, (Ibid 164).

What says the Vedanta philosophy to this most difficult of problems? "There must be a cause to the effect of wrong we clearly see in the world. That cannot be mere caprice or injustice in the Creator... It can only be the result of acts done in a former life."—Hère comes the great and awful doctrine of the migrations of the human soul, its repeated births and many bodily existences. This doctrine is to be found among nearly all ancient philosophers and mystics, Pythagoreans, Parsees, Platonists, Neo-Platonists, Jews, Christians, (John IX.) Qabbalists, etc. . . It is wonderfully and grandly rationalized by the Vedantist: You and I suffer or enjoy today, not alone for our own bad or good deeds, not for the personal acts of our own life, but you and I suffer or enjoy on account of the bad or good actions of ourselves, of our contemporaries, of our sires and the sires of our fellow-men—nay, we suffer for our fellow-creatures, too. Entire creation forms one great chain, by the ties of fellowship, of universal brotherhood. The virtues and vices, the merits and demerits of all are entailed upon every link in the chain, upon each and every member of creation. We, individually, enjoy and suffer by the virtues and the vices of our predecessors and of our contemporaries in this grand association. There is in this world one universal solidarity, each social member is co-responsible for every deed of every living fellow-creature until it is atoned and made good. Every deed, good or bad, has its inexorable, unalterable results and consequences, until atoned and obliterated. As Brāhman, and the Brahmān, too, is the only Essence and Soul of creation, as he pervades and energizes all, of this our own, and of every past generation of beings, as the same sap of the tree lives in each leaf, of each season and each vegetation, even so is Brahmān the soul and energy of every individual being, of you and me, of our predecessors and our neighbors' predecessors, we all being pervaded by that one and same World-Soul, God, Brahman, Isvara, etc.. Hence our mutual responsibility, our solidarity, our participation in the results, good or bad, of the entire creation. Hence you and I enjoy and suffer not only for our own deeds, but for those of all our former existences, of our one common, human existence.—Here is, I believe, the grandest doctrine, the most sublime and all-embracing scheme of the Vedanta philosophy. It is the grandest communism and solidarity, physical, mental, social, ethical, ever expounded by philosopher or religionist. Nay more. Not only does it tally perfectly with facts, it squarely answers the questions: Whence comes evil into the world, apparently made by combined Wisdom, Power and Goodness? Whence comes the evil into the human world, while the universe is full of beauty, harmony and happiness?[1] The answer is: Evil is the result of the shortcomings of all society, each individual suffers for those of his neighbors and predecessors, and each enjoys by the merits of the same. More, this bold and world-vast theory is verified. Daily, we are making the experience of benefits and of losses, of good and of ill-luck which we have not deserved. One is born strong, is well educated, has all social advantages, finds a paved road to walk on, travels smoothly, reaches old age and leaves his progeny to the same advantages. Another is born ill-starred, sickly, doomed early to wretchedness and neglect, next to vice and ignorance, then to temptation and crime, struggle, pain, disappointment, and premature, shameful death and ignominy—all that being the necessary results of his surroundings and conditions. They are not caused or created by that unhappy individual, but by superior forces, by a long line of antecedents, centuries before he was born! Is there not a strong presumption that the Vedantist is right, that his answer tallies with facts? Does not

[1] So Job XXI. 6-27: Why do the wicked exist; peacefully, fat and long-lived, they and their progeny?—while that other man never saw happiness, and dies in despair—yet both are bedded in the ground and worms cover both of them?

the Decalogue, too, state: (2 M. XX. 5)*Ihvh* Thy God is a zealous (exacting) God. He entails the sins of the fathers upon the children and children's children to the third and fourth generation; and is benign to thousands of generations, to those who keep the Commandments."—What Moses says of Ihvh, the Vedantist states of Brahman. It is the law of retaliation and retribution, pervading entire nature and history. While Jesus and Buddha taught that man should offer only good for evil, and thus mitigate the exacting law of talion, visible in nature, Moses taught not to be over-revengeful, nor over-sentimental, but to do justice, and no more than justice, to insist upon exact right and to punish "Eye for eye and tooth for tooth." . . That is true to nature. So too, Moses taught: Thou shalt love thy neighbor as thyself (III. M. 19) because thy neighbor's fate influences thine. He did not teach "Love thine enemy," for human society could not thrive by that method. Buddha, Nazareth and Spinoza advised to "love one's enemy" because they thought very poorly of the generality of men, and recommended to the sage the principle of self-sacrifice—the only way to get along in this world, not worth while fighting for. All three had renounced the world, the one hoping in Nirvana, the other in the "Kingdom of heaven," and the third identifying both: All is a bubble. God alone is real—a *"Salto mortale"* of philosophy. More quietly and rationally, but more boldly, solved the fourth moralist, Sankara, our problem, logically following up his theory of universal solidarity. If the tree could speak, it would say: My children, little leaves, do not quarrel; ye are all identically the same, a repetition of each other.—Even so the Vedantist bids thee, "Love thy neighbor" because he is but another thyself, his *Self* and thy own *Self* are one and the same *Self* of Brāhman.—"He is the sap and the seed of all of us, in which we all live and move and have our Being."—Therefore . . "in loving our neighbor, we really love God, and loving God, we really love ourselves." (Ibid. 169.)—This doctrine is called *"Karman,"* deed, viz: that human fate is the result of human deeds, and such human deeds are the seed of human fate.

"Yet their growth depends upon God, just as any other seed depends upon rain and sunshine for its growth." Here Sankara holds the door open for escape, since his theory will not always be borne out by facts, that theory being so vast that we cannot follow it up fully. "Si non e vere, e ben trovato."[1]

Quaintly F. Max Mueller remarks (165) "That the influence of such a theory must have been marvellous upon the Hindu character. He bore his fate and his troubles with more resignation, as if paying off an old debt. It induced him to lay by moral surplus-capital for the future, and that was a motive for goodness. The belief that no act is lost, but must have its consequences, is only the same belief in the moral world, as our belief in the preservation of force is in the physical world . . . There is no doubt that the doctrine of *"Karman"* has met with the widest acceptance and has helped to soften sufferings and encourage efforts and improvement."—With some, it may be. With many it has rather produced apathy, despair, yea, that oriental craving for total extinction, for annihilation, as emphasized by the Buddhists. It is a sad task to have to answer for the sins of millions and of milleniums, and it is a desperate effort to pay for such old, accumulated debts. Hence comes the Asiatic apathy and resignation in fate, Allah, Brahman, etc., while the Buddhists' hope is only in annihilation, for who can stand the chances of such a formidable responsibility? Even the Brahmanic *Nirvana,* viz: re-union with God, is scoffed at by the Buddhist. What will that help him? As Brahman, he will be born again, be once more responsible, and suffer again; for Brahman, the world-soul, abiding everlastingly in creation, is no refuge from tribulation. The Buddhist's only escape is: extinction, *Nirvana,* in his modified sense, total quenching of the flame, ceasing to exist. But we may like that doctrine of universal responsibility or not, comparing notes and facts, in history and in nature, we must acknowledge that it has great probability of being the true one. It solves the riddle. It is a desperate doctrine, but it offers also much real consolation: We do not only suffer, we also enjoy by the deeds of our fellow-

[1] הרוצה לשקר ירחיק עדותו is to the same point.

men, by the concatenation of the universal facts, and that, to all appearance, makes it even. Each is the heir of all, for good or for evil.—Now this last great feature of the grand Vedanta philosophy, in metaphysics and in ethics, is taught in the Qabbala, too, as verified in the coming volume. Metempsychosis, universal solidarity, ancestral responsibility and final return into the bosom of the Ain-Soph, the Soul of the universe—all that is Qabbala and is Vedanta.—(172) A Hindu philosopher has formulated his grand system in one short line: "Brāhman is true, the world is false (fleeting), man's soul is Brāhman . . There is nothing worth gaining, enjoying or knowing, but Brāhman alone . . for he who knows Brāhman is Brāhman."

We have given here an epitome of Hindu philosophy as, apparently, the oldest source from which contemplative thought started, and which, to my mind, appears to be the reservoir of the system, in grand outlines followed up by Qabbala, Zohar, old and modern philosophers. Next, it was with me a labor of love and veneration, executed in honor of a departed great teacher and a dear friend, the often-mentioned F. Max Mueller, whose work I have here reverently followed, a requiem to his manes!

Having thus carefully discussed the leading doctrines of philosophy; its metaphysics, mysticism, rationalism; starting with the Zohar and Qabbala, we have retraced our steps back to Maimonides, Gebirol, Saadia, the *Book of Creation* and that of *"Divine Height;"* to the Aggadas, the Talmud, the Bible and the Apochryphae; to Plato, Aristotle, Neo-Platonism and Philo; to the Greek and Egyptian mythologies, and the Persian Avesta; finally to the great reservoir, the Hindu Vedas, Upanishads and Vedanta philosophy and theology. We have there studied the elements of metaphysics and mysticism, of rationalism and supernaturalism, of reason and of creed, of religion and of superstition. We have reviewed the systems of the oldest thinkers, the Rishis, Manu, Zoroaster, Buddha, down to Böhm, Spinoza, Malebranche, Schelling, Hegel, etc. We shall proceed, in the second part of this labor, to the closer study of the *Zohar* proper and its theories, the bible of the Qabbalists and of all mystics, Christian, Mohammedan and Jewish. We shall find there the streams of nearly all the great systems, all philosophical thoughts and all popular beliefs, merged into one huge cauldron, one vast lake of philosophy. We shall find there an eclecticism of the best and of the weakest; the most rational and the most naive, the most sublime and the most futile, agglomerated into one curious and highly interesting collection of treatises, denominated the *"Zohar of Rabbi Shimeon ben Iohai."* We shall contemplate there the vast influence these purely theoretical doctrines of the Qabbala have exercised upon Judaism, Christainity and Mohammedanism. We shall elaborately discuss the Zohar's sociological and political schemes, its *Messianic* Ideal, its ethical and social aspirations in juxtaposition with history, science, our instincts, etc., the ameliorations they all hold in store for mankind. There we shall find, side by side with Vedantic, Greek and other Arian propositions, many derived from other sources, from Oriental, Semitic, etc., origins, some curious and others greatly interesting to the inquirer. Finally, we shall collect there all the leading ideas and rays of our series on the "Biblical Legislations and the Messiah Ideals" into one central focus, and thus offer a full, succinct tableau of the views advocated in these volumes. This will prove that Israel's thinkers are not isolated and sporadic in the mental laboratory of the human race, but an integral and sympathetic part, a necessary link in the golden chain of mankind's mental achievements. It will show humanity as one bee-hive, with many cells, parcelled out among its several tribes, who are all jealous and fighting, yet the common task of honey-making, the *human advance,* is never stopped, however retarded by envious misunderstandings. It will be cheering and optimistic. It will point out the philosophy of all philosophies to be, as in Ecclesiastes XII. 11-14: "The many sages and systems are but the spurs of the diverse peoples. They are all derived from one origin. Take no heed of the host of books and their conflicting schemes; they are but a waste of body and force. The result of all true philosophy, all being heard and pondered over, is: Venerate God and keep his commandments, for all our deeds, public or private, good or bad, are counted and judged and have their sure results, and this is the whole of man."

GREAT NINETEENTH CENTURY TEACHERS.

Reader! Having occupied our mind throughout this volume with theories, let us close with something concrete, live, personal. Let us do reverence to the bearers of those theories above elaborately discussed. Finishing the first part of this "Philosophy," let us bid adieu to our guides, and especially those with whom the writer of this had the honor to be in personal touch and to count among his great academic teachers, those who exercised upon his work a lasting influence.

We salute as such, first, our often-quoted master and greatly revered friend, Frederick Max Mueller, of the Oxford University. He has powerfully contributed and advanced the comparatively new Sanskrit science, Indian history, the Upanishad and Vedanta philosophy. He has warmly encouraged us in our labors. His venerated hillock is yet green and fresh. May these pages be the first flowers growing forth from it. They witness to his immortality, his *Nirvana*. His genius now is translated and united to mankind's genius. His work is resumed and continued under his own auspices. He advised this publication. It was he especially who unlocked to us the Vedanta philosophy, and this volume attempts to show its vast influence over Rishis, Kapila, Buddha, Zarathustra, Plato, Philo, Plotin, the Middle Ages, Spinoza, modern and present thought. Hence this volume may be considered as a new layer to his structure, as a shoot from his plant. Let us place a wreath upon his hillock!

Next, these pages have drawn from the "*Qabbala*," published half a century ago, by Adolph Franck of the Paris College de France. With a thrill of joy, I remember his all-embracing, thoughtful, spirited *seances,* emulating those of his colleagues and compeers, Laboulay, Saint-Marc Girardin, Renan, etc. Adolph Franck taught and exemplified to his crowding hearers how to grasp vast ethical themes, great philosophical problems, the objects and aims of great legislators, the intricate mechanism and spirit of government, and the scope of great institutions. Laboulay ever closed his seances with an appeal for liberty, for virtue, for unflinching truth. Girardin electrified his hearers with love of country and of glory. Renan incarnated the genius of religion without the smoke of bigoted sectarianism. Ad. Franck especially pointed out in his *Qabbala* how to treat such abstruse, intricate subjects, how to find out and grasp the grain of truth, hid in these riddles of oriental philosophy. Whether we shared or opposed his views, we ever respected them. A wreath to his manes!

Then I remember Professor Munck, of the same College de France. He, too, has a share in this present work. He rescued Gebirol from oblivion, from a manuscript-grave. He proved this illustrious thinker and master-mind to be one of the spiritual heroes of the Western Hebraic world. I remember Munck over thirty years ago, youthful at over sixty, cheerful, though blind, a noble exemplar of a scholar, a sage, after the heart of the Mishna and the Vedanta. A laurel to his brow!

Another leading man, a dear friend, a teacher and philanthropist I reverently and lovingly remember. It is Albert Cohn, of the Ecole Rabbinique of Paris, who has greatly influenced my entire career and my aspirations—a man of vast perspectives and humane sympathies, a noble type of manhood, a conciliating link between Arian and Semite, looking out from the watch-tower of Israel-humanity, a champion of universal good-will, in the wake of Adolph Cremieux, Moses Montefiore, Rieser and others. A garland to his liberating efforts!

Let us honorably remember Nehemias Bruell, Chief Rabbi of Frankfort, A. M., the flower of German scholarship—a man who had justly aroused bright hopes of great achievements, which premature death has nipped in the bud. A wreath to his name!

A kind and honorable reminiscence we entertain of the hoary Chief-Rabbi, Adler, senior; of the modest and suave Zedner, both of London, and of the brilliant, versatile Emanuel Deutsch, of British Museum, each great in his way, in the vast disciplines of the Jewish science. We salute them each and all, reverently and lovingly!

After the historical, ethical and philosophical views, criticisms and methods of the great Kant, Schiller, Lessing, etc., in the earlier period of our youth, the important theories of the Anglo-Saxon Darwin, John Stuart Mill and Herbert Spencer have greatly influenced our thought in riper years.—A laurel to the brow of these great leaders!

With deep respect I mention the venerable Professor of Philosophy, Drobisch, of the University of Leipzig, Germany, whose lectures I followed more than a generation ago, and whom I heard again, and with as much pleasure, fifteen years ago, at the same university of Leipzig. That was his last course of lectures, which he announced to be his one hundred and twenty-second semester of teaching philosophy.—An ideal of a Teutonic man of study and science, of modesty, simplicity, and virtue. Reverence to his memory!

Here is another glory of the Leipzig University, Professor *Franz Delitzsch,* a man of vast sympathies and profound erudition, an enthusiastic expounder of the Hebraic Scriptures, who aspired at the unification of the Spirit of Sinai, Karmel and Nazareth; the most Jewish Christian, and the most Semitic Arian. A laurel to his name!

Now let us honorably mention some of our living teachers; master-minds, who have spent each an honorable, laborious life in the university halls, in the service of science and higher education. I allude to Dr. Adolph Neubauer, of Oxford, who is about to celebrate his seventieth birthday, who has devoted half a century to assiduous and successful research in the fields of Hebraic literature, who has caught up many a pearl in the Ocean of the Talmud, and has deposited such in the storehouse of universal science. Offering him our hearty good wishes to his honorable jubilee, and thanking him for his encouragement in our work, we bid him good cheer on his earthly pilgrimage, and tender him a well-deserved wreath, coming from an old, warm friend across the ocean, flowers on the thorney path of scholarship.

We continue this galaxy of scientific celebrities with another great teacher, of whom I have greatly profited, viz: Roscher, at the Leipzig University, a glorious expounder of the economical, political, historical and sociological sciences.

Last, but not least, we remember with especial delight, our brilliant and erudite Professor of philosophy, W. Wundt, a favorite of the German students; strong in wisdom, science and honors, a scientific orator to whom nightly many hundreds listened enthusiastically, during this half-century; and whose modes of viewing and treating philosophy have wonderfully impressed and influenced me, to this day. I would say more, but I remember distinctly when, once on his arrival, the crowded hall of students received him with applause, he smilingly requested them to stop "for that creates dust," ("Das macht Staub;") a fine way of a philosopher to avoid jealousy. It is in such an atmosphere, in contact with such men that the students caught up the spark of inspiration, the delight in study, the cult of science, *for science sake,* the neglect of the vulgar instincts and ambitions. Such men were the models held up to our gaze. To these men may this work be dedicated as an offering of love, gratitude and veneration!

These pages are but a humble and weak echo of their teachings on the sciences of philosophy, history, ethics, laws, etc. It is their wisdom, which this volume attempts to transplant to these shores of the Atlantic, the Mississippi, the Rio Grande. A new people is arising here, a giant-people. It is as yet in its infancy, it is as yet occupied with its material interests. But it is growing apace, rapidly. Very soon higher maturity will be reached. Then the great American democracy will need its mental food—a giant's food! Then those illustrious men, our guides in these pages, will loom up and occupy the American mind. At that time, this hand, now penning these lines, will be stiff and gathered with those mentioned: *"Morituri salutamus!"*[1] So we deliver this volume cheerfully, con-

1 "Dying we salute you!" shouted the Roman gladiator to the attending spectators.

fidently, written expressly for you, American youth!—An oriental tale illustrates this:

A hoary man of four-score, busily planting a date-tree, was asked by his blooming grandchild:

"Who will enjoy of the fruit of this thy planting?"

"Thy children," the old man replied.

"What for then thy painstaking labor?"

"To prepare for thee and those after thee."

"What will that profit thee, grandpapa?"

"I profited by the labors of my grandfathers, and my grandchildren shall profit by my labors."

This is the *universal solidarity* taught by Philosophy, Vedanta and Qabbala.—With these words, *universal solidarity,* I take leave of you, my kind *Readers,* till we meet again in the solemn halls of the Alhambra of the *Zohar,* in the second part of this work, carrying over the seeds of the departed fathers as fruits for the learners of coming generations.

END OF VOLUME FIRST.

Errata.

PAGE	INSTEAD OF	READ
4—Middle	clearly retraced	traced
20—Below	the bees will	the bees would
21—Note	creation	creation, 92
39—Above	attain a	attain at
42—Above	the manifestations	manifestation
102—Middle	Indians	Indian
127—Id	prophesies an	prophesies as an
144—Id	attributes of	attributes or
151—Above	venerable page	venerable age
162—Middle	each in a light	are each in a
180—Above	light, cave	light-cave
185—Id	Mandala I, 11	Mandala V, 11
192—Middle	the Brāhman	the Brahmān
209—Below	Cordix Ioreh Deah	Codex Ioreh
230—Middle	is obliged	is obligated

COMMENTS ON MAURICE FLUEGEL'S WORKS:

ZEND-AVESTA AND EASTERN RELIGIONS.

Ambassador Andr. D. White, writes: "I have gone carefully over its contents. It contains a vast deal of matter suggestive of fruitful thought."

Count Leo Tolstoy, the Russian Liberal, Statesman and Author: "I read your excellent book with great pleasure and interest."

Prof. F. Max Mueller, of Oxford Univ.: "I hope it will be widely read, marked and inwardly digested."

Prof. E. Wilhelm, of Yena Univ. offers to review it in scientific Periodicals.

Dr. Isr. Levi, Editor of the *Etudes Juives*, Paris, offers the same.

Dr. A. Neubauer, of Oxford University, will do the same.

The London J. Chronicle: "The author has set a noble aim before himself . . . He deserves all encouragement—His standpoint is broadly liberal."

"*Ungarischer Israelit*", Pest: "The author has acquired a fine reputation. His immense readings and deep researches in comparative legislations, Religions, doctrines, rites, etc. in connection with Bible, Talmud, Gospel, Koran, etc. led him to new and surprising results . . . Leading scientists find there a pioneer of uncommon acumen, opening new paths, creating a school."

Rev. Dr. Kohler, New York, warmly recommends the work and the entire series for their scholarly caliber and originality."

Mr. Lipman Levy, Secretary of the Union American Hebrew Congations sends the expression of the best feelings of the Board."

Prof. Adams, of Johns Hopkins "hopes the author will continue his studies and publications."

MESSIAH IDEAL, VOL. I. and II.

Jesus' Ethics, Paul and N. Testament, Mohammed and Koran.

Prof. F. Max Mueller: "It contains a great deal that is not only good and interesting, but valuable and permanently useful."

Dean Farrar, Canterb. Engl.: "I read your book with the greatest interest. The Jewish writings are *invaluable* for their Gospel illustrations."

Rector A. Schwarz, of Vienna Seminary: "Your work gives me great pleasure. It is a gigantic labor. . . I congratulate you most heartily."

Ungar. Israelit reviews it enthusiastically in two successive leaders.

Dr. A. Neubauer, of Oxford Univ. in London *J. Quarterly Review*: "The analysis of the Gospel is the best part. The Chapters on Messiah Ideal are full of information . . Those on Mohammed and Koran are well arranged. . .

Baroness de Hirsch, *the Khedive of Egypt*, *Rector Ernst Curtius* of the Berlin Univ., *Dean Day* of Yale, etc., send encouraging letters.

Leading Dailies and Periodicals of New York, Philadelphia, Baltimore, Chicago, St. Louis, etc. reviewed the works most elaborately.

Universities, *Libraries* of America, England, Germany, etc., order them.

Dr. I. Hamburger, Germany, Real Encyclopaedie Article "*Jesus of Nazareth*," (1897) fully adopted the view of the author.

Dr. Isidore Loeb, Paris, declared his satisfaction with the authors' "*Reply to Franz Delitzsch*," setting forth that view in 1889.

COMMENTS ON MAURICE FLUEGEL'S LITERARY WORK.

"THE MESSIAH-IDEAL." VOLUME I.

"JESUS OF NAZARETH."

The first impulse to that work came from Professor FRANZ DELITZSCH of the Leipsic University, who amicably challenged the author to write on that subject. See above page 296.

President GEORGE E. DAY of Yale University wrote next: "Seeing your clear style of writing, I have strongly felt what a contribution it would be if you would undertake to show the teachings of the most distinguished of the Jewish nation . . . . . Such a presentation, I am sure, would be welcomed by all thinking men."

From the Mss. of this book the author has repeatedly lectured here before Ministers' Associations, who listened with kind attention. The Press reported most favorably. On such an occasion the late Rev. Dr. WILLIAMS, Baptist minister, said: "With the greatest interest have I followed the readings on that subject. More than ever I feel proud of my religion. I wish to see that book published."

Prof. MAX MUELLER, England, to whom an outline was sent, writes: "Your new work bids fair to bring out much interesting matter;" and referring to the numerous rabbinical excerpta therein, he adds: "The Talmud is a rich mine, by far not yet exhausted."

Provost UHLER, of Baltimore Peabody Institute, encouraged this study, allowing to the author the freedom of the library.

"THOUGHTS ON RELIGIOUS RITES."

To this, President W. H. GREEN of Princeton Seminary wrote: "This book seems to embody in an interesting way the results of extensive reading, study and careful reflection."

President GEORGE E. DAY, Yale University, had a continued correspondence, desiring the author to write on the doctrines of Jesus. (this volume).

President ANDREW D. WHITE, of Cornell University: "It interests me very much in my examination of it."

Cardinal GIBBONS sends his good wishes to its favorable reception by the Press.

FRIED. VON BODENSTEDT, Germany, Poet: "I have read it with lively interest, finding it most instructive and suggestive."

Professor FRANZ DELITZSCH, of Leipsic University: "It is likely to prove a real enrichment to science . . it is rich in contents, offering much material for reflection."

Professor W. WUNDT, of same University: "Your historical researches are calculated to vividly interest me. I shall utilize your remarks in my studies on Spinoza."

Professor ROSCHER, same University, contributed some historical suggestions to its composition.

Dr. M. HIRSCH, of the German Reichstag: "It interests me greatly, offering me useful information."

The Right Hon. W. E. GLADSTONE, London: "It appears to be a treatise of great interest. Being about examining into the character of the Mosaic System, *it is very welcome to me.*"

Professor MAX MUELLER, Oxford, England: "It is full of interesting information and I hope you will continue;" alluding to this "Messiah-Ideal."

Librarian Dr. A. NUSBAUER, Oxford: "I have just finished reading your interesting work, hearty thanks for it. I shall lend it to . . . . . who is writing on the "Avesta."

Grand rabbi ZADOC KAHN, Paris: "I have read your charming book with pleasure and profit."

Dr. A. SCHWARZ, Rector of Vienna Theological Seminary: "I have read already many fine passages therein."

Rabbi GUTTMAN, of Hildesheim, writes similarly.

The Morgenländische Gesellschaft in Leipsic and chief-rabbi Brüll, of Frankfort a./M., gave it an honorable mentioning in their respective scientific periodicals.

"Univers Israelité," Paris, reviewed it most cordially and elaborately.

Dr. Rahmer, Magdeburg, reproduces a large part thereof in his "Literatur Blatt."

Professor H. Graetz, of Breslau University, offered to superintend its publication.

"MOSAIC DIET AND HYGIENE."—OTHER TRACTS OF THE AUTHOR.

Professor H. Graetz wrote: "It pleases me very much and I request you to let me keep the copy." Further, your "*Shylock and Prejudice*" is beautiful. We dare not speak here so frankly.

Similar approving utterances by Drs. Chief-rabbi H. Adler, London; Isidor Loeb, Paris; Allgemeine Zeitung des Judenthums, of Dr. Philippson; Archives Israelités, Paris; Rahmer's Literatur Blatt; etc.

POLITICAL WRITINGS.

Right Hon. W. E. Gladstone: "Rev. Fluegel's articles on "*The Ottoman Empire*" gave me unqualified pleasure. I am desirous of expressing my gratification to him."

Letters from Adolf Crémieux, Lord Beaconsfield, Presidents Garfield and Hayes, Secretaries Evarts, Carl Schurz, etc., approving of articles on Political Questions.

Rev. Henry Ward Beecher: "I congratulate you on your command of the English language. Your work might make many a native proud."

Encouraging and approving letters came from Drs. L. Philippson, Bonn; David Einhorn, S. Adler, A. Hübsch and A. Kahut, N. Y., etc.; especially numerous, spirited and warm letters came from Albert Cohn and Adolf Crémieux, Paris.

"SPIRIT OF THE BIBLICAL LEGISLATION."

Cardinal Gibbons sent an autograph letter with a liberal subscription. Then, verbally, he said: "Your book contains new ideas . . . I shall continue my subscription to your continued work."

Right Hon. W. E. Gladstone sent a letter with his greetings.

Professor Max Mueller, Oxford, England, sent the same with his portrait.

Librarian Dr. A. Neubauer, Oxford, commented in the London Quarterly Review: "We have no doubt that this present study will be as favorably received as his "*Thoughts on Religious Rites.*" It is an original attempt at comparative legislation and the influence of religion on law."

Mr. Herbert Spencer wrote: "Your work contains much interesting matter which I should like to read when my health permits."

Dr. A. Schwarz, Rector of Vienna Theological Seminary, finds the book profound and has it reviewed in the "Ungar. Israelit," Buda-Pesth. It says:

"The erudite and sympathetic author of this work has already by other publications earned the warmest acknowledgment and approbation of leading scholars in Europe and America. — The reader of the present work finds there both instruction and enthusiasm. — The author has been very successful in bringing out therein the spirit and the principles of the Mosaic Institutions."

Rev. Dr. A. Kohut, New York: "It is the product of a systematically trained mind that has well mastered the philosophy of Jewish Legislation."

Bishops Drs. Paret, Kephardt and Wilson; ministers, lawyers, professors and leading merchants write approvingly.

Professor W. T. Harris of the Educational Bureau, Washington: "It aught to have a wide reading among students of religion, sociology and politics. . . . . . It is doing much good towards clearing up grave economic misgivings. I hope the author will further bring out his studies.

The Press, political, religious and scientific, here and abroad, has most kindly reviewed the above writings and frequently given them its cordial encouragement.

The author's and proprietor's address is:

M. FLUEGEL,
521 Robert Street, Baltimore, Md.